UFO
WITNESS
SIGHTINGS

D1363888

UFO

WITNESS

SIGHTINGS

AN ILLUSTRATED DOSSIER
OF ALIEN ENCOUNTERS

Peter Brookesmith

amber
BOOKS

This Amber edition first published in 2019

Published by Amber Books Ltd
United House
North Road
London N7 9DP
United Kingdom
www.amberbooks.co.uk
Instagram: amberbooksltd
Facebook: www.facebook.com/amberbooks
Twitter: @amberbooks

ISBN: 978-1-78274-890-8

Chapter 8 text written by Johnny Dee
Editor: Henry Russell
Designer: Lisa Rathgen and Andrew Easton

Printed in China

Picture Credits
Alamy: 148 (EDB Image Archive), 150 (AF Archive), 158 (Everett Collection), 164 (ITAR-TASS), 166 (Radius
Images), 167 (Sipa Asia/Zuma Wire), 171 (Ken Howard Images)
Via Stewart Campbell: 62/3
Mary Evans Picture Library: 6/7, 10, 14, 20, 27, 28/9, 30, 34/5, 40, 46/7, 48, 49, 50/1, 52, 56, 58, 64, 74, 75/7,
82, 93, 96, 114/5, 118, 125, 126, 154 (Michael Buhler), 172/3
Fortean Picture Library: 2, 8/9, 12, 16, 18, 22, 26, 36/7, 38, 42/3, 44, 54, 60/1, 66/7, 68, 70, 72, 78/9, 80/1,
84/5, 86, 87, 88, 90, 99, 100, 102/3, 104/5, 106, 109, 111, 112, 116, 120/1, 122, 130/1, 132, 134, 136, 137, 138,
142, 144/5, 146/7, 148
Johnson Space Center: 170
Los Angeles Times: 32/3
Mexican Air Force: 160
NASA: 156
Natural History Museum, London: 24/5
Range Pictures: 94/5
Shutterstock: 162 (Micha Weber)
Sidgwick & Jackson: 141
UFORSA/Zani: 151
U.S D.O.D: 140, 153, 161
U.S. National Archives: 128, 129

CONTENTS

A Secret History

Unrecognized, perhaps even disguised, the UFO has been with us for centuries

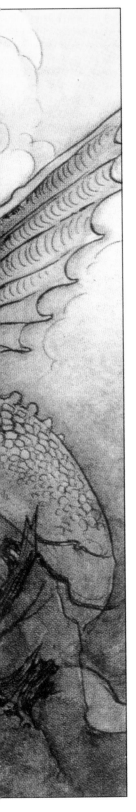

What is an unidentified flying object (UFO)? The late Dr J. Allen Hynek, who spent 40 years studying the enigma, would respond to such a question by posing another: 'Unidentified to whom?'

Hynek meant several things by this parry. He knew from long experience that well over 90 per cent of apparent 'UFOs' can be identified if the investigator has all the right information. In most cases, what has seemed to be a brilliantly-lit saucer-shaped craft with a dome on top turns out to be an especially bright planet, or an aircraft seen at an odd angle with its landing lights on, or some other everyday item. It is the element of surprise as much as anything that turns such things into exotic objects in the eye of the beholder.

Sometimes the knowledge required to identify an apparent UFO is not readily to hand. I know this from my own experience. On 31 March 1993, I was staying in a remote corner of Wales and gave the house dogs (and one determined cat) a final airing at about 1:00am. In the still, clear sky two golden blobs of light passed overhead, leaving long vapor trails. They were flying fast, keeping exact formation. I thought they were a couple of military jets, at maybe 2000ft (600m) altitude, probably on afterburners. Only when I realized

In the Middle Ages, and for centuries before, the untamed countryside was seen as dangerous and strange, a place full of legendary beasts where magical and fantastic events commonly occurred. Today, the realm of the alien and uncanny has retreated to the edge of space. Is the notion of 'flying saucers' carrying beings from the stars to Earth only the modern equivalent of the ancient belief in dragons and elves?

Close Encounters at a glance

- **Close Encounters of the First Kind:**
  UFOs are witnessed at close quarters
- **Close Encounters of the Second Kind:**
  UFOs cause physical effects on humans, animals and objects
- **Close Encounters of the Third Kind:**
  Entities are seen in or near UFOs
- **Close Encounters of the Fourth Kind:**
  UFOs abduct humans
- **Close Encounters of the Fifth Kind:**
  Humans contact UFOs by conventional signals or telepathy

that they made no sound did it dawn on me that I'd seen something very odd: two jets flying at that speed and altitude should have been deafening.

So what were those lights? Enquiries among aviator acquaintances, radar operators, even friends at the British Ministry of Defence, all came to a dead end. But a regional UFO investigator dug harder until he came up with the answer – which you can read in the last chapter of this book.

But there was apparently another strange object flying around the western British Isles that night, and there are yet others reported almost daily that seem not to be identified to anyone on Earth. Which was one of the subtler points Dr Hynek was making. And the scale of the phenomenon is extraordinary. In 1991 a Roper Organization poll found that 7 per cent of adults in the USA had seen a UFO. On the basis of the 1990 Census, this means that some 17.4 million Americans have had a UFO experience. If every one of their sightings were properly investigated, the chances are that around 850,000 of them would probably be classed as 'unidentified'.

Where do these objects come from? Who could identify them? It is here that the trouble starts. In the last 50 years, most people have associated UFOs with extra-terrestrial visitors. Yet several ufologists have protested that the number of alleged sightings, landings, encounters (with craft and aliens of all kinds) is simply too large to bear a purely extra-terrestrial explanation. The Universe is too big and the conditions in which life as we know it is likely to develop are too rare. Unless, as one commentator put it, for some bizarre reason Earth is the most popular tourist spot in the Galaxy. Even researchers who believe that aliens perform elaborate medical experiments on thousands of people each year, confess they have no idea where the aliens come from.

So ufologists have speculated that our mysterious visitors may be time travelers; or from societies that have discovered how to defeat the barriers of space and time, and intrude into our world from other dimensions; or they may be the product of unknown but human psychic energies. They may be life-forms that live in the atmosphere, or they may be produced by energies in the Earth itself, and are either conscious themselves or can respond to human thought. Any of these speculations may be true or, equally, utterly wrong.

My own conviction is that the human mind is inextricably involved with all UFO phenomena, from 'simple' sightings of flying disks to complex, full-blown abduction accounts. I say this partly because of the astonishing variety in UFO reports, and partly because UFOs and aliens seem to single out individuals or small groups of people to whom they reveal themselves – while remaining unseen by others close by. But mainly I say it because the secret history of the UFO stretches back into antiquity. The similarities between modern UFO reports and ancient tales of fiery wheels, dragons and portents in the sky are truly remarkable; moreover, there are extraordinary parallels between today's descriptions of abductions by aliens and archaic accounts of folk being 'stolen' by elves and goblins.

Does this mean that, before the space age, people mistook visiting alien craft for magic, fiery, flying beasts, and shining crosses in the sky? Or are dragons and flying disks, along with alien 'grays' and goblins, different forms of a phenomenon that adapts itself to the beliefs and preoccupations of each era? And is that phenomenon at least partly *created* by the mind?

The case histories collected here should help you ponder these problems for yourself. A book of this length cannot be an absolutely exhaustive compendium of UFO experiences – thousands are reported from all over the world every year. But the cases here have been chosen carefully for their historical significance – to show how the phenomenon has altered and developed over the years – and to show the amazing diversity of unusual features that every aspect of the phenomenon displays – from the endless variety of lights in the sky, to the off-beat forms and strange utterances of aliens. And some are here to show that UFOs are truly a global experience. Unless they illustrate some uncommon facet of that experience, I have avoided single-witness cases, as they are less reliable than those involving two or more observers. And, not least important, some cases, which have been repeatedly cited as 'proof' of the UFO mystery, are exposed for what they are – hoaxes, frauds, legends and, sometimes, honest mistakes.

The introduction to each historical era includes an overview of what ufologists and others concluded at the time. Not the smallest reason for my belief that a greater understanding of the human mind is central to solving the UFO enigma is the fact that the ufologists' conclusions have so often borne little or no relation to what people on the ground were actually experiencing. But that, perhaps, is another story.

Peter Brookesmith

This photograph, one of a series of a purported UFO that allegedly overflew the tiny, barren island of Trindade in 1958, typifies the problems faced by investigators who want to establish the real truth about UFO reports. No two accounts of the events during the sighting or its aftermath entirely agree – even on the name of the ship's captain – whether written by those who believe the pictures to be genuine or those who have debunked them. A complete, accurate assessment of all the claims and counter-claims made over this case is long overdue.

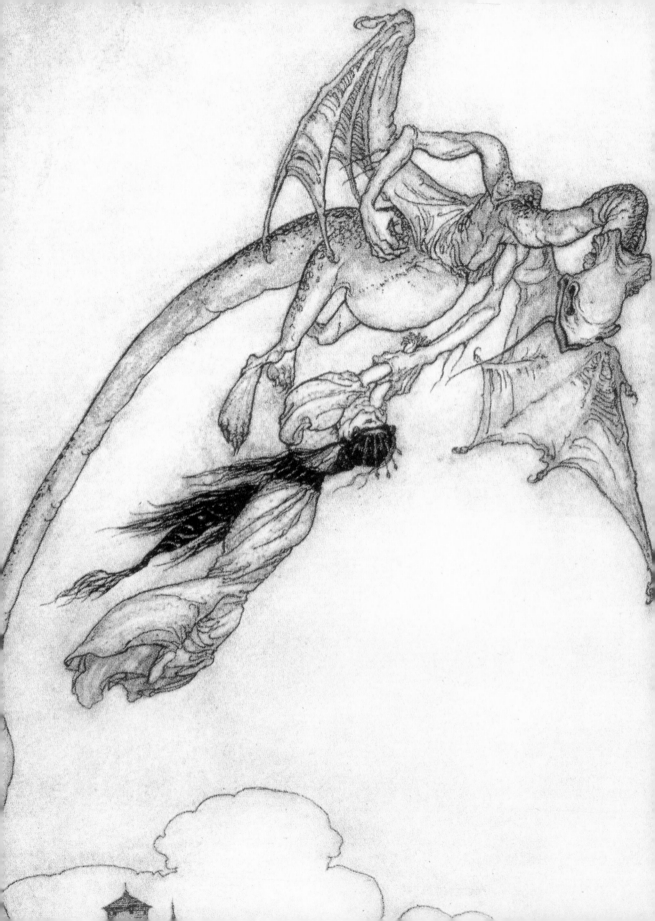

CHAPTER 1

Dragons and Demons

A SUPERNATURAL HISTORY OF THE UFO

The unidentified flying object, or flying saucer, seems a uniquely modern phenomenon. Most people assume — rightly or wrongly — that UFOs are some kind of manifestation from extra-terrestrial intelligences, and that they are peculiar to our time. And yet, if we examine these assumptions more carefully, we may be struck by how odd they are. Surely it is too much of a coincidence that extra-terrestrials should start to visit our skies just when we ourselves were beginning to look to the stars and think about colonizing other worlds? After World War II, with the rapid, exciting development of rocket technology, this seemed to many people a real possibility. And then, what appeared to be alien spacecraft suddenly began to appear around the world.

Within a few years of the first 'flying saucer' sightings in 1947, a number of researchers had concluded that this was indeed too much of a coincidence, and began to look at ancient chronicles, religious writings, epic poems and folklore in

Arthur Rackham's illustration of the abduction of the king's daughter in 'The Four Clever Brothers', one of the folk stories collected by the Grimm brothers. Claims of abductions by bizarre otherworldly creatures are not an exclusively modern phenomenon, and the underlying pattern in both ancient and modern stories is strikingly consistent.

a new light — uncovering evidence that strange phenomena had been appearing in our skies for centuries, indeed for millennia. Sedulous reading by investigators such as Harold T. Wilkins, W. Raymond Drake, and Jacques Vallée threw up a wealth of evidence for the existence of UFOs in former times.

Some of that evidence has been found to be dubious: for example, many medieval European chroniclers embellished their accounts of heroic occasions with miraculous events almost as a matter of course, especially when the occasions had taken place long before the time of writing. Signs and wonders in the skies would be wheeled out as verbal special effects to indicate divine approval of military victories or the deaths of enemies, or even to enhance a royal wedding. Some tales, too, if read objectively, are clearly dramatizations of violent weather or the passage overhead of a comet or meteorite. Nevertheless there remains a hard core of contemporary accounts that can't be rendered down like this, and that do seem to describe some genuinely puzzling aerial phenomena.

The theme of 'ancient UFOs' was reworked and richly embroidered in the late Sixties and early Seventies into the claim that alien astronauts visited the Earth in ancient times. Apart from accelerating our technological development, they may also have interbred with our ancestors to produce the human race as we know it. The best-known, if by no

means the first, writer to propose this idea was Erich von Däniken. But the 'evidence' these writers offered was soon shown by historians, archaeologists and other experts to be incredibly flimsy, often wildly inaccurate, and sometimes simply untrue. Of course, demolishing bad evidence does not prove that, when the Old Testament says 'The sons of God came in unto the daughters of men', it does not mean that aliens fathered offspring from whom we are all descended. But it does mean that the case for 'ancient astronauts' remains pure speculation, without scientific foundation.

THE REAL EVIDENCE

This book is a catalogue of UFO experiences and reports, and so does not delve any further into the 'ancient astronaut' hypothesis. Nor do the vast majority of the case histories in this book deal with the indirect evidence that UFOs like those we know today were seen in prehistoric times, before the advent of written records. But there are signs in early records that, well before the earliest specific account of a UFO in ancient Egypt, UFOs were not unknown.

Two paleolithic cave paintings at Niaux in southern France, which are at least 30,000 years old, depict elongated, perhaps disk-shaped objects topped with a dome; one trails a series of dotted lines, which may represent movement. In the Altamira caves near Santander, northern Spain, are paintings at least 15,000 years

This 'flaming celestial object', pictured by Hermann Schaden in 1463, is typical of the strangely-shaped objects witnessed in European skies during the Middle Ages. It also bears an interesting general resemblance to the cigar-shaped UFOs reported in the 20th century.

old showing disks, ovals, and what may be 'spacemen'. However, it must be said that archaeologists and art historians have made far more prosaic and mundane interpretations of these images, and not even all ufologists accept the ufological interpretation as valid.

Several ancient Indian texts describe extraordinary flying machines called *vimanas*, which are controled by the pilots who usually number among the 330 million gods of the Hindu pantheon. There are a number of lengthy descriptions of

how the *vimanas*' various power systems work, but these are tantalizingly obscure. The devices are mentioned in the great Sanskrit epics, the *Mahabharata* and *Ramayana*, where they are described as military machines with the range to 'carry death' anywhere in the world. One commentator even went so far as to say that 'we cannot but be struck [when reading these works] by the modernity of certain passages, where we seem to be reading an account of a nuclear war.'

In other respects the *vimanas* bear some resemblance to UFOs. Some are small, single-seater craft; others are enormous. Some, in a manner that recalls accounts of UFOs by abductees, have a remarkable capacity to seem infinitely spacious inside, while showing only modest exterior proportions. One account in the *Mahabharata*, of the kidnapping of King Duryodhana by a demonic female entity named Krtya exactly parallels the

modern accounts of abductions by aliens, even down to hints of genetic manipulation. Once again, scholars of Vedic literature dispute that the *vimanas* are to be taken at their literal face value. The myths of most human societies, from the legend of Hiawatha to the tales of the Greek gods, include stories of magical flight and extraordinary powers, and even abductions. Skeptics would say that this only indicates that UFO lore is itself a kind of folklore. Others would argue the opposite – that such widespread themes demonstrate that folklore and myth are based on actual events – in these cases, on actual UFO experiences.

THE EYE OF THE BEHOLDER

We are on stronger ground in justifying the suspicion that UFOs have a very long history when we come down to actual cases. And then, as we noted in the Introduction, it becomes clear that in former times people rarely saw UFOs as a 20th-century person would see them. Indeed they did not even see fearsome weather in the way we do.

For example, a chronicle from Melrose Abbey in Scotland records that in York, England, in 1165, 'Many people in this year saw a black horse of large size.... It always kept hurrying toward the sea, while it was followed by thunder and lightning and fearful noises, with destructive hail.'

That, surely, describes a particularly dramatic thunderhead being blown out to sea. But what are we to make of this report from an ancient Celtic source? A star 'of wonderful magnitude and brightness suddenly appeared in the skies over Wales' giving out a bright ray of light, and 'toward the ray, a fiery globe in the likeness of a dragon was stretched out. Out of the mouth of [the dragon] proceeded two rays, and the length of one... was seen to stretch out beyond the region of Wales.'

This sounds like the visitation of a comet and, in the tradition of the ancient epics, it appeared in the midst of a battle being waged by Uther Pendragon, father of the legendary King Arthur. But note that the comet, a bright, unusual (and portentous) light in the night, is seen *with* a dragon. There is a clear distinction between the two. And when dragons in particular (and other curious shapes and signs too) appear in the sky in medieval times, the accounts are sometimes so strange that is difficult to believe that comets, meteors or fireballs are what lie behind them.

Like UFOs today, dragons occupied a strange no-man's land between humdrum reality and the Otherworld. Most people had never seen a dragon, but medieval people would have had no trouble identifying one if it landed in a bustling market place and snorted smoke and flame. Even so, actual dragons remained elusive and magical, perhaps possible but definitely improbable. Today, much the same thing could be said of UFOs, except that they are magical only in the sense that they could be 'other-worldly' – that is, either extra-terrestrial or paranormal.

THE FIRST SIGHTING ON RECORD

Fire circles in Ancient Egypt

TYPE: **Daylight Disk**
PLACE: **Egypt**
DATE: **Reign of Pharaoh Thutmose III**

BACKGROUND

Thutmose (also known as Thothmes) III ruled Egypt jointly with his wife, his half-sister Queen Hatshepsut, from about 1501 Before the Common Era (BCE) and after her death as sole pharaoh from the year 1479 until 1447 BCE. Thutmose is widely regarded by historians as having been one of the greatest of all the rulers of ancient Egypt.

THE EVENTS

According to a papyrus allegedly found among the papers of a director of the Vatican's Egyptian Museum, 'In the year 22, of the third month of the winter, sixth hour of the day... the scribes of the House of Life found there was a circle of fire coming in the sky... It had no head, the breath of its mouth had a foul odor. Its body was one rod (16.5ft [5m]) long and one rod wide. It had no voice.' On hearing of the event, the pharaoh meditated on it, but after some days 'these things became more numerous in the sky than ever. They shone more in the sky than the brightness of the sun, and extended to the limits of the four supports of the heavens.... The army of the pharaoh looked on with him in their midst. It was after supper. Thereupon, these fire circles ascended higher in the sky toward the south....'

ASSESSMENT

The circular appearance of the objects, their peculiar smell, and their silence are all paralleled in modern UFO reports. However, there are striking similarities between this account and the vision of Ezekiel (see below): the Vatican cannot trace the Tulli manuscript and suspects it was a fake.

UFOS IN THE BIBLE

Visions of other realities

TYPE: **Hypothetical daylight disk and close encounters**
PLACE: **Middle East**
DATE: **14th to 6th century Before the Common Era**

BACKGROUND

Several passages in the Bible, particularly the Old Testament, have been seized on by some ufologists to support the theory that they are descriptions of sightings of or encounters with UFOs. Such interpretations, however, are a minority view.

THE EVENTS

- *Book of Exodus* – Scholars date the Exodus at about the 14th century BCE. In *Exodus* Chapter 13, verses 21-22, as Moses leads the children of Israel out of Egypt toward Mount Sinai and the Promised Land, '...the Lord went before them by day in a pillar of a cloud, to lead them the way; and by night in a pillar of fire, to give them light; to go by day and night.' This, according to Brinsley le Poer Trench, is 'a wonderful description of a modern flying saucer.'

- *Second Book of Kings* – In Chapter 2, the prophet Elijah – who lived around 900 BCE – crosses the River Jordan with his son Elisha; in verse 11, 'it came to pass, as they still went on, and talked, that, behold, there appeared a chariot of fire, and horses of fire, and parted them both asunder; and Elijah went up by a whirlwind into heaven.' This is seen by some commentators as a description of the prophet being taken aboard a flying saucer.

- *Book of Ezekiel* – This Hebrew prophet was a captive of Nebuchadnezzar, King of Babylon, and was transported to Mesopotamia (modern Iraq) in 597 BCE. On four occasions he had visions that some writers think were of extra-terrestrial spaceships. These are recounted in Chapters 1, 8, 10, and 43. The first description reads in part as follows: 'A whirlwind came out of the north, a great cloud, and a fire infolding itself, and a brightness was about it, and out of the midst thereof as the color of amber, out of the midst of the fire.' From this, Joseph F. Blumrich, a senior executive at NASA's Marshall Spaceflight Center, reconstructed the 'spacecraft' Ezekiel saw: according to Blumrich, it was an elaborate device like a quadruple helicopter.

ASSESSMENT

Of the pillars of cloud and fire in *Exodus*, Ronald Story notes that the Bible says that, when the Hebrews arrived at Mt. Sinai, they found it 'altogether in a smoke, because the Lord descended upon it in fire... and the whole mount quaked greatly' – which Story considers more likely to be a volcano than a UFO.

Elijah's translation to heaven by fiery chariot is, of course, purely symbolic. Many critics have pointed out that even before Ezekiel begins his account of the 'UFO' he specifically states that 'the heavens were opened, and I saw visions of God.' In short, Ezekiel is describing mystical revelations, not material objects.

THE EMPEROR'S EXPERIENCE

UFOs aid a mighty king of the ancient world

TYPE: **Daylight disk**
PLACE: **Jaxartes River, India;**
       Tyre, Phoenicia
DATE: **329 BCE and 322 BCE**

BACKGROUND

Alexander (born 356 BCE), son of King Philip of Macedonia, built a gigantic empire throughout the Mediterranean and as far east as India between 336 and his death in 323 BCE. He was an explorer as much as a general; his conquests enormously increased the influence of Greek ideas on the ancient world.

THE EVENTS

- In 329 BCE, while Alexander and his army were crossing the river Jaxartes into India, two 'shining silver shields' dived repeatedly from the sky onto the military columns, causing soldiers, elephants and horses to disperse.
- In 322 BCE, Alexander was besieging Tyre, a city in Phoenicia (modern Lebanon). Soldiers on both sides watched in astonishment as a large 'flying shield', moving in a triangular formation with four smaller 'shields', circled over the embattled city. Suddenly the largest UFO shot a beam of light at the city wall in front of the army, and drove a hole right through it. Further beams were fired from the UFO and these shattered towers and other defenses of the citadel. Alexander's troops quickly took advantage of the situation and poured into the city, and the UFOs remained overhead until the army had fully secured the town. The UFOs then took off together and disappeared.

ASSESSMENT

These reports may be the typical stuff of legend – in which various supernatural phenomena aid a great general to victory or, by harassing his army, serve to show how great were the odds he overcame. It is impossible to tell, 23 centuries after the events, how true these reports are.

THE SIRIUS MYSTERY

The Dogon tribe of Mali and visitors from the Dog Star

TYPE: **Close encounter of the**
       third kind
PLACE: **Mali, Africa**
DATE: **200 BCE**

BACKGROUND

In 1976, Robert Temple published *The Sirius Mystery*, the result of his researches into the beliefs of the Dogon people who

live on the Bandiagara plateau, about 300 miles (500km) south of Timbuktu, Mali. The Dogon believe that they received their culture from the Nommo, an amphibious race of space beings who came from the star system Sirius, 8.7 light years from our Sun.

THE EVENTS

In 1946, French anthropologist Marcel Griaule was initiated into the secrets of the ancient Dogon religion. Central to it is the belief that Sirius, the Dog Star, has an invisible companion star, many times denser than Earth, that travels in an elliptical orbit around Sirius once every 50 Earth years. The existence of this companion, an enormously dense 'white dwarf' known as Sirius B, was first suspected by astronomers only in the 1830s, and first seen through a telescope in 1862. It was not until 1926 – just five years before Griaule arrived in Mali – that its superdense nature was revealed. The French anthropologist was certain that the Dogon already knew the details of Sirius B when he arrived among them. To him and to Temple there appeared to be no way in which the Dogon tribesmen could have discovered these things except in the way they claimed – from the Nommo, who arrived on Earth in 'arks' centuries before.

ASSESSMENT

Dogon knowledge of the Sirius system is not as accurate as Temple claims. They actually say that Sirius B orbits Sirius A

A startling hybrid of female human and giant bird, from Indian folklore. Such creatures appear in the myths and legends of every continent, but in Hindu tradition they exist on numerous levels of 'higher dimensions'. Many UFO reports today also tell of human crossbreeding with alien beings, and hint that the ufonauts originate from beyond the known dimensions of our Universe.

once every 60 years, not 50, and astronomers have found no evidence for the Dogon belief that a third star, as well as several planets, also revolve around Sirius A. Temple's reproduction of a sand drawing of Sirius B in orbit is a partly blanked-out rendition of 'the egg of the world' that in the original contains eight more symbolic worlds, such as 'The Sun of Women'. The Dogon have been exposed to Western education since 1907, and Timbuktu has an Islamic university – where astronomy has been taught since the 16th century. The tribe is not a collection of primitive savages, but a sophisticated people who took rapidly to Western-style education. They would have had no difficulty in incorporating modern knowledge into their established religion, especially as the new information strengthened their existing belief that the gods came from Sirius.

REPORTS FROM ROMAN TIMES

Classical writers record strange aerial phenomena

TYPE: **Daylight disk, lights in the sky**
PLACE: **Italy**
DATE: **216-66 BCE**

BACKGROUND

A number of Roman writers noted visitations by what seem today to be UFOs: a selection of these accounts follows.

THE EVENTS

• Julius Obsequens, a pagan Roman of the 4th century of the Common Era, recorded in his work *Prodigia* that in 216 BCE, 'things like ships were seen in the sky' over Italy. The same phenomenon then reappeared over Rome in the following year, and it was seen again over the town of Lanupium (16 miles [25km] from Rome) in 170 BCE, according to a 16th-century German account.

• Livy (respected Roman historian Titus Livius, 59 BCE-17 CE) described a reported sighting in 213 BCE at Hadria, in the Gulf of Venice, Italy, in which what looked like an altar in the sky was surrounded by 'the strange spectacle of men in white clothing.'

• Julius Obsequens noted that in 203 BCE, 'At Setie (about 50 miles [80km] from Rome), a dazzling light like a torch was seen, going east to west in the sky' and that it was accompanied by another object. He also recorded that:

• In 90 BCE, 'In the territory of Spoletum, a globe of fire, golden in color, fell to the Earth from the sky, was seen to gyrate... became greater in size, was seen to rise from the Earth, was borne east, and obscured the disk of the sun with its magnitude'.

• Pliny the Elder (23-79 CE) refers to 'gleaming beams in the sky' in his *Historia Naturalis*, and tells how in 66 BCE a 'spark' fell from a star to Earth, became as large as the Moon, and then, shrinking in size, returned to the sky.

• In his *Historia Naturalis*, Pliny asserts: 'A light from the sky by night, the phenomenon usually called "night suns", was seen in the consulship of Gaius Caecilius and Gnaeus Papirius and often on other occasions causing apparent daylight in the night. In the consulship of Lucius Valerius and Gaius Marius a burning shield scattering sparks ran across the sky at sunset from east to west.'

ASSESSMENT

There are many more such descriptions of sightings in Roman times, and it has to be admitted that many of them are undoubtedly nothing more than awed accounts of normal astronomical events such as fireballs and comets. But no matter how skeptical one may be in response to such anecdotal evidence, it still remains very difficult to disregard the extraordinary 'ships', the 'altar' or the objects that fell to earth and rose again and dismiss them all as the fantasies of an ancient people. The words 'usually called'

A contemporary woodcut by Hans Glaser of the 'very frightful spectacle' seen in the morning sky over Nuremberg, Germany, on 4 April 1561.

in the last passage of Pliny are particularly fascinating. This may mean either that such celestial phenomena occurred frequently during the period, or that the idea was at least well enough known to have a name that was common parlance in Roman civilization.

MYSTERIES FROM MEDIEVAL EUROPE

One thousand years of UFO sightings

TYPE: **Daylight disk, lights in the sky, close encounters**
PLACE: **Europe**
DATE: **5th to 16th century CE**

BACKGROUND

Throughout the medieval period, the literature of all the countries of Europe abounds in UFO reports. Most reflect the prevailing notions of the day and Christian imagery is prevalent: medieval UFOs often appear as crosses in the sky (and sometimes still do: see Chapter Four), or seem to be dragons.

THE EVENTS

- Conrad Wolffart, known as Lycosthenes, a professor at the University of Basel, Switzerland, from 1539, recorded that in 457 CE, over Brittany in northern France, 'a blazing thing like a globe was seen in the sky. Its size was immense, and on its beams hung a ball of fire like a dragon out of whose mouth proceeded two beams, one of which stretched beyond France, and the other reached toward Ireland, and ended in fire, like rays.'
- St Gregory, Bishop of Tours in France, relates in his *Historia Francorum* ('History of the Franks'), how in 584 CE 'there appeared in the sky brilliant rays of light which seemed to cross and collide with one another,' while in the following year, 'in the month of September, certain people saw signs, that is to say rays or domes such as are customarily seen... to race across the sky.' Elsewhere, St Gregory describes 'golden globes' that, on several different occasions, were seen

flashing at enormous speeds across the skies of France.

- In 793, the *Anglo-Saxon Chronicle* reported: 'In this year terrible portents appeared in Northumbria, and miserably afflicted the inhabitants; these were exceptional flashes of lightning, and fiery dragons were seen flying through the air.' These events were also recorded by Roger of Wendover, who wrote: 'Fiery dragons in the sky alarmed the wretched nation of the English.'
- Wolffart noted that in Switzerland in 1104, 'Burning torches, fiery darts, flying fire were often seen in the air this year. And there were, near stars, what looked like swarms of butterflies and little fiery worms of strange kind. They flew in the air and took away the light of the Sun as if they had been clouds.'
- In England in 1113, a group of churchmen from Laon in France were going from town to town in Wessex (south-west England), bearing with them relics of the Virgin Mary, which they used to perform miracles of healing. At the coastal town of Christchurch, Hampshire, they were astonished to see a dragon come up out of the sea, 'breathing fire out of its nostrils.' (Reports of UFOs coming up out of the sea form a virtual subsection of modern ufology.)
- The 12th-century chronicler Ralph Niger recounts that on 9 March 1170, at St Ostwyth in Essex, south-east England, 'a wonderfully large dragon was seen, borne up from the Earth through the air. The air was kindled into fire by its motion and burnt a house, reducing it and its outbuildings to ashes.'
- During a Sunday mass at Gravesend, Kent, England in 1211, it is said that the congregation saw an anchor descend and catch on a tombstone in the churchyard. The churchgoers rushed outside to see a strange 'ship' in the sky, with people on board. One occupant of the vessel leaped over the

side, but did not fall: 'as if swimming in water' he made his way through the air toward the anchor. The people on the ground tried to capture him. The man then 'hurried up to the ship' – presumably still 'swimming'. His companions cut the anchor rope, and the ship then 'sailed out of sight.' The local blacksmith made ornaments from the abandoned anchor to decorate the church lectern.

- In his *Historia Anglorum* ('History Of The English'), the English chronicler Matthew of Paris tells how at sunset on 24 July 1239, 'a great star like a torch appeared' over Hereford and Worcester (western English cities near the border with Wales) and 'rose in the south and climbed the sky giving out a great light. It was shaped like a great head, the front part was sparkling and the back part gave out smoke and flashes.' And, he noted, 'It turned toward the north... not quickly, nor, indeed, with speed, but exactly as if it wished to ascend to a place in the air.'
- Matthew of Paris also recorded that over St Albans in southern England, at midnight on 1 January 1254, 'in serene sky and clear air, with stars shining and the Moon eight days old, there suddenly appeared in the sky a kind of large ship elegantly shaped, well equipped and of marvelous color.'
- Martin Cromer's *History of Poland* records the story that on 6 December 1269, 'at twilight, a strange brightness shaped like a cross gave light from high in the air and shone down on the city of Cracow.'
- At Byland Abbey, Yorkshire, England, one day in 1290 the abbot and monks saw 'a large round silvery thing' fly over; it 'excited the greatest terror'. The story (including the 'original' Latin) was a hoax by two schoolboys in a letter to the London *Times* in 1953.
- Henry Knighton's *Continuation of the Chronicle of Leicester* says that in November and December 1388, 'a fire in the sky, like a burning and revolving wheel, or round barrel of flame,

emitting fire from above, and others in the shape of a long fiery beam, were seen through a great deal of the winter in the county of Leicester, and also in the county of Northampton.'
- The same source notes that in the following year (1389), in the city of Leicester, 'A flying dragon was seen in April in many places.'
- In his memoirs, the French Duke of Bourgogne recalled that on 1 November 1461 an object appeared in the night sky that was 'as long and wide as a half-moon; it hung stationary for about a quarter of an hour, clearly visible, then suddenly... spiraled, twisted and turned like a spring and rose into the heavens.'
- In 1528, Wolffart reports, while Utrecht, Holland, was under siege, 'a strange and cruel sight was seen in the sky' – the form of a Burgundian cross, directly over the city, 'yellow in color, and fearful to behold.'
- In the morning of 4 April 1561, blue, black and blood-red balls, along with disks and blood-red crosses that emerged from two huge black cylinders, battled together in the skies over Nuremberg, Germany. To judge from the contemporary woodcut made by Hans Glaser, some of the spheres crashed on the ground outside the city.
- There seems to have been a similar aerial conflict a little more than five years later in the skies over Basel, Switzerland, between black spheres that appeared at sunrise: 'Many became red and fiery, ending by being consumed and vanishing,' wrote Samuel Coccius, the 'student in sacred writings and the liberal arts' who reported the weird events of 7 August 1566 in the city's gazette.
- In *Histoires Prodigieuses* (1594), Pierre Boaistuau records the story that at 7:00am on 5 December 1577, a few miles outside Tübingen, Germany, local people witnessed strangely colored, 'fiery' clouds that seemed to gather around the sun. 'Out of these clouds [came] forth reverberations resembling

large, tall and wide hats, and the Earth showed itself yellow and bloody, and seemed to be covered with hats... which appeared in various colors such as red, blue, green, and most of them were black.'

ASSESSMENT

St Gregory wrote seven volumes concerning miracles and – in keeping with his devout Christianity – seems to have been in little doubt that the 'UFOs' he records were heavenly signs. As so often, the interpretation of the events fitted the preconceptions of the chronicler.

In contrast, the *Anglo-Saxon Chronicle* was written by secular scribes, and their report reflects the still thickly pagan atmosphere of 8th-century England. What today would be called a UFO or even a 'flying saucer' was to them a dragon. It flew in the air, it lit up the sky, and it was fearsome and inherently inexplicable; it was a dragon because that was the nearest thing in human knowledge to match what people actually saw. And whatever form UFOs take, they are always perceived as being on the very edge of knowledge in any particular era, and exhibit some alluring extras that we can imagine but cannot yet achieve – such as faster-than-light travel today, or heavier-than-air flight in the Middle Ages.

British researcher Paul Devereux has suggested that dragon sightings show a close correlation with ancient religious sites, and that these in turn were often built where unusual geological formations caused anomalous lightforms to emerge into the atmosphere. These 'earthlights' are certainly UFOs, if not off-world or alien in kind, for scientists understand almost nothing about them. It is certainly possible that some such phenomena were responsible for the aerial 'battles' at Basel and Nuremberg, and for the bizarre 'hats' of Tübingen.

Perhaps the most intriguing of these medieval accounts are those featuring ships in the sky. According to Agobard, Bishop of Lyons, France, from 816 CE, the belief in 'a certain region, which they call Magonia, whence ships sail in the clouds' was so strong that fairs were known to exhibit people who were said to have fallen from the Magonian sky-ships. It is possible that the witnesses saw strange, graphic cloud formations and, in some cases, were so disturbed by the sight that an 'Oz factor' (see Glossary) created the subjective impression of a close encounter. Some ufologists have argued that this in itself is a psychic means used by aliens to communicate with humanity. Other interpretations of the available facts include the possibility that the witnesses were deluded or else that they simply made it all up to impress and draw attention to themselves. And yet there remain too many variables, too many occurrences and sightings that cannot be fully explained by scientists or skeptics, for all these events to be dismissed out of hand or to be rationalized

away with a single blanket interpretation. Whether all or any of them were UFOs or the manifestation of an earthlight or some other unexplained earthly phenomenon must remain a matter of conjecture.

UNREASONABLE EVENTS IN THE AGE OF REASON

A strange 'meteor' in the 18th century

TYPE: **Light in the sky**
PLACE: **England, Ireland, Romania**
DATE: **9-10 December 1731**

BACKGROUND

In the 18th century, observers (including the renowned astronomer Edmund

Halley) continued to note a host of bizarre aerial phenomena. But now the tone of the reports changed yet again: as the 'Age of Reason' dawned in the late 17th century and rigorous scientific observation became the order of the day, so different explanations for sightings of what we would now call UFOs begin to creep in to the accounts.

THE EVENTS

● At Sheffield, England, on 9 December 1731, at about 5:00pm, Thomas Short saw what he later described as 'a dark red cloud, below which was a luminous body which emitted intense beams of light. The light beams moved slowly for a while, then stopped. Suddenly it became so hot that I could take off my shirt even though I was out of doors [this in the dead of winter!]. This meteor was observed over Kilkenny,

Ireland, where it seemed like a great ball of fire. It was reported that it shook the entire island and that the whole sky seemed to burst into flames.'

- The next afternoon, local manuscript records show, this 'meteor' appeared over Romania: '...there appeared in the west a great sign in the sky, blood-red and very large. It stayed in place for two hours, separated into two parts which then rejoined, and the object disappeared towards the west.'

ASSESSMENT

To the Romanian mind of the time, this was 'a sign'; to the cultured gentleman of Augustan England – in the so-called 'Age of Reason' when virtually any anomalous item in the sky tended to be explained away with an off-the-peg rationale – it was a 'meteor'. But if it was a meteor it was a very strange one, because it remained stationary for two hours.

THE FIRST 'FLYING SAUCER'

John Martin coins a phrase

TYPE: **Daylight disk**
PLACE: **Denison, Texas, USA**
DATE: **2 January 1878**

BACKGROUND

The term 'flying saucer' was brought into widespread popular usage by a journalist covering Kenneth Arnold's sighting of nine flying disks in June 1947. But farmer John Martin had used the same term 70 years earlier to describe what he saw on a hunting expedition in rural Texas .

THE EVENTS

On 25 January 1878, the *Denison Daily News* ran this account under the headline

Citizens of Basel, Switzerland, gape in astonishment at large black globes infesting the sky over their city on 7 August 1566.

'A STRANGE PHENOMENON':

'Mr John Martin, a farmer who lives some six miles north of this city, while out hunting, had his attention directed to a dark object high in the northern sky.

'The peculiar shape and the velocity with which the object seemed to approach, riveted his attention, and he strained his eyes to discover its character. When first noticed it appeared to be about the size of an orange, after which it continued to grow in size.

'After gazing at it for some time, Mr Martin became blind from long looking and left off viewing to rest his eyes. On resuming his view, the object was almost overhead and had increased considerably in size and appeared to be going through space at a wonderful speed. When directly over him, the object was the size of a large saucer and... at a great height.'

ASSESSMENT

Strikingly, this UFO is dark – not silvery, or reflective, or a mysterious light. If Martin is reported accurately, he must have seen a solid object against the sky, with the light behind it.

THE FUTURE KING'S UFO

Two British princes see a bizarre light

TYPE: **Light in the sky**
PLACE: **At sea between Melbourne and Sydney, Australia**
DATE: **11 June 1881**

BACKGROUND

In 1881, the Princes Albert Victor and George, sons of the then Prince of Wales (later King Edward VII) were cruising on the ship *Bacchante* in Australian waters.

THE EVENTS

As the Princes described the event in their book *The Cruise of The Bacchante*, they were alerted to a peculiar sight in

the air by the lookout at about 4:00am on 11 June 1881. The sailor described it as 'a strange light, as if of a phantom vessel all aglow.' Twelve other members of the crew of the *Bacchante* also witnessed it.

ASSESSMENT

We can assume the 'phantom vessel' was not a ship. It may have been some unusual natural phenomenon, although this seems unlikely in cold water in the Antipodean winter. In his commentary, Charles Fort notes: 'Whether there be relation, or not, five hours later, the lookout fell from a crosstree and was killed.'

THE ICEMEN'S REPORT

A hint of UFOs to come

TYPE: **Cylindrical Ufo**
PLACE: **Crawfordsville, Indiana, USA**
DATE: **5 September 1891**

BACKGROUND

As reported in the *Brooklyn Eagle* newspaper of 10 September 1891, two icemen were working outside in Crawfordsville at about 2:00am five nights previously, when a bizarre object sailed overhead.

THE EVENTS

The icemen described the UFO as a 'seemingly headless monster', although there is no reason to believe that it was an animal of any kind. It was about 20ft (6m) long, and 8ft (2.5m) wide, moving in the sky toward the two men, and 'seemingly propelled by fin-like attachments.' The men moved, and the UFO flew off. The noise awoke Methodist pastor G.W. Switzer, who saw it circling in the sky.

ASSESSMENT

Charles Fort tracked the Rev. Switzer down in Michigan, but never got his account of the sighting. The UFO resembles phantom airships that plagued the Mid-West five years later – as described in the next chapter.

A STREET & SMITH PUBLICATION

ASTOUNDING

STORIES

JUNE
20¢

CONTENTS
COPYRIGHTED
1935

THE INVADERS
by
DON A. STUART

ALAS,
ALL THINKING
by
HARRY BATES

CHAPTER 2

From outer space?

THE FIRST 50 YEARS OF ALIEN ENCOUNTERS

As society has changed, so has the appearance of UFOs. Where a medieval monk, confronted by strange aerial phenomena, saw them as signs, wonders, dragons or the work of Satan, the rational man of the 18th or 19th century saw an innocuous material object – which he called a meteor.

Towards the end of the 19th century, the nature of that 'material object' altered yet again. The Victorian era witnessed astonishing accomplishments in engineering, especially in transport – from the spread of railways around the globe and the launch of ocean-going iron steamships, to the production of the first automobiles. But if land and sea had been conquered, the air had not. Balloons could rise from the ground, but they could not undertake predictable journeys. Steerable ('dirigible') airships seemed the most promising way to achieve sustained,

Extra-terrestrial aliens make a physical examination of humans. Such events form the backbone of accounts of alleged alien abductions that have surfaced in ever-increasing numbers since the late Seventies. Yet this edition of *Astounding Stories* was published in 1935, and the story made no pretense to be true – a fact that raises many questions about the ultimate source of many of the more recent abduction claims.

controled flight, but the problem was how to power them. It was not until light, compact internal combustion engines appeared in the late 1890s that dirigible airships became practicable.

By then, dirigibles had been discussed everywhere – for the idea of manned flight was more than the next great advance for engineering to achieve. It was also a matter for wonder – a matter of mastering nature, of realizing a dream at least as old as Ancient Greece. So when, in November 1896, the citizens of Sacramento, California, saw a light moving sedately through the night sky, apparently borne on a vast, cigar-shaped craft, the thing was at once reckoned to be an airship. Even when, among the dozens of visits of these monstrous aerial vessels that followed, some of their occupants claimed to be from Mars, they were still referred to as airships – not spacecraft.

AHEAD OF THEIR TIME

Nonetheless, this wave of sightings fundamentally altered the way in which people thought about unidentified aerial objects. They were no longer as-yet-unexplained natural objects, but the product of a secret technology – one that was clearly superior to anything publicly known or officially admitted. Although not all UFOs in their various disguises were yet seen as extra-terrestrial craft, the two notions of superior technology and strange, sentient visitors in the skies first came together in the momentous sightings of 1896-97.

They have been inextricably intertwined ever since.

As the 20th century progressed, so did the technology that UFOs apparently employed. Curiously, this always seemed to be one jump ahead of current Earthly achievements. From about 1910 to the mid-Thirties, mystery aircraft filled the sky. In the Forties, there were 'ghost rockets', before the flying disks made their dramatic impact on the public consciousness when reports of Kenneth Arnold's sighting took the media by storm in 1947 – by which time the context had changed yet again. The disks' unusual shape and astonishing maneuvers fused with a popular belief (and hope) that space travel was just within humanity's reach, and produced the assumption that these were spacecraft.

In among the pre-1947 reports, however, were some of UFOs that, as it were, got away. These were the disk-shaped 'flying saucers' that did not go in contemporary garb as dragons, meteors, airships, or whatever, and were seen for what they were – or at least as we might see them today. Yet, nearly a century after achieving controled flight, human ingenuity has still not managed to make a disk airworthy, let alone make one perform the aerobatics typical of a UFO.

These two facts continue to feed the tenacious belief – or hope, or fear – that UFOs are extra-terrestrial in origin. They seem to have been with us for a very long time, which would indicate that the aliens'

It is noteworthy that the sightings increased in the 10 days before Arnold's historic flight, and that his were by no means the only UFOs seen over Washington State on 24 July. It is as if the UFO phenomenon was like a secretly rising river, stretching the dam of public awareness ever nearer to breaking point. Kenneth Arnold's report added the final, irresistible few pounds of pressure, and the dam burst.

But what the range of cases described here also shows is that the modern UFO phenomenon had been 50 years in the making.

GIANT PHANTOMS

The mystery airship wave of 1896-97

TYPE: **Close encounters of the first, second and third kind**
PLACE: **USA**
DATE: **17 November 1896- 6 May 1897**

BACKGROUND

The wave of sightings of Winter 1896 to Spring 1897 was preceded by a number of incidents involving what the witnesses believed to be hot-air balloons but in fact turned out to be rather more mysterious (see Chapter One). In July 1896, there were similar incidents in Canada. On 1 July, citizens of Winnipeg, Manitoba, reported sighting what they presumed was the balloon of Saloman A. Andrée, who was known to be planning a flight across the North Pole from Spitsbergen, Norway, to Canada. Two days later a black balloon was spotted over Hazelton, British Columbia, Canada at 7:35pm; at about the same time of day, 500 miles (800km) to the north, Indians reported

The very first mystery airship of the wave of 1896-97, as depicted by an artist for the San Francisco *Call* in November 1896.

technology is very old. And we can't reproduce it – which serves to reinforce further the impression that it is far in advance of our own.

If UFOs are controled by an alien intelligence, and are technological in nature, then they are extraordinary, capable of defying the known laws of physics. But that does not mean that UFOs are extra-terrestrial. Indeed, the striking physical likeness of reported alien biology to our own would support the hardly less remarkable notion that we share our planet with another highly intelligent life-form – albeit an elusive, enigmatic one.

Whatever they are, UFOs have come in clever disguises: just far enough within the bounds of human understanding, and carefully matched to the mood of the times, to be acceptable, if strange – and just far enough beyond normality to preclude the possibility of direct investigation or interference.

1947 – YEAR ZERO

Although naked, undisguised flying disks, spheres, triangles and 'cigars' were reported from time to time down the centuries, Kenneth Arnold's seminal sighting of July 1947 was by no means the first of that year. Arnold's 'flying saucers' certainly captured the imagination of the world, but it is clear that UFOs had, apparently permanently, adopted their characteristically modern guise at least three months earlier.

what looked like a lighted balloon over the Blackwater Lake, North-West Territory. But Saloman A. Andrée made no flights in 1896, and no balloon launches were reported at around the time of these sightings.

THE EVENTS

On 17 November 1896, between 6:00 and 7:00pm, hundreds of people reportedly saw an 'electric arc lamp' pass over Sacramento, California. A huge dark shape loomed behind it. Some witnesses heard music coming from it, others heard a voice say, 'Well, we ought to get to San Francisco by tomorrow noon.' During the month further reports of this machine poured in from all over California. From March 1897, the American Great Lakes states, the Midwest and Texas were plagued by reports of lights in the sky, some colored, some like searchlights, others shaped like balls or wheels, that were attached to craft – which were at once dubbed airships ranging in size from 12ft to 70ft (3.5-20m) long, shaped variously like a cigar, an egg, or a barrel, and apparently powered by propellers. Estimated speeds ranged from 5mph to 200mph (8-320km/h). Some of these objects made hissing or humming noises, others were entirely silent.

Among the more outlandish tales connected with the airship wave were those from Sioux, Iowa, where at the end of March 1897 Robert Hibbard maintained his trousers were caught by the anchor of one of the craft; Alexander Hamilton's claim that one of his heifers was stolen from his farm near Vernon, Kansas, on 28 April; and the alleged destruction of a windmill by a crashing airship – whose dead pilot was deemed to be a Martian – at Aurora, Texas, on 17 April. There was also a handful of mysterious persons who claimed to attorneys and reporters that they had invented the airship(s) – although none of them ever filed a patent.

The final report came from two peace officers from Garland County, Arkansas, who published an affidavit in which they testified that they had come across a landed airship on 6 May, and that they heard its occupants explain that they were en route to Nashville, Tennessee, 'after thoroughly seeing the country.'

ASSESSMENT

It was not until 1900 that a dirigible first flew, and that was in Germany. The first dirigible to fly in the United States was Thomas Baldwin's *California Arrow*, which took off from Oakland, San Francisco, California, in 1904. Research by Jerome Clark, Bob Rickard and others has proven that many of the printed airship reports were the work of humorous reporters maintaining a long tradition of tall tales in local newspapers. Telegraph operators, whiling away the hours between genuine messages, may have originated many reports. Some were straightforward hoaxes. But the wave made a crucial contribution to the mythology and assumptions surrounding UFOs and indicates the part that suggestibility can sometimes play in UFO witnesses' reports.

FROM PARIS TO TEXAS

Object of undisguised strangeness

TYPE: **Lights in the sky, daylight disk**
PLACE: **South-western states, USA, and various locations, France**
DATE: **1898 and 1899**

BACKGROUND

These sightings from 1888 and 1899 represent a selection of UFOs that did not take the form of futuristic aircraft, and were seen in widely spread locations.

THE EVENTS

- 4 September 1898 – Lille, France: An astronomer saw through his telescope a rectangular object with a violet colored band on one side, the rest

being striped red and black. It was not in the position of any known planet. It remained stationary for 10 minutes, then 'cast out sparks and disappeared.'

- 2 March 1899 – El Paso, Texas: A luminous object was seen in daylight from 10:00am to 4:00pm; Venus was two months past its secondary phase of maximum brilliance.

- 8 March 1899 – Prescott, Arizona: Dr Warren E. Day observed a luminous object that 'travelled with the Moon all day' until 2:00pm. A similar object had been observed the day before from Tonto, Arizona.

- 28 October 1899 – Luzarches, France: At 4:50pm, M. A. Garry observed a round luminous object rise above the horizon and shrink in size as it moved into the distance over 15 minutes.

- 15 November 1899 – Dourite, Dordogne, France: An object 'like an enormous star' was seen from 7:00pm, 'at times white, then red, and sometimes blue... moving like a kite' in the southerly sky.

ASSESSMENT

The reports were made by astronomers and other trained and experienced sky-watchers, and reported in academic or professional journals. They do appear to represent genuine anomalies.

NAKED LIGHTS

The first sightings of the 20th century

TYPE: **Lights in the sky**
PLACE: **England, Denmark, France, USA, Wales**
DATE: **May 1902-July 1908**

BACKGROUND

Reactions to the sightings of the early part of the century were an interesting mix of dismissal (the planet Venus, then as now, took much of the blame) and mild paranoia. Another accusation, also to become a litany in the history of UFOs, was that secret weapons were being tested. In the prelude to World War I, an arms race was under way between the British and German empires, and the Russo-Japanese war of 1905 raised the specter of what was demonized as the 'yellow peril' in the USA.

THE EVENTS

- 10 May 1902 – Devon, England: A Colonel Markwick reported a sighting of numerous 'highly colored objects like little suns or toy balloons.'
- 9 August, 1903 – Argenteuil, France: At 11:00pm, M. Desmoulins and four others saw a red object travel over 4 miles (6km) in 20 minutes. Seen through field glasses, the object did not appear to be a balloon.
- 28 February 1904 – California, USA: Lt. Frank H. Schofield and three others, aboard the USS *Supply* off the California coast, saw three 'meteors' at 6:10am, 'traveling in echelon' toward the south-east. The largest object was egg-shaped, and 'had an apparent area of about six suns.' The formation came below the clouds, changed direction and soared out of sight. (Schofield rose to become Commander in Chief of the US Pacific fleet in the Thirties.)
- 29 March 1905 – Cardiff, Wales: Witnesses reported 'an appearance like a vertical beam of light, which was not due to a searchlight, or any such cause.'
- 2 April 1905 – Cherbourg, France: First sighting of an oval, reddish-colored object that hung in the sky over this northern French port until 11 April. It was not in the position of the planet Venus, and was not reported from other towns. At midnight on 9 April a similar object was seen for several minutes over Tunis, North Africa. Some ascribed the Cherbourg sighting to a British torpedo boat experimenting with signal lights attached to a balloon.
- 2 August 1905 – Silshee, California, USA: At 1:30am, J.A. Jackson noticed a bright light heading toward him in the sky. The light was also seen by the postmaster at the nearby town of

Imperial. As the light neared him, Jackson made out the form of an 'airship' (although it had no gas balloon), showing several lights and apparently propelled by flapping wings.
- 2 September 1905 – Llangollen, Wales: Several witnesses saw a dark object in the sky that, observed through binoculars, had short wings and legs, and moved 'casually inclining sideways.' It reminded some witnesses of 'a huge winged pig, with webbed feet.'
- 28 January 1908 – Norfolk, England: Night workers at the Norwich Transportation Company saw a 'dark, globular object, with a structure of some kind upon the side of it, traveling at a great pace.' The object was 'too large for a kite, and… it was traveling against the wind.'
- 1 February 1908 – near Tacoma, Washington, USA: Between 7:00 and 9:00pm on this and the following night, a reddish cigar-shaped object 'two or three times as bright as Jupiter' flew over Kent, Washington; the same week, colored lights and a rocket were seen 'at high altitudes'. Some newspapers proposed that a Japanese spy device was involved.
- June and July 1908 – Denmark: Many reported sightings of an 'airship' – 'an object with lights and wings' – were made in the skies over Denmark. Some commentators held that the object had been launched by British warships which were known to have been on exercise at the time in the North Sea.

The forest in Stony Tunguska canyon, still devastated in 1929 (when this picture was taken) from the explosion of a mysterious fireball there in June 1908. A number of ufologists have suggested that the impacting object was a manned spacecraft, but there is little objective evidence to support their case.

ASSESSMENT

These sightings cannot all have been misidentified astronomical objects. Many have the hallmarks of the modern UFO.

THE DESTRUCTION AT TUNGUSKA

Huge, mysterious object shatters the Siberian forest

TYPE: **Impact and explosion**
PLACE: **Stony Tunguska Valley, Siberia, Russia**
DATE: **30 June 1908**

BACKGROUND

The gigantic explosion at Tunguska has regularly featured in UFO literature, and

several bizarre explanations have been proposed for it.

THE EVENTS

Citizens of Vanavara saw and felt the heat from an enormous, blindingly bright, blue fireball streaking through the northern morning sky. Seconds later, a huge explosion came from the north-west, damaging buildings and knocking people flying. The object had detonated 40 miles (65km) away in the heavily wooded Stony Tunguska River valley, sending up a sinister mushroom-shaped cloud. The blast felled trees for up to 20 miles (32km) around and turned the forest into an inferno. The shock waves shook houses and knocked over animals as far as 400 miles (650km) away, and were powerful enough to circle the Earth twice. The dust from the explo-

sion created unusually bright nights and extraordinary colors in the skies of Europe and western Asia for days afterward. Around Tunguska, a black rain fell. In the 1960s scientists estimated the force of the blast at between 2 and 30 megatons – that is, between 10 and 1500 times more powerful than the nuclear bomb dropped on Hiroshima in 1945. Amazingly, no human beings died as a result of the explosion.

ASSESSMENT

A scientific expedition to the area in 1927 found the forest still devastated, but perfectly preserved at the center of the impact zone. The fireball had exploded above the ground. The sheer size of the explosion, the 'black rain' that fell afterward, and increased radioactivity in the

Tunguska valley led some to speculate that a nuclear-powered interplanetary spacecraft weighing 50,000 tonnes had come to grief three miles (5km) above Siberia in 1908. Others proposed that a miniature black hole had ripped into the Earth, but such an event would have caused an equally destructive 'exit wound'. Another hypothesis said that anti-matter had leaked into this Universe from another dimension.

The truth is probably more prosaic. The Tunguska explosion is entirely consistent with the impact of a carbonaceous chondrite (a type of fragile stony meteorite), as Soviet scientists showed in 1977. The comet would have shattered in mid-air from the force of its deceleration in the atmosphere. The apparently high radioactivity at Tunguska in 1908 is well within normal year-to-year fluctuations. The meteorite was probably a fragment, perhaps 100 yards (90m) across and weighing one million tonnes, from the comet Encke, which passed close to Earth on 30 June 1908.

BRITISH IMPERIAL SCARESHIPS

Mystery craft in the northern and southern hemispheres

TYPE: **Close encounters of the first, second and third kinds**
PLACE: **United Kingdom and New Zealand**
DATE: **March–May and July–August 1909**

BACKGROUND

The phantom airships of the closing years of the 19th century reappeared in 1909 in two entirely different parts of the world.

THE EVENTS

- In the UK, the first mystery airship – or 'scareship', as it has since become known – was seen in Peterborough,

the men 'jabbered furiously to each other in a strange lingo', leapt in the 'carriage' suspended from the craft and flew off toward Cardiff, showing lights. Residents there said that they saw an airship pass overhead at about the same time. Later, ground markings and papers that referred to airships and the German army were found at the site.

- In New Zealand, from mid-July, residents of the Blue Mountains, South Island, repeatedly saw an airship that 'did not appear to be very long but was very broad' flying in the daytime, as well as mysterious lights at night. On 6 August, 10 'hitherto skeptical' workmen saw a cigar-shaped airship showing a powerful headlight.

ASSESSMENT

Neither Britain nor New Zealand possessed an airship at this time. There were only three functioning Zeppelins in Germany, all at an experimental stage. Thus the sightings must either have been hallucinations or what we now call UFOs. There were similar reports at about this time from Gothenburg, Sweden, Reval, Russia and New England, USA. Whatever they were, the mystery airships became a worldwide phenomenon in 1909.

A contemporary artist's impression of the mystery airship reported by two Peterborough police officers, in widely separated parts of the city, on 23 March 1909. The sighting was the first of many in the British Isles that year. No entirely satisfactory explanation has ever been offered for this wave of UFO events.

Cambridgeshire, by two police officers in different parts of the city, at 5:10am on 23 March. A long oblong body with a light attached passed overhead at speed, making 'the steady buzz of a high power engine.' After a six-week long investigation, a Peterborough police spokesman claimed implausibly that the officers had seen an illuminated kite.

- The sightings began in earnest in early May, being reported at first from all over south-east England from Northampton, Northamptonshire to Southend, Essex. The furthest north they were seen in May was Hull, in Yorkshire. The furthest east was on the coast at Ipswich; the furthest west was Belfast, Ireland. There were numerous reports from widely separated locations on the same nights. Many of the craft reportedly carried out elaborate, high-speed maneuvers.
- The most bizarre event of the UK wave was the encounter with the two-man crew of a large airship by a Mr Lethbridge on Caerphilly Mountain, south Wales. The meeting occurred at about 11:00pm on 18 May, on the top of the mountain. On seeing Lethbridge

VISITING THE BIG APPLE

Long black object flies over Manhattan

TYPE: **Close encounters of the first kind**
PLACE: **Manhattan Island, New York, USA**
DATE: **30-31 August 1910**

BACKGROUND

In January 1910 there were several daylight sightings of mystery dirigibles over Chattanooga, Tennessee, and Huntsville, Alabama. The New York events involved a UFO that took on the shape of a winged aircraft.

THE EVENTS

A 'long black object' with red and green lights appeared low in the sky over Manhattan at about 8:45pm on 30 August, and passed over Madison Square and around the Metropolitan Life Insurance Company building. Hundreds watched as its 'vague bulk... took on the semblance of a biplane.' The craft circled the Metropolitan building, 'its outlines standing out clear in the lights from many windows.' The UFO flew toward the Flatiron building before returning for

The British Army's airship Beta made its maiden flight in 1910 – too late to be a suspect in the 1909 wave of sightings and, like its successors, too small to be a realistic explanation for any of the second British wave of 'scareships' of 1913.

another lap of Madison Square. It flew so low that it 'seemed to brush the tops of the trees.' Next night, it returned at 9:00pm and performed similar maneuvers. All over Manhattan, there were hundreds of witnesses to both episodes.

ASSESSMENT

In 1910 there were only 36 licensed pilots in the USA, and none of them was flying in New York on the nights in question. The description of the craft is unlike any plane known at that time. This would appear to be the first instance of that curious UFO-related phenomenon, the phantom aircraft, which have included 'Flying Boxcar'-type planes and the mysterious helicopters often associated with cattle mutilations. These craft are usually gray or black and unmarked, and the authorities invariably deny all knowledge of them.

THE UFOS OF ST CYRIL

Mystery object cruises down the Americas

TYPE: **Lights in the sky**
PLACE: **Central Canada, USA, Cape São Roque, Brazil**
DATE: **9 February 1913**

BACKGROUND

The UFOs in this event in Brazil have come to be known as the 'Cyrillids' because 9 February is the feast day of St Cyril of Alexandria.

THE EVENTS

A series of fiery red and orange lights was seen traveling slowly and at low altitude on a roughly north-west to south-east course, from central Canada, down the USA to Cape São Roque in eastern Brazil.

The lights maintained a constant formation throughout and flew parallel to the horizon across the evening sky.

ASSESSMENT

The behavior of these objects was quite unlike that of meteors. The most widely accepted explanation for the Cyrillids is that they were space debris that had been captured by the Earth's gravitational field and gradually burned up in the atmosphere. However, some ufologists have proposed that these were the same as the group of UFOs seen the following night from Toronto, Canada, maneuvering over Lake Ontario, and that they were an extra-terrestrial mission investigating the aftermath of the Tunguska explosion in Siberia. Few share this belief.

THE WILTSHIRE SHADOWS

Triangular objects and an invisible light

TYPE: **Daylight disk**
PLACE: **Chisbury, Wiltshire, England**
DATE: **8 April 1912**

BACKGROUND

Charles Tilden Smith reported the following case to the respected British science journal *Nature*.

THE EVENTS

For over half an hour Smith observed two fan-shaped or triangular 'heavy shadows' cast onto clouds overhead. The clouds were moving rapidly, but the shadows remained stationary in the sky. From time to time the unidentified apparitions varied in size. Smith concluded that two large unseen objects in the west were intercepting the Sun's rays.

ASSESSMENT

If the Sun had been the light source that the objects were intercepting, then the shadows should have moved higher on the clouds as the Sun declined in the sky. But they did not. Therefore there must have been a separate light (which Smith did not see) maintaining a constant position in the sky. The changes in size were probably caused by shadows falling at different angles on the cloud surfaces. Which does not explain the objects or the light source.

THE FINAL AIRSHIP SCARE

Sightings over Britain on the eve of war

TYPE: **Close encounters of the first kind**
PLACE: **United Kingdom, Belgium, Holland, France, Germany**
DATE: **October 1912–March 1913**

BACKGROUND

Political tensions in Europe immediately before the outbreak of World War I produced a rash of airship sightings over countries that felt threatened by German military might – and, eventually, even in Germany itself.

THE EVENTS

- The scare started with the sighting of a large, dark object making a strange buzzing sound that passed over Sheerness, Kent, on the evening of 12 October 1912. Nearby was the Eastchurch Naval Flying School. Reports of the incident led to a strengthening of air defenses.
- The British wave began in earnest on 4 January 1913, when three witnesses saw an airship, showing a light, approach from the sea at Dover, and fly north-east. It was traveling at high speed despite a strong west wind.
- On 17 January at 4:45pm, Captain L. Lindsay, Chief Constable of Glamorganshire, saw an airship flying over Cardiff, trailing 'a dense volume of smoke' and noted it was much bigger and faster than the locally-built Willows airship. Half an hour later Steven Morgan saw a similar ship, trailing smoke, over Merthyr, 30 miles (48km) away – a very high speed for airships of the era.
- In February there were numerous sightings in Yorkshire, and on the night of 21 February lights and engines were seen over Warwickshire and Norfolk.
- Belgium and Holland had their first airship sightings in February 1913 and in France, German airships were reputedly spying on the eastern border.
- On 4 March, sightings began in Germany. An airship visited Tarnowitz, Prussia, while at Lake Schwielow there was a foretaste of the 'crashed UFO'

syndrome, when a burning airship was seen to crash in the nearby forest – but, after extensive searches, no wreckage could be found.

ASSESSMENT

Many of the 1913 sightings may have been due to misidentifications fueled by fear of war. Others are less easily dismissed. The British cases cannot be attributed to the few known airships in the country at the time, and most Zeppelins were in regular commercial service and their where-abouts known. The reported speeds of the 1913 airships (60mph [100km/h]) are also far higher than those known to be operating. The true origins of the 1913 wave remain a mystery.

THE REGIMENT THAT VANISHED

Cloud-shaped UFO abducts a British unit at Gallipoli

TYPE: **Close encounters of the fourth kind**
PLACE: **Suvla bay, Gallipoli, Turkey**
DATE: **28 August 1915**

BACKGROUND

In one of the most famous and ill-starred actions of World War I, French, British, Australian and New Zealand troops first landed on the Gallipoli peninsula in April 1915, in an attempt to seize Turkish forts

overlooking the narrow Dardanelles entrance to the Black Sea. The mysterious events related below were first reported as late as 1965.

THE EVENTS

According to three eyewitnesses serving with the New Zealand Army, 28 August 1915 was clear and bright but for a group of clouds that, oddly, did not move despite a breeze of about 4-5mph (6-8km/h). One cloud – an 'absolutely dense, solid-looking structure' – seemed to be resting on the ground across a creek near Hill 60 on Suvla Plain. A battle was raging between Turkish and British troops for possession of the hill. The New Zealanders, whose post was on Rhododendron Spur, some 300ft (100m) above the hill, then observed the following:

'A British regiment, the First-Fourth Norfolk... marching up this sunken road or creek towards Hill 60. However, when they arrived at this cloud, they marched straight into it, with no hesitation, but no one ever came out to deploy and fight at Hill 60. About an hour later, after the last of the file had disappeared into it, this cloud very unobtrusively lifted off the ground and, like any cloud or fog would, rose slowly.... As soon as the singular cloud had risen to their level, they all

Troops go 'over the top' during the disastrous Gallipoli campaign of 1915. The disappearance of a Norfolk infantry unit's colonel, with 16 other officers and 250 men, during a battle in August 1915 has been promoted for years as a mass abduction by UFOs, but the grim truth is that at least half the missing men died in battle, and the rest were probably taken prisoner and shot in cold blood by their Turkish captors. The British, intent on fostering good relations with Turkey after the war, kept the soldiers' murder secret for many years – and so gave the UFO myth fertile ground in which to grow.

An artist's highly stylized impression of the vision of the Blessed Virgin Mary as allegedly seen by a crowd of 70,000 people at Fatima, Portugal, on 13 October 1917. Several commentators have noted the similarities between this event and some UFO sightings, and have further suggested that the two kinds of visionary experience may have a common origin.

Turkey never captured that regiment, nor made contact with it.'

ASSESSMENT

Records show that two of the three 'eyewitnesses' had been evacuated from Gallipoli by 28 August because of illness. The First-Fourth Norfolks was not a regiment but the First Battalion of the Fourth Norfolk Regiment. The unit did not disappear on that day or any other, but went on to fight with distinction in Gallipoli until the end of 1915, when it was evacuated. However, on 12 (not 28) August, the First Battalion of the Fifth Norfolk Regiment's Colonel, 16 officers and 250 men did vanish. They were in hot pursuit of the enemy when night fell; the next day, there was no trace of them. Sir Ian Hamilton, the commanding general, called the incident 'a very mysterious thing.' But they were operating over four miles (6km) from the New Zealanders, and nowhere near Hill 60.

New Zealand researcher I.C. McGibbon suggested that the memory of Frederick Reichardt, the main witness (who had indeed been on Rhododendron Spur), became confused. He concludes that at some point Reichardt did see soldiers disappear into a (normal) mist on the battlefield – for instance, one official report noted: 'By some freak of nature Suvla Bay and Plain were wrapped in a strange mist on the afternoon of 21 August.' He also probably heard of the 'disappearance' of some of the First-Fifth and conflated the two events. His imagination supplied the rest. In the early

moved away northwards.... In a matter of about three quarters of an hour they had all disappeared from view.

'The regiment mentioned is posted as "wiped out" and on Turkey surrendering in 1918, the first thing Britain demanded of Turkey was the return of this regiment. Turkey replied that she had neither captured this regiment, nor made contact with it, and that she did not even know that it existed.... Those who observed this incident can vouch for the fact that

Eighties, however, one of Reichardt's sons stated that he had heard his father tell the story 'from the earliest days I can remember (I was born in 1932).'

WERE THERE UFOS AT FATIMA?

The connection between UFOs and miraculous events

TYPE: **Close encounters of the third kind**
PLACE: **Fatima, Portugal**
DATE: **13 October 1917**

BACKGROUND

On 13 May, 10-year-old Lucia dos Santos and her two cousins saw strange aerial phenomena, including a glowing, buzzing globe, and in it a white-robed lady. These visions or apparitions continued monthly at Fatima until October, attended by ever larger crowds. The three children predicted that a miracle would occur at the October apparition.

THE EVENTS

On 13 October, 70,000 people had gathered despite heavy rain. The 'usual' vision appeared and departed, and then the rain stopped abruptly. The clouds parted to reveal a brilliant pearly disk that was spinning and emitting rays of colored light. It stopped spinning and fell toward the ground with a typical UFO-like 'falling leaf motion'. The crowd, thinking the Sun was falling from the heavens, fell to its knees. The disk then rose and disappeared into the Sun. The soaked ground and people's clothes were now completely dry.

ASSESSMENT

The parallels between religious experiences like this and many UFO encounters raise the possibility that a common phenomenon is at work in both, but is interpreted differently by religious and secular or agnostic people. To those with no specific faith, the root of these experiences remains an enigma.

THREE BIZARRE ENTITIES

TYPE: **Close encounter of the third kind**
PLACE: **Bolton, Lancashire, England**
DATE: **November 1926**

BACKGROUND

Henry Thomas, the young son of a policeman, had been put to bed early. He wanted to be with his friends who were playing outside. So he slipped out of the house to join in with them. Together they started a game of hide-and-seek in the alleys. Seeing a back gate ajar, Henry entered the yard in the hope of finding one of his friends hiding there.

THE EVENTS

In the yard were what Henry took to be three people, of normal height, who were looking into the back window of the house whose yard they were in. The trio was dressed in strange suits that seemed to be made of silver-gray tubes of rubber, with dark boots. They looked like thin versions of the Michelin Man. On their heads were 'transparent, dome-like helmets'. Tubes came from these and joined tanks that the creatures carried on their backs. The 'men' then turned to face the boy. They had pale heads 'shaped like lightbulbs', dark, slit-like eyes, scarcely any nose and no apparent mouth. Henry had the impression that they were wise, if frightening. One made a gurgling noise, and all three began to move forward toward the boy. He fled in terror.

ASSESSMENT

Single-witness UFO reports always present problems of assessment and none more so than close encounters (of any kind). And in this case there was no UFO reported. One reason to believe the witness is that he immediately ran home and told his parents of what he had seen; the beings he had seen became known as the 'three wise men' in his family. Jenny Randles comments: 'We might speculate

[that] the boy had seen rat catchers and fumigators and misinterpreted their strange garb for something more mysterious'. In the dim light he may simply have imagined the unusual clothing and inhuman features, whoever it was he disturbed. It is intriguing, however, that both the 'Michelin Man' suits and, in particular, the facial features of the entities have cropped up in many close encounter reports since the 1940s. Both may have a psychological explanation.

UFOS BY THE SEA

Three reports from the Twenties

TYPE: **Mystery aircraft, daylight disk, light in the sky**
PLACE: **Wales, California, USA, Atlantic Ocean**
DATE: **22 September 1922, early 1927, 29 August 1929**

BACKGROUND

UFO reports of any kind from the Twenties are very rare. The few that do exist reflect the 'mystery aircraft' theme and more modern UFO forms.

THE EVENTS

• 22 September 1922 – Barmouth, Merionethshire, Wales: John Morris, coxswain of the local lifeboat, and another witness saw what they thought was an aircraft falling, with extraordinary slowness, into the Irish Sea. They took a motorboat out to investigate but found nothing. There were no reports immediately afterwards of any terrestrial aircraft having gone missing.
• Early 1927 – Sausalito, Marin County, California: Writer Ella Young said that while sitting outside the Madrona Hotel she saw 'a cigar-shaped craft shoot out of a cloud beyond the bay, and across the sky toward Tamalpais.' It was not shaped like any airship she knew. 'It was long and slender, of yellow color, and traveling at great speed... it

UFO

seemed to progress by alternately contracting and elongating its body.'

- 29 August 1929 – North Atlantic: Thomas Stuart, third mate of the SS *Coldwater*, reported that at 400 miles (640km) off the coast of Virginia he saw a light traveling at an estimated 100mph (160km/h) toward Bermuda. 'There was something that gave the impression that it was a large, passenger craft,' he said, though investigation failed to show any airship or airplane on that course at that time.

ASSESSMENT

The 'features of an aeroplane' seen on the UFO in Wales are like the 'flying crosses' reported at other times. The California and Atlantic sightings conform to common patterns of UFO reports.

THE LONE FLIER'S SIGHTING

Famous airman encounters UFOs

TYPE: **Close encounter of the first kind**
PLACE: **Tasman Sea, between Australia and New Zealand**
DATE: **1931**

BACKGROUND

Although Francis (later Sir Francis) Chichester will always be best remembered for his epic 119-day single-handed round-the-world voyage in the yacht *Gypsy Moth IV* in 1966-67 when he was nearly 65 years old, he began his career as a pioneering aviator, and in 1931 he made the historic first solo flight from Australia to New Zealand across the Tasman Sea.

THE EVENTS

During the course of the flight, Chichester was suddenly startled by flashing lights moving erratically at high speed in the sky. He described one of them as

being 'like a silver pearl', and flashing 'like a searchlight or a heliograph.' This strange object approached his aircraft, moved in front of the engine nacelle, then faded away again as suddenly and unaccountably as it had appeared.

ASSESSMENT

Although Chichester could not explain what he had seen, he did not attribute the sighting to fatigue during his long, demanding and undoubtedly dangerous flight from Australia to New Zealand.

THE FIRST SCANDINAVIAN FLAP

Ghost fliers and Sunday sightings

TYPE: **Close encounters of the first and second kinds**
PLACE: **Finland, Norway and Sweden**
Date: **1932-1937**

BACKGROUND

Reports of mysterious aircraft in the remoter regions of Scandinavia began in 1932, but reached a peak in 1934. Enigmatic radio signals often accompanied the sightings. After a lull, the 'ghost fliers' returned in 1936 and 1937, following the same routes as before.

THE EVENTS

There were hundreds of reports of gray, unmarked aircraft over Scandinavia in the five years from 1932 to 1937. A number of clear patterns emerged from this welter of reports:

- The aircraft were uniformly large, single-winged 'machines' with multiple engines. On one occasion five witnesses saw a giant plane with eight engines, unlike any known to conventional aviation history.
- The fliers frequently appeared in the kind of bad weather that would normally have grounded the airplanes of the time.

- Despite the fearsome weather conditions, the pilots would cut their engines at low altitudes and circle several times without power. As one researcher put it: 'Try this is in a conventional airplane, and you'll end up a basket case.'
- Like the mystery airships, the aircraft often used powerful searchlights to scan the ground below, making no secret of their presence, although (like later UFOs) they made an alarming habit of surveying military installations, forts, railways and other strategic sites.
- The low-flying aircraft were often seen in the company of strange red, white and green lights that flew at much higher altitudes and performed apparently intelligent maneuvers. On one occasion a mystery aircraft, a seaplane of some kind, made a classic UFO-like ploy – on being approached by a fishing boat, it suddenly vanished in a cloud of smoke.
- The sequence of sightings during any given week followed a route south

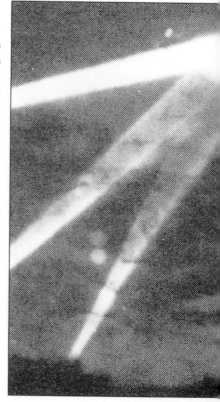

through Norway, across Sweden, then north into Finland. The inference was of an air base somewhere inside the Arctic Circle.

- All attempts to find the source of the aircraft ended in failure. In December 1933 the Swedish Air Force ordered Flying Corps No 4 to Törnaby to look for the fliers' bases, lost two aircraft in the ensuing searches, and found nothing at all. Similar searches by the Norwegian and Finnish military were equally fruitless.

ASSESSMENT

The Swedish military suspected at first that the aircraft must have belonged to smugglers, but they found no evidence to support the theory, and none to suggest they belonged to any foreign power on an espionage mission. There were too few private planes in Scandinavia to account for the number of reports that were filed, and none of the planes matched the descriptions or was remotely capable of

the preternatural performance reported by witnesses. The futuristic designs of the aircraft will immediately strike commentators by their similarity to those of the airship sightings of 1909 and 1913. These ghost planes remain a mystery to this day.

IN BASQUE COUNTRY

A sighting in the midst of the Spanish Civil War

TYPE: **Daylight disk**
PLACE: **Guipuzcoa, Spain**
DATE: **2 October 1936**

BACKGROUND

English novelist and former soldier Valentine Williams and two others were driving from General Franco's headquarters in Burgos to Biarritz, France. The sighting occurred at 4:18pm in the Basque province of Guipuzcoa, about 75 miles (120km) from San Sebastian.

THE EVENTS

Williams's companions gasped in amazement; he turned to see what he thought was a flare or tracer round on a course at right angles to the road, heading northward at an amazing velocity. Williams later described it as 'like a streamer of white smoke.... As it went, it burst into a bright orange flame. There was no sound or explosion.'

When they reached Biarritz, they told their story. Tom Dupree, from the British Consulate at Hendaye, said that he had been at San Sebastian (about 30 miles [48km] west of Biarritz) at the same time that day and had seen the same object.

ASSESSMENT

This UFO could have been a particularly large fireball, burning brightly enough to be visible by daylight. However, the accounts give the impression that the object was traveling parallel to the ground, not falling towards the earth.

THE LOS ANGELES AIR RAID

Unknown intruders run into an anti-aircraft barrage

TYPE: **Lights in the sky**
PLACE: **Environs of Los Angeles, California, USA**
DATE: **25 February 1942**

BACKGROUND

Less than three months after the Japanese attack on Pearl Harbor, the US military forces could not rule out an aerial attack on the continental USA. Tension on the Pacific coast was running high.

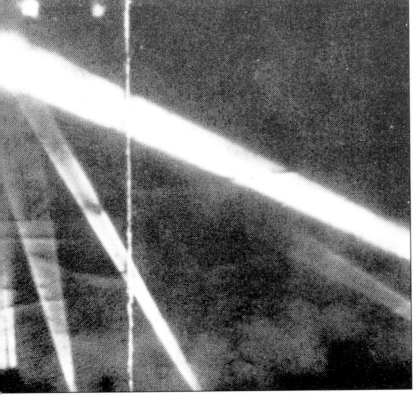

Just visible in this rare photograph is a large UFO that reputedly took numerous direct hits from AAA barrages over Culver City during the 'air raid' on Los Angeles, California, USA on 25 February 1942.

THE EVENTS

At 2:25am on 25 February air raid sirens sounded over Los Angeles. The city blacked out, and at 3:16am anti-aircraft artillery (AAA) batteries began firing at 'unidentified aircraft' coming in over the ocean, as searchlight beams pursued them through the sky. There seemed to be at least two types of craft involved in the incident. Witnesses saw fast-moving, high-flying small objects, red or silver in color, that arrived in formation and then appeared to dodge their way through the AAA salvos at speeds of up to five miles (8km) per second – 18,000mph (29,000km/h). There was also a large object that remained stationary for some time, was caught in searchlights over Culver City, and then moved at a stately 60mph (100km/h) to the coast at Santa Monica and then southward toward Long Beach, before being lost to sight. This large object reportedly took numerous direct hits. The AAA continued firing until 4:14am, using 1430 12.8lb (6kg) shells in all. No bombs were dropped and no aircraft were downed.

ASSESSMENT

On 26 February, General of the Armies George C. Marshall informed President Franklin D. Roosevelt that as many as 15 unidentified aircraft had been logged over Los Angeles, flying at speeds of up to 200mph (320km/h) and at altitudes of between 9000 and 18,000ft (2700-5400m). General Marshall surmised that the enemy had used commercial aircraft operated by enemy agents to spread alarm, locate AAA positions in California, and slow up US war production.

Artist's impression of a B-24 Liberator bomber pursued by 'foo fighters' in the closing months of World War II. Both Allied and Axis air crews reported seeing these strange lights, which both believed were secret weapons belonging to the other side. No entirely satisfactory explanation of the mystery light balls has yet been made.

No proof that any of these conclusions was accurate has ever been forthcoming. Official estimates of the UFOs' speeds are hugely and worryingly at variance with those of witnesses, and the behavior of the objects was unlike that of any conventional aircraft of the period – it is very difficult to imagine why hostile aircraft would show their lights during an air raid over enemy territory.

There has been speculation among many commentators that the US military was aware all along that these were unusual targets, because in the 50 minutes between the time they were first alerted and the time they opened up the AAA barrage, aircraft of the 4th Interceptor Command had not been sent to engage the intruders. Furthermore, for reasons that have never been explained, the US Department of Defense strenuously denied having any record of the Los Angeles Air Raid until 1987.

BRITAIN'S FIRST ABDUCTION?

A lone sentry and lost time

TYPE: **Close encounter**
PLACE: **Newbiggin-on-Sea, Northumberland, England**
DATE: **September 1942**

On an unseasonably cold night, Albert Lancashire, aged 27, armed with a rifle with bayonet fixed, was guarding a radar base on the North Sea coast.

THE EVENTS

A light appeared on the horizon, and then disappeared behind a cloud. A second, yellow light then appeared, apparently throwing a beam from the rim of a round object. The beam, which was about 1ft (30cm) in diameter, swung around and shone straight into his face. The soldier

let go of his rifle and threw his hands in the air. He felt a strange floating sensation, and then blacked out. When he came to a few minutes later he was lying a few yards from the spot where he had seen the light. He lay, 'shocked and dazed' for 'five or 10 minutes' before he felt fully recovered and well enough to resume his vigil. In the years following this episode Lancashire experienced a number of unusual dreams. In one, he recalls being on board the object he saw and looking down at the sea through a large window. A man in white is present in the dream, and he tells him that he had to be carried aboard the craft. In another dream, Lancashire is on board the craft and meets a red-haired woman in a calf-length skirt (fashionable in 1942) who hands him a pair of goggles. In later years Lancashire came to believe that an abduction by aliens was the best explanation for his wartime experience.

ASSESSMENT

Apart from its inherent difficulty as a single-witness case, there are several problems with Lancashire's account. According to him he was guarding the base against the Luftwaffe (German Air Force). One would have thought that the station's radar would have detected enemy aircraft more effectively and brought more efficient defenses to bear than Lancashire's rifle and bayonet. He also claimed he was under orders not to fire at enemy aircraft as that would 'only give away the position of the base', a statement that does not bear rational examination. By the time Lancashire reported his alleged experience he was in his 70s, and had 'devoured every piece of UFO literature he could get hold of.' There is at least a possibility that in this intervening period he had confabulated, if not actually invented, details of his sighting and his dreams in the light of his reading. However, Lancashire's account did follow a common psychological pattern for abductees in that he developed an intense interest in religious matters after his experience. But whether that represents an 'abduction' or not has to remain open to question.

THE FOO FIGHTERS

Unexplained lightballs track warplanes

TYPE: **Close encounters of the first kind**
PLACE: **European, Asian and Pacific theaters of war**
DATE: **1943-45**

BACKGROUND

The 'foo fighters' were balls of light, varying in color and in size from several feet to a few inches across, that pursued warplanes in the later stages of World War II. Allied pilots assumed they were enemy inventions, either reconnaissance drones or psychological warfare weapons. Reports of foo fighters were also made in

the Korean War. A short selection of World War II sightings follows.

THE EVENTS

- In 1943, US bomber pilots flying missions from Burma to China reported being buzzed and circled by 'glittering' objects. Instruments failed to operate until the objects flew off.
- On 14 October 1943, US B-17s of the 348th Bomb Group had started a bombing run over Schweinfurt, Germany, when they ran into a formation of 'scores' of small, silvery disks, about one inch (2.5cm) thick and four inches (10cm) in diameter, flying toward the bombers. Major E.R.T. Holmes reported that one struck the tail of one aircraft, but without effect.
- On 10 August 1944, Captain Alvah M. Reida was piloting a B-29 bomber based at Kharagapur, India, on a mission over Palembang, Sumatra, when his right gunner and co-pilot noticed a sphere 'probably five or six feet (1.5-1.8m) in diameter, of a very bright and intense red or orange in color' that constantly throbbed, about 12,500ft (3750m) off the starboard wing. It paced the B-29, then flying at 210 mph (340km/h) at 14,000ft (4200m). Reida jinxed his plane to shake it off, but it stayed in the same relative position until, after eight minutes, it 'made an abrupt 90° turn and accelerated rapidly, disappearing in the overcast.'
- On 22 December 1944, Lt. David McFalls of the US 415th night-fighter squadron was over Hagenau, Germany. At 6:00am, he saw two 'huge, bright orange lights' climbing toward the plane. McFalls dived, banked and turned his plane, but the UFOs stuck with him for two minutes, then peeled off and blinked out.

ASSESSMENT

Interrogation of captured enemy aircrew revealed that both German and Japanese fliers had also been pursued by foo fighters. Donald H. Menzel proposed that these fighters were light reflections from tiny ice crystals formed by super-cold air eddying around battle damage on the aircraft (hence their reappearance in Korea). However this does not account for the reported arrivals from elsewhere of foo fighters, or their effect on aircraft electro-magnetic systems. Many modern ufologists now believe that the foo fighters are a form of plasma or ball lightning.

GHOST ROCKETS

Another phantom invasion centers on Scandinavia

TYPE: **Lights in the sky, close encounters of the first and second kind**
PLACE: **Denmark, Finland, Greece, Norway, Sweden**
DATE: **June-August 1946**

BACKGROUND

On 13 June 1944 an off-course German V-2 rocket exploded harmlessly near Böckebo in southern Sweden. By analysing the fragments, Swedish scientists soon had a precise idea of what had landed on their soil. The authorities were then in a good position to judge the 997 reports of rocket sightings they received in the summer of 1946. A selection follows.

THE EVENTS

- Early May – Sweden: At night, dark, rocket-shaped objects showing intermittent bursts of flame from the tail were seen; in daylight, slow-moving cigar-shaped objects were reported.
- 10 June – Finland: Objects 'resembling German V-weapons' were seen in several locations.
- 12 June – Sweden: The Defense Staff secretly ordered police, home defense and customs officers to gather rocket sighting reports.
- 18 July – Norway: Two 'ghost rockets' were seen crashing into Lake Mjösa.
- 19 July – Sweden: At 12:00 noon, witnesses saw a 6ft (2m) long ash-gray

rocket plunge into Lake Kölmjörv and explode with 'a heavy detonation'. An investigation by the military over three weeks found no trace of the object.
- 11 August – Sweden: Over 400 witnesses saw luminous objects traveling north in the the sky. In their trail several heaps of slag fell to the ground.
- 13 August – Finland: In the afternoon, a 'flying bomb' exploded over the city of Tammersfors; in the west, a rocket was seen over Helsinki that night.
- 15 August – Denmark: The latest in a series of Danish rockets was seen over Copenhagen during the evening.
- 20 August – Sweden: The Air Force F1 Wing at Vösterös reported a radar confirmation of a visual sighting of a vague luminous object.
- 1 September – Greece: Mystery projectiles were seen by British Army units over Macedonia in general and particularly the city of Thessalonika.

ASSESSMENT

In October the Swedish military issued a report that attributed 80 per cent of the sightings to 'celestial phenomena', but admitted that the remainder 'cannot be the phenomena of nature or products of the imagination, nor can be... Swedish airplanes.' Nor, the report added, were they German V-weapons. On 23 December a final report was issued that concluded 'there is no actual proof that a test of rocket projectiles has taken place over Sweden' but hinted strongly that secret weapons of some sort had been involved in the unexplained sightings.

In Greece, the country's top scientist, Prof. Paul Santorini, was put in charge of the investigation, but the project was abruptly terminated on the orders of the Greek Army shortly after it had conclusively established that, whatever the objects sighted may have been, they were not missiles. The behavior of the 'rockets' – traveling at estimated speeds as low as 200mph (300km/h), and changing direction in mid-flight – resembles that of cruise missiles many years before they were invented or even technologically

possible. Another odd aspect of this wave is that the sightings stopped as soon as they were officially declared inexplicable.

THE RISING TIDE

Early appearances of UFOs in 1947

TYPE: **Daylight disks**
PLACE: **France and USA**
DATE: **April-June 1947**

BACKGROUND

As noted in the introduction to this chapter, Kenneth Arnold's was not the first sighting of silvery flying disks, or indeed of other kinds of UFO, in 1947.

Karl-Gösta Bartoll investigates Lake Kölmjärv, Sweden, after several witnesses saw a rocket plunge into its waters and explode on 19 July 1946. This was just one of almost a thousand sightings of mystery rockets over Scandinavia that year. No physical trace of any of the 'rockets' has ever come to light.

- 10 June: At 11:00pm, at Douglas, Arizona, Mrs Coral Lorenzen watched a light rise from across the Mexican border, assume a spherical shape and disappear among the stars. The sighting lasted 10 seconds.
- 10 June: According to the files of the USAF's Aerospace Technical Intelligence Center, some 50 reports were made across Hungary of 'silvery balls' flying at great speed in daylight.
- 12 June: Witnesses saw a 'chain' of UFOs above Weiser, Idaho.
- 14 June: Richard Rankin was flying from Chicago, Illinois to Los Angeles, California when at about 2:00pm, over Bakersfield, California, he saw a triangular formation of ten 'saucers' heading north. He estimated their size at 100ft (30m) in diameter, their speed at 600mph (1000km/h).
- 21 June: At 11:50am eight disks 'the size of a house' were seen near Spokane, Washington, flying at an estimated 600mph (1000km/h). They descended with a 'falling-leaf motion' and landed across the nearby state line, in Idaho.
- 21 June: A salesman passing through Yukon, Oklahoma, reported seeing six strange objects in the sky at dusk. 'They appeared as large as washtubs, and were very high up, flying in formation and at an incredible speed.'
- 24 June: The day of Arnold's sighting, prospector Fred M. Johnson was also in the Cascade Mountains, about 12 miles (20km) from Mount Rainier. According to a USAF Project Sign report, 'he saw a strange reflection in the sky, and... grabbed his telescope. He saw six disks

Several other reports were made earlier in 1947, at least two from professional, trained observers – a meteorologist and a pilot – and not all reports came from the USA. There were also sightings on the same day as Arnold's.

THE EVENTS

- April: In Col de Serres, France, a M. Orliange reported seeing a 'disk with a cupola' about 100ft (30m) in diameter flying at low altitude over the valley of the River Clarry.
- Mid-April: Meteorologist Walter A. Miczewski and his staff at the US Weather Bureau in Richmond, Virginia, were tracking a weather balloon with a theodolite. They then noticed a silver disk, flat-bottomed, with a dome on top, crossing the sky from east to west. The object was larger than the balloon and was tracked for about 15 seconds before it was lost to view.
- 5 May: A silvery object was reported to have fallen out of the sky and disintegrated over Washington State.
- 18 May: Several observers again in Richmond, Virginia, saw a flat, white, cigar-shaped object speed across the sky at sunset, heading north-west.
- 19 May: between 12:15 and 1:15pm, a silvery object was seen approaching from the north-east toward Manitou Springs, Colorado. It halted, remained motionless for some minutes, and then started 'dancing' – performing complex aerobatics. Finally it rose and flew out of sight, against the wind.

about 30ft (9m) in diameter. He watched them for approximately 50 seconds while they banked in the sun. 'They were round, but with tails, and they made no noise and were not flying in formation.' While the disks were in sight, the needle on his compass 'weaved wildly'. It is possible, then, that an independent witness saw Arnold's flight of UFOs.

- 24 June: Between 9:15pm and 11:00pm, seven hours after Arnold's sighting, dozens of witnesses watched as light blue and purple balls of light performed formation aerobatics over Seattle, Washington State.

ASSESSMENT

Psychological 'contamination' by UFO lore cannot be called to account for these sightings, since there was no UFO lore at the time. It is noticeable too that the reported size of the objects is surprisingly consistent through almost every one of these sightings. And it is intriguing that these early UFO reports often mention apparent groups of 'craft' that appear to be flying together in formation, a characteristic rarely noted in modern accounts of unidentified flying objects and disks of all kinds.

THE MAURY ISLAND AFFAIR

Six UFOs, two deaths and a man in black

TYPE: **Close encounter of the second kind**
PLACE: **Maury Island, Puget Sound, Washington State, USA**
DATE: **21 June 1947**

BACKGROUND

A US Coast Guard launch commanded by Harold A. Dahl, with Dahl's 15-year-old son, his dog, and one other crew member on board, was patroling Puget Sound. The day was bleak and overcast, with low cloud. At about 2:00pm, the boat put into a bay on Maury Island, about three miles (5km) out from Tacoma.

THE EVENTS

Those on board the launch saw 'six very large doughnut-shaped machines' directly overhead, about 2000ft (600m) up. None of the craft made any sound. Five UFOs began circling around the sixth, which lost height until it stopped, hovering, about 500ft (150m) above the water. Dahl estimated its diameter as 100ft (30m), and the hole in the middle as 25ft (8m) across. Around its shiny metallic rim were 6ft (2m) portholes; around the inner circumference were dark, circular windows. Fearing it was about to crash into the water, Dahl pulled the boat over to the beach. From here he took four photographs of the objects. The central UFO then 'spewed out' molten metal fragments into the water and onto the shore. One killed the dog; another severely burned Dahl's son. Then the UFO rose, joined the others, and all six sped out over the Pacific. The men gathered samples of the still-hot metal.

On returning to harbour, Dahl reported the events to his superior officer, Fred L. Crisman. The next morning, a dark-suited individual arrived at Dahl's house in a black Buick sedan and invited him to breakfast – at which, he made it plain that he knew exactly what had happened at Maury, and told Dahl: 'Silence is the best thing for you and your family. You have seen what you ought not to have seen!' Dahl established later that no one on the boat had told anyone else of their strange experience.

The following day, 23 June, Crisman went out to Maury to see the metallic debris for himself. While he was there, a doughnut-like flying disk appeared, flew around the bay and disappeared into a stormcloud. He then developed the photographs: they were covered in white spots, 'as though they had been exposed to some radiation.' Two days later, the papers were full of Kenneth Arnold's sighting over the Cascade Mountains.

Crisman decided to talk to a local reporter about what Dahl and his crew had witnessed.

Word of the case reached Arnold through a journalist friend. On 30 June he went to Tacoma and spoke to Crisman. Next day he called Lt. Frank Brown, an intelligence officer at Hamilton Army Air Force Base, California, to ask him to join the investigation. Within the hour, Brown and a Captain Davidson were on their way by B-25 bomber. That afternoon they interviewed Crisman in Arnold's hotel room. Brown said he had to return to California that night, so could not visit the island. But he filled a large carton with the metal fragments before leaving.

Early next morning, Crisman was on the phone to Arnold. The B-25 with Brown and Davidson aboard had crashed. Both were dead. One of the plane's engines had mysteriously caught fire, 20 minutes after take-off. Arnold arranged to go out to Maury Island with him and Dahl, but then the boat's engine turned out to be dead. Crisman promised to call Arnold as soon as it was fixed. He never did. Nor did he hand over the photographs. He couldn't be found – according to Dahl, he had left town on business; according to other sources, he was last seen boarding an Army plane bound for Alaska. Then, Dahl's son disappeared.

On top of all this, someone, it seemed, was bugging Arnold's hotel room and passing the local newspaper details of his conversations, even when he was alone with Brown and Davidson. He called another intelligence contact, a Major Sanders, who stonewalled him. Arnold, now thoroughly shaken, left town. Somebody seriously did not want the Maury Island case investigated, and would apparently kill to make sure it was not.

ASSESSMENT

This version of the Maury Island events has been repeated in countless UFO books, and the story is one of the best known UFO sightings. Another version, the result of detective work by ufologist John Keel, was published in 1987.

According to Keel's account, Crisman had been in contact for years with Ray Palmer, publisher of the science fiction magazine *Amazing Stories*. When Arnold's story first hit the headlines, he dreamed up the whole Maury Island saga. Then he enlisted his colleague Harold Dahl in the conspiracy, and tried to sell the story to Palmer. But Brown and Davidson very quickly saw through the hoax, and did not even bother to take the 'space debris' on the plane with them. When their B-25 crashed, Crisman and Dahl, afraid that they would be blamed for the deaths, confessed to the USAAF. Both then made themselves scarce around Tacoma. The Air Force ignored the confession, because they were able to satisfy themselves from other evidence that the B-25 crash was a genuine accident. (False confessions to crimes – and indeed to tragic events for which no one is responsible – are, regrettably, increasingly commonplace the world over.)

Far from being worthless or fake, the 'slag' allegedly spewed from a UFO was in fact the key to the whole case. Crisman and Dahl were not Coast Guards, but co-owners of an old boat they used to tramp lumber around Tacoma Harbour.

But it is beyond dispute that something odd did happen on 23 June off Maury Island: two or more aircraft flew over the boat, and one, clearly in trouble, began dumping radioactive slag into the water and, inadvertently, onto the boat. The dog died, and Dahl's son was injured – these are facts. But the son did not 'disappear' during Arnold's visit: he was in hospital throughout that period.

Dahl's photographs were genuinely ruined by radioactivity, Keel maintains. He claims the slag came from the Atomic Energy Commission (AEC)'s plutonium processing plant at Hanford, Washington. Dahl was warned off not by a mysterious Man In Black but by a security agent of the AEC, which had traced him through his son's hospital records. The AEC was also in the midst of a major counter-espionage operation at the time; its agents routinely bugged hotel rooms in Tacoma. Details of Arnold's investigation

were passed to the press in the hope of covering up illegal dumping of nuclear waste under a spurious UFO story. Keel speculates that Crisman may himself have been working for the AEC, or that he may have tried to make a fast buck out of someone else's misfortune by inventing the 'saucer' yarn.

But despite the fact that the Maury Island event was a hoax, it is certain that, in terms of the effect the story had, the legend might as well be true. Because it injected into UFO folklore a number of motifs that resurfaced repeatedly in later cases. The sinister Men In Black, for example, the determination of those in the know (be they human or alien) to go to any lengths to maintain the 'cover up', the mysterious traces left behind by the UFOs after their landings, the evidence of radioactivity – all these undoubtedly

What appears to be a giant flying disk – but is in fact a giant 10-engined Convair B-36 bomber, seen in profile and reflecting light so that its airfoils are lost to sight. In the late Forties the US Air Force released several such pictures in the forlorn hope of convincing the public that most 'flying saucers' were similar misidentifications.

colored the way in which later UFO witnesses interpreted and reported their own experiences.

So what happened at Maury Island was not a true close encounter of any kind. And yet the story has had a deep impact and lasting repercussions on the later history of ufology, because the story has provided a framework for describing subsequent experiences.

CHAPTER 3
Contact
FROM FLYING SAUCERS TO THE FIRST ABDUCTIONS

The year 1947 saw the dawn of the modern UFO era. As far as the general public was concerned, it opened with Idaho businessman Kenneth Arnold spotting nine curious flying disks as he cruised in his private plane over the Cascade Mountains in Washington State. This was the sighting that caught the public imagination, and virtually everyone who heard or read about it in the next few days assumed that Arnold had seen extra-terrestrial craft.

This idea was not a creation of the media: it was a large-scale, world-wide, public perception by ordinary people. The reaction to Arnold's experience showed that the world was ready for the idea of visitors from outer space. Ever since, whatever line the argument has subsequently followed, every discussion of UFOs has started with the question: Are they extra-terrestrial?

It is not difficult to see why people, especially in America and Europe, were so ready in 1947 to assume that the 'flying saucers' were from outer space. The notion that space might be explored, possibly even settled, had been mooted before World War II. During the war rocket technology advanced spectacularly

An artist's impression from the French UFO magazine *Soucoupes Volantes*, liberally interpreting reports of Kenneth Arnold's epoch-making sighting of nine mysterious flying disks on 24 June 1947. His was not the only UFO sighting in the area that day, and news of Arnold's experience set off a deluge of claims that others had seen similar 'flying saucers'.

in Germany. As soon as hostilities ended, both the USSR and the USA rushed to recruit or coerce German scientists and technicians to work on their own rocket programs. But while space was the 'last frontier' for humanity to conquer, there was a more urgent requirement. That was to provide vehicles to deliver weapons of mass destruction in minutes rather than hours. Achieving such a capability was deemed crucial in the dawn of the nuclear age, with its 'balance of terror' and its strategy of Mutually-Assured Destruction, or 'MAD'.

In 1947, Americans were deeply concerned that the USSR would soon develop its own nuclear weapons – which would, in theory, make an invasion of the United States feasible. Kenneth Arnold's UFO sighting came at a time when the Western world, and the USA in particular, was obsessed with a fear of Communist invasion. Besides the military threat, there were fifth columnists, agitators, sympathizers and spies – 'the enemy within' – to beware of. The junior Senator from Wisconsin, Joe McCarthy, did not lack public sympathy when he began his crusade against communist subversion at home.

McCarthy's campaign reflected another fear: that the Reds could invade your mind. Since the 1930s it had been suspected that Communist regimes used far-reaching psychological techniques to remould the opinions of dissidents. Veterans of the Korean war, which broke out in June 1950, were to confirm the reality of this nightmare, with reports of the most soul-destroying, violent attempts to 'brainwash' Western prisoners of war into parroting like zombies the evils of the imperialist West and the

wonders of Marxist-Leninism. And in some cases, the brainwashing succeeded.

In 1947, then, and in the years immediately after, the intriguing notion of life in space made an odd marriage with political anxieties about invasions of all kinds – but especially an invasion of the unknown. And this union brought forth a 'logical' conclusion about Arnold's sighting: if these silvery disks were not from an Earthly power, they had to be invaders from outer space.

The Extra-Terrestrial Hypothesis (ETH) has remained popular ever since, partly because the media have usually ignored the alternative interpretations of UFO events – and partly because the kinds of fears and uncertainties that were common in 1947 have remained with us ever since.

HOSTILE OR BENEVOLENT?

Regardless of whether or not the ETH is correct, in many ways the years between 1947 and 1960 are the richest period of the modern UFO era in terms of the experiences that were reported (if not always published). In the first decade of the phenomenon, virtually every aspect of the subject as we know it today manifested itself. There were sightings of daylight disks, lights in the night, abductions with explicit sexual scenes, crashed saucer stories, landing traces and contactees with reassuring messages from benevolent beings in space, sieges by ferociously hostile aliens, and photographs both authentic and faked. If, as inexplicably as it had begun, the UFO phenomenon had ground to a halt on 31 December 1960, even in that case it would still be providing us with a wealth of material for awe, analysis and wonder.

Naturally, Arnold's sighting attracted the attention of the US military, who were of course concerned that he had seen some kind of Soviet secret weapon or reconnaissance craft, as yet unknown to them. In that sense, the USAF formed the world's first body of ufologists. As early as 22 January 1948 the USAF set up Project Sign to collect, evaluate and report on UFO sightings. Although the project foundered because it supported the hypothesis that UFOs were extra-terrestrial, the view was forming within the USAF and other interested agencies such as the CIA that the phenomenon was not a military menace. There had been rumors in intelligence circles in 1948 that UFOs gave out lethal radio-active clouds, and in 1949 it was even suggested that the armed forces be put on permanent alert against UFOs.

But these were exceptions. That UFOs were harmless became official policy after a group of eminent scientists reviewed the evidence in January 1953 at the CIA's request and found no reason to suspect a 'direct physical threat to national security.' But the panel did consider that UFO reports, 'in these parlous times', could distract the military from its proper functions, and in decorous language recommended a program of debunking. Thereafter the USAF investigatory effort was reduced to little more than a fact-gathering exercise.

For much of the period, civilian ufologists endorsed the official view, if from a somewhat different perspective. The initial assumption among commentators was that UFOs were extra-terrestrial, and that their intentions were peaceful, even benevolent. This view echoed that of the general public. When Washington, DC, suffered a plague of UFOs in July 1952, the White House mail room and switchboard were jammed by writers and callers pleading that the military refrain from shooting at the saucers.

Ufologists had taken a similar pacific view of the incident in which Captain Thomas Mantell, an Air National Guard pilot, died while pursuing a UFO over Godman Air Force Base, Kentucky, in January 1948. Major Donald Keyhoe, perhaps influenced by his Marine Corps training, suggested that the aliens had acted simply in self-defense, and Gerald Heard doubted a UFO invasion was likely, since they had thrown away the advantage of surprise. Even the aliens themselves reportedly regarded Mantell's death as a misfortune.

George Adamski said the Venusian he allegedly met in 1952 'regretted' the episode, and explained that Mantell had fallen foul of the 'power field' of a large manned spacecraft. Orfeo Angelucci said that 'space people' told him in 1955 that the UFO was 'remotely controled', and had fired on Mantell's P-51 fighter automatically. Whomever you believed, there was general agreement that Mantell's death was an unfortunate accident.

A CHANGE IN THE WEATHER

The fretful temper of the times was reflected in films that showed aliens in flying saucers as ready to colonize the world and even more ready to enslave humanity in the process. As early as 1948 the matinée serial *Bruce Conrad – Daredevil of the Skies* was portraying flying disks as hostile: in the movie, a demented scientist exploited these disks to wreck the Panama Canal.

But Hollywood was quick to catch the public mood. The message of one quintessential UFO movie of the early Fifties, *The Day the Earth Stood Still*, is that humanity, not the aliens, threatens peace and stability in the Universe. Five years later, in 1956, the equally notable *Invasion of the Body Snatchers* showed parasitic alien minds taking over living human flesh – a direct metaphor for the Red Menace and its brainwashing objectives. The gulf between these two films reflects the uncertain light in which UFOs were seen. But the five years that separated them also saw a crucial shift in the political atmosphere in the West, as the long winter of the Cold War set in.

Ufologists reflected this divergence in their commentaries, although from 1955

the UFO phenomenon itself developed in its own way, regardless of terrestrial opinions – as it continued to do for the next 30 years. But for the first seven or eight years of the phenomenon, ufology as such barely existed: the analysts were few and far between, and the 'contactees' who claimed to have met aliens and to have been for trips in flying saucers were probably, in the eyes of the public, as 'expert' as the writers attempting to interpret UFOs in general. But by the middle of the decade, commentators were beginning to have doubts about the good intentions of the ufonauts, no matter what the contactees themselves had to say.

One of the earliest to reveal suspicions that ufonauts had ulterior motives was Donald Keyhoe. In *Flying Saucers From Outer Space* (1953) he gave considerable space to the argument that UFOs boded no good, especially as they so persistently

 This UFO, photographed by W.D. Hall in Australia in 1954, was long known as the 'petrol tank saucer'. Taken by many as proof of the international nature of the saucer phenomenon, the picture was eventually admitted to be a fake. Hall had painted the UFO on to an original print, and then re-photographed the result.

cropped up in the vicinity of strategic sites. Keyhoe concluded, however, that there was 'at least an even chance' that the 'space race' meant no harm: 'they may be waiting only for proof that landing here is safe.' Yet Keyhoe typifies the era's confusion about UFOs, and about their connection to the Soviet menace (he wrote his book in the months of uncertainty following the death of Stalin). Noting that in 1954 the USSR might well become capable of a mass attack on the USA, he felt the Soviets might start rumors of a UFO invasion and use that as a cover for their own actual nuclear attack. 'It is imperative that we end this added danger,' wrote Keyhoe, pleading

for openness about the 'interplanetary' nature of UFOs.

By 1955, Keyhoe was seeing signs of UFO aggression everywhere: an air disaster is attributed to the aliens' 'heat beams', the disappearance of Flight 19 (later a keystone of the 'Bermuda Triangle' myth) is an abduction; he even claims a hole in a billboard is caused by a missile from outer space. But the British commentator Waveney Girvan saw little evidence of hostility in UFO reports, and in France Aimé Michel noted the saucers' 'inoffensive nature' and suggested it was the ufonauts who feared humanity and its 'murderous tendencies'. As the decade wore on, however, this variety of opinion gave way to a sense, expressed by writers such as Gray Barker, Harold T. Wilkins, and Leonard Stringfield, that UFOs were sinister, malevolent, even evil. By 1960, Keyhoe was urging Congress to fund a crash program to defend the USA against extra-terrestrials. This mood was to continue through the Sixties.

VISIONS FOR THE FUTURE

The most renowned individual to analyse UFOs in the Fifties (and perhaps at any time) was the distinguished psychologist C.G. Jung. In his 1958 book, *Flying Saucers: A Modern Myth of Things Seen in the Sky,* Jung called UFOs a 'visionary rumor', and noted: 'The present world situation is calculated as never before to arouse expectations of a redeeming, supernatural event,' while 'anything that looks technological goes down well with modern man.' Jung tended to an impartial, psychological interpretation of UFO reports not least because of the saucers' contradictory behavior: 'Their flights do not appear to be based on any recognizable system. They behave more like groups of tourists... viewing the countryside, erratically following first one interest then another.' Nearly 20 years were to pass before ufologists, especially in Britain and Europe, took heed of Jung's diagnosis, and at last began to develop the 'psychosocial' approach to interpreting the UFO phenomenon.

UFO

Cover illustration from Kenneth Arnold's *The Coming of the Saucers*, the book he co-wrote with *Fate* magazine publisher Ray Palmer in 1952. Like other contemporary attempts to depict Arnold's sighting, the impression makes the UFOs much more like conventional images of 'flying saucers' than Arnold's own description of his experience.

The change in ufology's general attitude across the decade, from cautious welcoming to outright suspicion, was barely visible among UFO witnesses. The most famous in the Fifties were the contactees, who claimed to have met extra-terrestrials and even to have taken trips in their craft. They uniformly described the aliens as friendly, caring folk, concerned for the future of humanity. This bore out Jung's remark that UFOs represented the possibility of a 'redeeming, supernatural event', and it was only late in the decade (when most analysts had, in effect, rejected the contactees' optimistic accounts) that the first abduction was reported – the Villas Boas case – and that was so bizarre that even ufologists were reluctant to publish it. Abductions that allegedly took place in the Fifties have been reported since, and have been investigated using hypnotic regression; but they did not influence attitudes at the time.

The COMING of the SAUCERS

$2.50

By Kenneth Arnold & Ray Palmer

THE DAWN OF AN ERA

Kenneth Arnold's historic sighting

TYPE: **Daylight Disks**
PLACE: **Cascade Mountains, Washington State, USA**
DATE: **24 June 1947**

BACKGROUND

Idaho businessman Kenneth Arnold was an experienced pilot. He was flying east across the Cascade Mountains from Chehalis to Yakima, Washington, enticed by the offer of $5000 reward to spend an hour or so searching for a Marine Corps C-46 transport aircraft that had recently come down near Mount Rainier with 32 men on board. Arnold's aircraft was specially designed for working in mountainous terrain. He took off from Chehalis airport at 2:00pm.

THE EVENTS

Kenneth Arnold was in the midst of his search at an altitude of about 9200ft (2750m) above the town of Mineral (about 25 miles [40 km] south-west of the peak of Mount Rainier), and was making a 180° turn when 'a tremendously bright flash lit up the surfaces of my aircraft.' Arnold looked for the source of the flash, but the only other plane in the vicinity was a Douglas DC-4 airliner. Arnold then figured he had seen a flash of sunlight off his wings of a close-flying fighter; he speculated that he had been buzzed by a P-51 Mustang, the most powerful fighter then in common service with the USAF.

Before he had time to look for a fast-moving Mustang, however, Arnold saw another flash – and where it came from. 'I observed,' he reported, 'far to my left and to the north, a formation of very bright objects coming from the vicinity of Mount Baker, flying very close to the mountain tops and traveling at a tremendous speed.' They were moving almost directly across Arnold's own flightpath, which made it easy to calculate their speed. Arnold was amazed to discover that the nine craft were traveling at over 1700 mph (2750km/h), well beyond the capability of any conventional aircraft at the time. What made this phenomenal speed all the more extraordinary was the way the craft were flying.

Arnold said later: 'They didn't fly like any aircraft I had seen before... they flew in a definite formation, but erratically... like speed boats on rough water or similar to the tail of a Chinese kite that I once saw blowing in the wind... they fluttered and sailed, tipping their wings alternately and emitting very bright blue-white flashes from their surfaces.'

Arnold decided to abandon his search for the missing C-46 and make for Yakima to report what he had seen. Landing there at about 4:00pm, he told his story to an airline manager and discussed it with other professional fliers, before taking off once more for Pendleton, Oregon. The news flew ahead of him: among the crowd to greet him there was reporter Bill Becquette, from the East Oregonian newspaper. Arnold described the craft he had seen as flying 'like a saucer would if you skipped it across the water.' From these words came the term 'flying saucers'. By now Arnold was sure that he had seen a flight of guided missiles, 'robotly controled'. He

concluded that the government had chosen this way to announce the discovery of 'a new principle of flight'.

Becquette put the story on the Associated Press wire. For three days at Pendleton, Arnold was beseiged with enquiries. Finally, exhausted and unable to work, Arnold flew the 200 miles (320km) across the state line to his home in Boise, Idaho. Shortly after arriving there, Arnold had a telephone call from Dave Johnson, aviation editor of the Idaho Statesman newspaper. The conversation changed everything for Arnold: 'I am sure he was in a position to know... that it was not a new military guided missile and... if what I had seen was true, it did not belong to the good old USA. It was then that I really began to wonder.'

ASSESSMENT

Though the immediate assumption was that Arnold had seen extra-terrestrial craft, Paul Devereux believes that Arnold saw a spectacular electromagnetic display created by faults and pressures in the Earth's crust, while Arnold himself came to believe that he had seen a hitherto unknown species of animal that inhabits the stratosphere. Hans van Kempen suggested that the UFOs were a flight of secret Republic XP-84 Thunderjets, which had a top speed of 605mph (975km/h) and had first flown in early 1946; but there is no evidence to support this.

THE WAVE OF SUMMER 1947

After Arnold, the deluge

TYPE: **Daylight disks UFO landings and lights in the sky**
PLACE: **Perm, Russia and USA**
DATE: **June-August 1947**

BACKGROUND

No sooner had Arnold's experience hit the headlines than UFO reports flooded in from all over the USA. By the Fourth

of July weekend, UFOs had been seen in every state except Georgia and West Virginia. By 16 July, the USAAF alone had received over 850 reports of UFOs. By then, the wave had peaked, and the number of sightings dropped to a trickle by the middle of August. A brief selection of the more intriguing typical reports of the period follows.

THE EVENTS

- 27 June: A housewife saw disks 'like silver plates' flying at high speed over the Cascade Mountains. They wavered from side to side in their flight, and changed formation.
- 28 June: At 2:00pm, USAAF jet pilot Lt. Armstrong, in the air 30 miles (48km) north of Lake Meade, Nevada, observed a formation of 'five or six' white disks flying at an estimated altitude of 6000ft (1800m).
- 28 June: At 3:45pm, Mr M. Beuscher saw 'more than seven' blue, soundless disks fly over his farm at Rockfield, Wisconsin, heading south. Evening radio newscasts said similar UFOs were later seen over Illinois that day.
- 28 June: At 9:30pm, at Maxwell Air Force Base, Montgomery, Alabama, two pilots, two intelligence officers and four other witnesses watched a bright light that 'zigzagged, streaked about at high speed, and made a sharp 90° turn before disappearing.'
- 29 June: At White Sands Proving Grounds, New Mexico, US Naval Laboratory rocket expert Dr C.J. John and two other scientists saw a silvery disk that they estimated was moving faster than sound through the sky.
- 29 June: At 4:45pm, the driver of a Des Moines-Mason City bus was about seven miles (10km) from Clarion, Iowa, when a group of five UFOs crossed his vision. They were followed by 13 more white, oval UFOs that came from the opposite direction, making a noise like a dynamo, and flying north-west.
- 30 June: Police officers in Portland, Oregon, watched five disks 'like shiny chromium hub caps' appear, disappear

and reappear in a wobbling flight. Said Patrolman K. McDowell: 'I saw five large objects in the sky, disk-shaped, and of no pronounced color. They dipped up and down in an oscillating motion at great speed. and vanished quickly.' Two other patrolmen and a private pilot reported seeing only three disks at the same time, flying 'at a terrific speed in straight line formation. The last disk fluttered sideways in a sideway arc, very rapidly. They were soundless and showed no vapor trails.'

- 30 June: At 9:10am, a US Navy pilot flying south near Williams Field, Arizona, saw two gray spheres about 10ft (3m) in diameter diving at 'inconceivable speed' and appear to land about 25 miles (40km) south of the Grand Canyon.

- 4 July: United Airlines Captain E.J. Smith, about to take off from Boise, Idaho, for Seattle, was asked about flying saucers. 'I'll believe them when I see them,' he answered. Eight minutes after take-off, at 7000ft (2100m) over Emmett, Idaho, nine circular objects flew into view; co-pilot Ralph Stevens and stewardess Martie Morrow also saw them. Over a period of 15 minutes, the UFOs performed aerobatics, merged together and split up again, and disappeared and reappeared, before vanishing.

- 4 July: Picknickers at Twin Falls, Smoke River Canyon, Idaho, saw at least 35 disks 'putting on a real Independence Day display' in the afternoon.

- 4 July saw the height of the wave, with 88 sightings by 400 people in 24 states. About half were of single objects; the rest were of two or more, some flying in formation. Two thirds of these sightings were made in daylight, and involved round, spherical or disk-shaped UFOs.

- 7 July: The phenomenon became international. From the beach at Brighton, Sussex, UK, a married couple saw 'something like a moon, only bigger, fly over Black Rock cliffs and out to sea' at 4:00pm. Astronomers at Del Salto

Observatory, Chile, reported a UFO discharging white gases move across the horizon at an estimated 3000mph (4800km/h). It remained visible for some minutes. In Naples, Italy, numerous witnesses saw a slow-moving 'shining disk' cross the night sky. On the same day, UFOs were also reported in Japan and Holland.

- 8 July: At 9:10am, three officers at Muroc Field (now Edwards AFB), in the Mojave Desert, California, spent 10 minutes watching three silver-colored UFOs heading west. At 9:20am, Lt. J.C. McHenry, who was warming the engine of a Republic XP-84 Thunderjet, spotted another sphere, yellow-white in color, moving in the same direction

(against the wind) at a speed of about 300mph (480km/h) and an altitude of 8000ft (2400m).

At 11:50am at White Sands, five Air Force technicians including a major were watching two P-82s and one A-26 aircraft conduct an ejection-seat experiment at 20,000ft (6000m). They saw a 'round object, white aluminum in color, which at first resembled a parachute canopy' come into view. The ejection-seat canopy opened 30 seconds later. The UFO was clearly nearer the ground, which it approached three times faster than the parachute, rotating or oscillating. The men noted no 'smoke, flame, propeller arcs, engine noise or other plausible means of

Artist's rendition of a UFO downed in the desert near Aztec, New Mexico, in 1947. This event, reported by Frank Scully in his 1950 book *Behind the Flying Saucers*, was the first of many claims that flying saucers have crashed in remote regions of the USA. Unfortunately for Scully, the story was a hoax played on him by two con-men who elaborated on the plot of a movie script then being touted around Hollywood.

propulsion.' The UFO reached ground level, and rose again. A USAAF captain at Rogers Dry Lake, immediately east of Muroc, also witnessed the object.

At 3:50pm, a pilot in a P-51 Mustang at 20,000ft (6000m) sighted a wingless 'flat object of a light-reflecting nature' above him some 40 miles (65km) south of Muroc. The UFO was too high for the P-51 to close with it. No air base in the area had aircraft in that vicinity.

- 23 July: John Jenssen was piloting a private plane over New Jersey when he saw a flash high above him. The engine cut out but the plane continued in level flight. Jenssen then saw to his left a 'strange, wraith-like' craft with 'portholes' around its flanged rim. A quarter

mile (0.4km) beyond it a second UFO hung motionless in the sky. Jenssen then restarted his engine and escaped the UFOs.

- 23 July: Survey workers at Bauru, near Pitanga, Brazil, fled when a disk landed 150ft (45m) from them. Jose C. Higgins returned to the site and encountered three entities, each over 6ft (1.8m) tall, in translucent suits, with bald, oversized heads and huge round eyes, as they emerged from the craft. They indicated that they had come from Uranus.

- 13 August: At Twin Falls, Smoke River Canyon, Idaho, a man and his two sons observed a sky-blue UFO, shaped like an inverted plate and about 20ft (6m) in diameter and 12ft (3.5m) thick. The object was 300ft (90m) away, flying about 75ft (22.5m) from the ground and causing the treetops beneath it to spin wildly.

- 14 August: At Raveo, Italy, Signor R.L. Johannis discovered a grounded disk, near which stood two dwarf-like, helmeted creatures less than 3ft (1m) tall. They had oversized heads, huge eyes with no lashes or lids, greenish skin, and eight talon-like fingers on each hand. They shot a vapor at Johannis from the center of their belts; he felt an electric shock and then passed out.

ASSESSMENT

Four things are notable about these sightings. First, most took place in daylight. Second is the sheer number of UFOs that

suddenly appeared after Arnold's experience made news. Was this a demonstration by whatever creates UFO incidents? Or had UFOs always been there, but now simply started to be noticed? Third, the proportion of pilots, military personnel and others who might be relied on to tell an aircraft from a UFO (especially in daylight) is remarkably high. Fourth, the events gain rapidly in complexity and strangeness. Within a month of Arnold's sighting, the first close encounters were reported. It may be significant that they occurred in countries steeped in religious tradition. It may be even more significant that each involved entirely different kinds of entity. What is clear is that within a few weeks the outlines of the UFO experience as we know it today had already begun to fall into place. Within five or six years they would be complete. After that, there would be only variations and developments of these related themes.

WHAT HAPPENED AT ROSWELL?

The most controversial crashed saucer case

TYPE: Crash/retrieval episode
PLACE: Foster Ranch, near
             Corona, Lincoln County,
             New Mexico, USA
DATE: 2 July 1947

BACKGROUND

At about 9:50pm on 2 July, Roswell hardware dealer Dan Wilmot and his wife were sitting out on their front stoop when they saw a 'big glowing object' traveling at speed through the sky out of the south-east. It was, they said, like 'two inverted saucers faced mouth to mouth.'

The Foster Ranch, 'Mac' Brazel's rough, isolated spread, lay 30 miles (48km) from Corona, and 75 miles (120km) north-west of Roswell. It was stormy there on the night of 2 July. Brazel thought he heard an explosion above the sound of thunder.

THE EVENTS

Warrant Officer Irving Newton with the wreckage of a weather balloon at Fort Worth, Texas, on 8 July 1947. Newton, a weather expert, said he had giggled at the suggestion that this was from a downed flying saucer. He also disputed the claim that the Army had replaced real UFO wreckage with some innocuous material. In September 1994 the US Air Force stated that the 'UFO' was most likely an experimental balloon array built for the top-secret Project Mogul, designed to detect Soviet nuclear tests. In 1995 it was revealed that Major Jesse Marcel, the Roswell intelligence officer, had lied about his qualifications and service record, discrediting his claims about the Roswell 'UFO'.

Next day, checking his sheep, Brazel came across some wreckage that spread in a 400-yard (365m) trail across his land, pointing due west, toward Socorro, a town on the Rio Grande about 100 miles (160km) distant. The debris was a 'metallic, foil-like substance', which was very thin, pliable, and tough. He could not crease it or give it a permanent bend. On it were some obscure markings. Some fragments had a 'tape-like material' attached to them, which showed a floral pattern when held up to the light. Shortly after this, in Corona, he heard for the first time about the rash of UFO sightings in the area. Wondering if the wreckage on his land was connected, he told the US Army at Roswell of his find. Major Jesse Marcel and a Counter-Intelligence Corps agent went with him to inspect the

debris, and next day, 8 July, troops descended on the site, keeping everyone off the land until they had cleared it. Marcel stated in 1978 that the wreckage he saw was like 'nothing made on Earth'. It resisted prolonged attack by blowtorch and 16lb (7kg) sledgehammer, despite its thinness and, if crumpled, slowly but surely reverted to its original form.

On 8 July, too, civil engineer Grady L. Barnett of Socorro was working in the desert about three miles (5km) from where the debris was scattered when he saw what he thought might be a crashed aircraft. He found 'some sort of metallic, disk-shaped object', about 30ft (9m) in diameter, split open. Inside it, and beside it on the ground, were a number of bodies. They were small, hairless humanoids with large heads, wearing gray, one-piece suits without fasteners. Barnett was soon joined by a group of archaeology students. Shortly after, a US Army jeep roared up. The officer on board declared the area off limits and under military control. The area was cordoned off, the civilians told to leave – and to say nothing of what they had seen – and troops began to move in. The crashed disk had been detected from the air.

The same day a statement printed in the *Roswell Daily Record*, authorized by the base commander at Roswell, announced that a flying disk had been found and recovered from a ranch 75 miles (120km) from Roswell. Later that day, the Army called two press conferences, proclaiming that the debris found on Brazel's ranch was the remains of a weather balloon. Reporters saw and photographed it.

There is considerable testimony that secret cargoes were flown under heavy guard from Roswell to Forth Worth, Texas, and Wright Field (now Wright-Patterson AFB) at Dayton, Ohio, over the next few days.

ASSESSMENT

That something, which the military establishment wanted to keep very secret, came down from the sky that night seems beyond doubt. But the evidence will fit several scenarios, none involving extra-terrestrial craft or aliens.

First, the US Army may have told the truth when it said the debris was from a balloon, even if the fragments of Rawin radar target balloon shown to the press were not from the balloon that actually crashed. The US Navy and the CIA were planning the Moby Dick program, which sent high-altitude Skyhook balloons drifting over the Soviet mainland on spy missions. There was every reason to keep these secret. The material that so astonished Marcel may have been an early form of polythene; White Sands Proving Ground launched the first polythene balloons for the US Army on 3 July. Aluminized Saran, which behaves in just the way Marcel describes, was also available then.

Researcher John Keel has noted that in World War II the Japanese had developed *fu-go* balloons, made of very tough paper, that carried incendiary bombs. A *fu-go*

An artist's impression of the 'Roswell UFO' that allegedly crashed in July 1947 on the Plains of St Agustin, New Mexico. According to some accounts, a group of archaeology students from the University of Pennsylvania came across the wreckage only moments before the military arrived to take charge – although no reliable witness has yet come forward to give a first-hand account of this event.

balloon was huge, filled with 19,000 cu. ft (5700 cu. m) of gas. The top was silvered to reflect sunlight and stop the gas overheating and lifting the balloon too high. In 1945 over 9000 of these devices were launched from Japan into the jetstream, and between 300 and 500 of the weapons reached the USA. But they could stay in the air for a very long time. Witnesses said the 'hieroglyphs' on the Roswell debris were 'like the writing on firecrackers', and were arranged in columns. They were, most likely, Japanese pictograms.

The Army was interested in Brazel's find for two reasons. The 509th Bomb Group at Roswell was then the world's only nuclear-equipped attack unit, and any hint that it was being spied on would have brought a very swift reaction. But if the threat turned out to be a leftover from World War II, the cover-up may have been to avoid admitting that the USA was still being bombed by Japan two years after the war had ended.

None of the skeptical explanations covers every aspect of the Roswell case. But testimony gathered since the Seventies is largely hearsay and circumstantial. Supporters of the crashed saucer hypothesis fail to consider that atomic weapons, or parts of them, were the most likely cargo to move from Roswell under heavy guard. Even so, the authors of the study published in 1991 for the J. Allen Hynek Center for UFO Studies favor an extra-terrestrial solution.

FATAL PURSUIT

The death of Captain Thomas Mantell

TYPE: **Daylight disk, multiple witnesses**
PLACE: **Godman Field near Fort Knox, Kentucky, USA**
DATE: **7 January 1948**

BACKGROUND

According to some, but not all, accounts, the Kentucky Highway Patrol alerted the control tower at Godman Field near Fort Knox that residents at Maysville, Owensboro and Irvington had reported a UFO moving west at an erratic pace. Numerous witnesses including the base commander observed it from about 1:20pm onward. Descriptions agree the object was white, but vary as to shape, from 'like an upside-down ice-cream cone' to 'umbrella-shaped'. The sky was clear, but with considerable haze. At 2:45pm, six F-51s of the US Air National Guard arrived at Godman on a ferrying flight, and were asked to investigate. One, low on fuel, landed. The others, led by Captain Thomas Mantell, went after the UFO.

THE EVENTS

At 15,000ft (4500m), two of Mantell's wingmen peeled off and returned to

Artist's impression of the standard tale of Captain Thomas Mantell's encounter with a UFO in January 1948. According to this, his F-51 Mustang aircraft was 'shot down' by a UFO, and his body never found. The facts of the case are less dramatic, if no less tragic.

Godman. Their aircraft lacked oxygen, which USAF regulations demanded be used over 14,000ft (4200m). Mantell radioed the control tower that the UFO was 'metallic and tremendous in size', and 'appears to be moving about half my speed.' At 22,000ft (6600m), the two remaining wingmen dropped out. One, Lt. B.A. Hammond, informed Mantell that they were abandoning the intercept, but Mantell failed to respond. He made no

weather conditions) and then as a weather balloon – or two balloons and Venus. It seems reasonably certain that Mantell was chasing a balloon. In the early Fifties the US Navy stated it had secretly sent Skyhook balloons over the area. The appearance of these balloons – they were 450ft (135m) tall and 100ft (30m) across at the top – matches descriptions by witnesses at Godman. Mantell's 'UFO' had probably been launched from Camp Ripley, Minnesota.

PROJECT TWINKLE

The mystery of the green fireballs

TYPE: **Lights in the sky**
PLACE: **Centered on New Mexico, USA**
DATE: **1948-51**

BACKGROUND

Green fireballs were seen in the skies over New Mexico, in 1948. Reports soon came from neighboring states. The USAF at first attributed the sightings to flare guns: thousands were in private hands after World War II.

THE EVENTS

At about 9:30pm on 5 December 1948 a bright green light flashed past a USAF C-47 Dakota and another airliner over New Mexico. The crewmen on the C-47 saw the light arc toward them – something no meteor would do. They agreed with the captain of the airliner to report the sighting to Kirtland AFB. This was the second mysterious green light they had seen on the flight. A few minutes later, a Pioneer Airlines DC-3 Dakota radioed Kirtland with a similar report. The green light had headed straight for the plane at 9:35pm, forcing the pilot to take evasive action. When the plane finally landed at Albuquerque, the crew were grilled by USAF intelligence officers.

The USAF was particularly interested in the above events because these

'unusual' UFOs had been seen skimming around in New Mexico, an area of high sensitivity because it was home to the greatest concentration of secret military installations in the continental USA. Dr Lincoln La Paz, an expert at tracking meteors, was called in to head the investigation. If the fireballs were meteors, he would be able to find their points of impact and fragments. Investigations showed five green fireballs had been seen on 5 December. La Paz calculated the impact zone of the largest, investigated that zone thoroughly and found nothing. At a conference of scientists held at Los Alamos, New Mexico, in February 1949 it was concluded that the fireballs were a natural phenomenon, but an unknown one. La Paz was then put in charge of Project Twinkle, to be funded by the USAF, to discover more.

La Paz's plan was to set up three cinetheodolite stations to film and record the fireballs' precise location, altitude, size, speed and chemical structure. But only one camera was made available to them, the investigating team always seemed to arrive at sighting locations after the local 'flap' was over, and the USAF failed to come up with all the required funds. Although many fireballs had been seen in New Mexico, and 165 people witnessed a giant green fireball explode silently over Arizona on 2 November 1951, none of these occurrences was ever caught on film. On 27 December 1951, La Paz declared Project Twinkle a failure, and closed it down. By the end of 1952, the fireballs themselves had stopped appearing.

ASSESSMENT

In 1952, the USAF Directorate of Intelligence recommended that Project Twinkle remain classified, as it had found no scientific explanation of the fireballs, and 'some reputable scientists still believe [they] are man-made.' The speculation was that they were some kind of spy device. More than 40 years later, there is still no convincing answer to the riddle of the green fireballs.

further calls, but continued to climb. By 3:15pm his plane was lost to sight. A search was launched almost immediately. Just after 5:00pm the wreckage of Mantell's P-51 was found on a farm near Franklin, Kentucky. His body was inside it. His watch had stopped at 3:18pm, which was taken as the time of impact.

ASSESSMENT

Rumors began almost at once that Mantell had been shot down by the UFO. It seems certain that Mantell died because for some reason he persisted in the chase even though his plane had no oxygen. He would have blacked out while his plane continued to climb until the engine itself died of oxygen starvation. The USAF first explained the UFO as the planet Venus (which would have been invisible in the

THE ASTRONOMER'S REPORT

The case of the luminous rectangles

TYPE: **Lights in the sky**
PLACE: **Las Cruces,**
        New Mexico, USA
DATE: **20 August 1949**

BACKGROUND

Clyde W. Tombaugh was familiar with the night sky. At the age of 24, in 1930, he had discovered the planet Pluto. In 1949 he was working at White Sands Missile Range (WSMR) and living in Las Cruces, 40 miles (65km) away.

THE EVENTS

Tombaugh was with his wife and mother-in-law in Las Cruces; all three saw a group of between six and eight rectangular UFOs in an ellipsoid formation. The UFOs were yellow-green, and traveling from north-west to south-east. In 1957 Tombaugh said of the experience: 'I was so unprepared for such a strange sight that I was really petrified with astonishment.' Tombaugh saw UFOs on two other occasions, but he did not report them at the time, because he was afraid that to do so would jeopardize his professional reputation.

ASSESSMENT

Skeptic Dr Donald H. Menzel suggested that what Tombaugh saw might have been reflections of city lights on a temperature inversion, but Tombaugh himself commented: 'I doubt the phenomenon was any terrestrial reflection.' From his work at WSMR, Tombaugh said he knew 'we didn't have anything that could do that.' And yet despite his refusal to accept Menzel's rationalization, Tombaugh still did not have any fixed opinion of his own about what the ellipsoid formation might really have been. 'It is still a very open question,' he commented.

THE TRENT PHOTOGRAPHS

Experts still argue about their authenticity

TYPE: **Daylight disk**
PLACE: **McMinnville, Oregon, USA**
DATE: **11 May 1950**

BACKGROUND

UFO sightings occurred frequently in the McMinnville area, and Mr and Mrs Paul Trent had previously observed a number of them from their small farm.

THE EVENTS

Mrs Trent was outside feeding her rabbits at about 7:45pm when she saw a very bright, 'almost silvery' object silently approaching the farm. She called to her husband, who was inside the house. He didn't answer, so she ran in to get him, and to fetch a camera. She took two shots before the UFO rapidly accelerated

and sped away out of sight in a north-westerly direction.

ASSESSMENT

In some ways, the Trents behaved rather surprisingly after the events of 11 May. To begin with, they waited until the whole reel of film was finished before having it processed. Then at first they showed their extraordinary pictures only to friends, and they never took very good care of the negatives.

When astronomer William Hartmann came to analyse the shots for the Condon Committee he concluded they were probably genuine. Robert Sheaffer's analysis, however, found that the pictures had been taken in the early morning, not in the evening, and minutes rather than seconds apart – findings that were at variance with the Trents' own account of the sighting. Furthermore, Sheaffer concluded that lens smudges accounted for the UFOs' apparent brightness. Now skeptical, Sheaffer speculated that the UFO was a model suspended on a string. Hartmann accepted this point of view, and so did the Condon Committee. But when Ground Saucer Watch (GSW) digitally enhanced the original photographic negatives they found no trace of a string, and calculated that the object must have been 65-100ft (20-30m) in diameter. However, GSW agreed with Hartmann that the photographs must have been taken in the morning.

A detail from one of the two photographs taken at the Trent farm near McMinnville, Oregon, on 11 May 1950. Computer enhancement revealed no sign of a fake, but the pictures still draw the wrath of skeptics. They point to the discrepancies in the Trents' accounts of the event, the fact that they were 'repeater' witnesses with a record of many claimed sightings, and telephone wires (not visible in this cropped version of the picture) from which a model UFO could have been suspended.

THE LUBBOCK LIGHTS

UFOs in V-formation over Texas

TYPE: **Lights in the sky**
PLACE: **Albuquerque, New Mexico, Lubbock, Texas, USA**
DATE: **August-October 1951**

BACKGROUND

At roughly 9:00pm on 25 August, a guard at the secret Sandia base, and another witness with his wife, saw a huge V-shaped craft pass silently over Albuquerque, heading south. Eight soft blue lights glowed along the trailing edge of the flying wing. Estimated speed was 400mph (650km/h), and altitude 800-1000ft (240-300m).

THE EVENTS

At approximately 9:20pm, four Texas Technical College professors watched a semi-circular formation of 20-30 lights flying fast north to south over Lubbock, Texas. Before midnight, they saw two more similar formations flying in the same direction at the same speed. The lights were yellowish white, and glowed softly. A neighboring USAF radar station picked up an 'unknown' flying at 900mph (1450km/h) at 13,000ft (3900m) at about the same time. The blips were on the screens for six minutes, and an F-86 Sabre was scrambled, but failed to make contact with the UFOs.

On 31 August, college freshman Carl Hart presented the *Lubbock Evening Avalanche* with five photographs, allegedly taken the previous night, of V-shaped light formations. In September and October the four professors went skywatching and saw 12 random light formations moving north to south.

ASSESSMENT

USAF investigators found a rancher 30 miles south of Lubbock who had also seen the three V-formations of lights on 25 August. He recognized them as flights of plovers, whose white breasts can reflect city lights. The Hart photos do not match witnesses' descriptions, and many suspect them of being a hoax. It is remotely possible that an experimental, eight-engined jet bomber, the Northrop YB-49 'flying wing', was responsible for the Albuquerque sighting and the Lubbock radar 'unknown'. Otherwise, these events remain unexplained.

THE 1952 WORLDWIDE WAVE

UFOs appear all over the planet

TYPE: **Daylight disks, lights in the sky, close encounters**
PLACE: **Africa, the Americas, Asia, Europe**
DATE: **1952**

BACKGROUND

The UFO experience in all its manifestations became a global phenomenon in 1952. Within the overall pattern was the 'flap' over Washington, DC, in July. Sightings worldwide intensified in April, rose to a peak in July, and began to fall away again in November. There were hundreds of sightings reported every month, and the figure reached thousands at the height of the wave. A brief selection of them follows.

THE EVENTS

- 30 January – Korea: A UFO 'like a large horizontal wheel', radiating orange light and emitting blue flames from its rim, was visible for several minutes.
- 10 May – France: At La Roche-sur-Yon, 12 witnesses saw a flat, brightly-lit disk flying silently to overtake a second UFO hovering above it.
- 31 May – Korea: Two military guards at Chorwon observed a UFO with a dull center and bright rim darting around the sky. An F-94 Starfire fighter sent to intercept the UFO found itself in a dogfight, until the UFO accelerated

away. The pilot could not describe it or its size 'due to blinding light of object'.

- 15 June – Brazil: At Itenhaem, a woman woken at 3:00am by an explosion and a powerful blue light saw a 'fleet' of disks hovering 3ft (1m) from the ground, 600 yards (550m) from her house. They remained there for 30 minutes, while two figures stood on one of the UFOs and observed the sky, then took off one by one.

- 2 July – Utah, USA: Navy Chief Warrant Officer and expert aerial photographer Delbert C. Newhouse, driving near Tremonton with his wife and two children, saw 12 objects, each 'like two pie cans, one inverted on top of the other', flying west in changing formation. He shot 40ft (12m) of color 16mm film of the objects. They seemed huge and very high, but Newhouse could not accurately guess their size,

speed, distance or altitude, but did say 'if they had been the size of B-29s they would have been at 10,000ft (3000m) altitude.' The USAF decided the objects were birds. Ground Saucer Watch's 1976 computer analysis concluded that they were disks about 50ft (15m) across, between five and seven miles (8-11km) distant.

- 1 July – Germany: At Hasselbach, local politician and former Wehrmacht Major Oskar Linke and his 11-year-old step-daughter Gabrielle had to abandon their motorcycle; walking near a wood, they saw among the trees a grounded 50ft (15m) wide saucer with a 10ft (3m) conning tower on top. Linke said: 'Standing by it were two figures… in shimmering metal dress.' Gabrielle called to them, and they hastily climbed into the UFO and took off toward Stockheim. A shepherd, a mile from the

wood, saw the UFO fly away, as did the watchman at a nearby sawmill.

- 20 July – Morocco: A M. Petijean saw a saucer take off at Dai-el-Aouagri; it gave out blue flashes and a powerful smell of burning sulfur.

- 12 September – Flatwood, West Virginia, USA: Mrs Kathleen May, her five children and National Guardsman Gene Lemon, set out to investigate her sons' report that a UFO had landed on Flatwood Hill. The party reached the hill but fled in terror from a hooded monster 'worse than Frankenstein' – half man, half dragon, with a blood-red face and green eyes and 'terrible claws'. A sickening stench came from the thing. Local people confirmed the landing of a sphere-shaped UFO on the hill, and the stench it left behind.

- 20-24 September – English Channel and North Sea, north-west Europe:

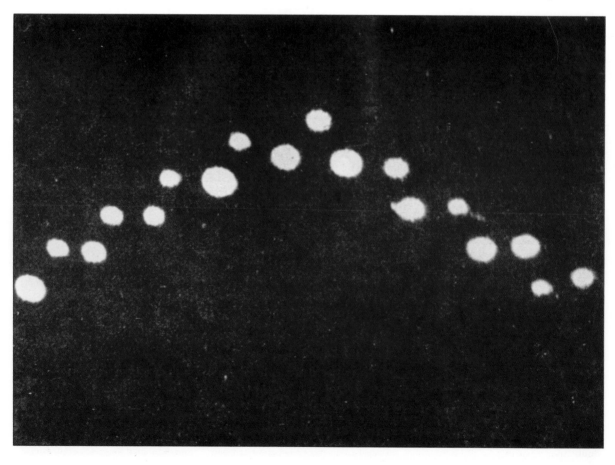

Operation Mainbrace, a huge NATO naval exercise, was plagued by UFOs. On 20 September, three photographs were taken from the aircraft carrier USS *Franklin D. Roosevelt* of a UFO that was flying behind the NATO fleet. The next day, six seaborne NATO fighters chased a bright spherical UFO. On 24 September, a UFO was sighted at sea and chased by a Royal Air Force Meteor fighter flying from RAF Topcliffe on the mainland.

- 21 September – Morocco: UFOs appeared over Tangier, Marakesh, and Casablanca. One extremely fast flying disk changed shape to an ellipse west of Nefik, and stopped briefly while explosions came from it. It then proceeded at the same pace, in the same direction, and as luminous as before.
- 28 September – Scandinavia and northern Europe: Dozens of reports involving hundreds of witnesses were made of UFOs of all shapes and sizes over Denmark, Sweden, northern Germany and northern Poland.
- 2 October – Australia: At Sunshine Road, Melbourne, two teenagers out for an evening stroll heard a whistling sound and then saw a low-flying, red and blue UFO hurtling straight toward them. The pair fled for cover.
- 7 October – France: At about 12:50pm, M. Prigent, the headmaster of a school at Oloron-Sainte-Marie, Pays Basques, and his family saw a fleet of UFOs and a 'mother ship', flying a zig-zag course. The latter was a white cylinder, tilted at 45° into the sky, at an altitude of 8000ft (2400m). (The objects were also seen on radar at the nearby Mont-de-

One of five photographs taken by student Carl Hart of the 'Lubbock lights' seen in Texas in August 1952 (see account on page 53). The patterns of the UFOs in these pictures do not match the formations of unidentified lights seen by other witnesses, but there seems little doubt that something physically real was behind the sightings.

Marsan station.) Traveling in pairs ahead of it were some 30 spherical objects that, M. Prigent saw through binoculars, were red spheres with a yellow planetary rings around them, like small versions of Saturn. All the UFOs gave out occasional puffs of smoke, and left long trails of a substance that drifted to the ground. Many witnesses testified that the material kept falling for hours afterwards; it was gelatinous at first, but eventually vaporized. In the early Fifties UFO events were frequently accompanied by such curious precipitations; they were dubbed 'angel hair'.

- 18 November – Italy: Farmer Nello Ferrari of Castelfranco found himself flooded in red light; looking up, he saw 30ft (9m) above the ground a 70ft (20m) wide copper-gold disk with a rotating cylinder beneath; from it came sounds like an electric motor. On the upper surface was a turret from which three beings observed him directly. They looked 'perfectly human'. The cylinder was retracted and the craft took off vertically at high speed.
- 6 December – Gulf of Mexico: A B-29 bomber at the end of a night practice flight to Florida was heading for its base in Texas. At 5:24am the plane was 100 miles (160km) south of the Louisiana coast and 100 miles (160km) from Galveston, cruising at 18,000ft (5400m) in bright moonlight. One minute later, the first of three 'unknowns' appeared on the B-29's radar, heading directly for the bomber. They passed safely by as the crew computed their speed as 5240mph (8440km/h). Moments later, four more UFOs appeared on the same heading: this time the crew made visual contact as they passed. At 5:31am, two more UFOs bore down on the B-29 at the same speed and passed by. Then five UFOs appeared on the radar, behind the bomber and flying across its course. They suddenly swerved, headed for the B-29, and abruptly slowed to pace it for 10 seconds before veering away. Next, a huge blip came into view

on the radar. The smaller UFOs, without slowing, seemed to merge with it. And then the giant blip picked up speed, flashing off the screen at a computed 9000mph (14,500km/h). All three radar sets aboard the B-29 were working perfectly and showed exactly the same returns.

ASSESSMENT

Many of the sightings in 1952 were doubtless misidentified aircraft and natural phenomena, induced by a contagious fascination for UFOs. But it seems equally reasonable to say that many witnesses were not mistaken. At the time, the USAF actually encouraged interest in the UFOs to increase recruitment into its newly formed Ground Observer Corps!

UFOS OVER THE WHITE HOUSE

The first Washington flap

TYPE: **Daylight disks and lights in the sky**
PLACE: **Washington, DC, USA**
DATE: **19-20 July and 26-27 July 1952**

BACKGROUND

For Americans, the two sets of events recounted here formed perhaps the most dramatic part of the 1952 global wave.

THE EVENTS

- 19-20 July: Between 11:40pm and 5:00am, two radars covering Washington picked up eight UFOs in restricted air space. They flew at between 100 and 300mph (160-480km/h), suddenly accelerating to phenomenal velocities. Airline pilots were also reporting strange lights in the sky over the capital, behaving in the same fashion. Jet interceptors, delayed by an earlier investigation of UFOs over New Jersey, arrived at 3:30am; the UFOs disappeared, then reappeared after the jets departed. At one point, radar controlers following events at Andrews AFB saw a large, blazing orange sphere hovering over the base.

- 26-27 July: From 9:00pm, between six and 12 UFOs performed similar maneuvers. At 2:00am, interceptors from Wilmington, Delaware, were scrambled, but again the UFOs disappeared from sight and from radar screens as soon as the jets came within radar range, and reappeared 10 minutes later, when the planes were returning to base. However, at about 3:20am a fresh flight of fighters came on the scene and the UFOs remained visible. Lt. William Patterson was surrounded by a ring of enormous blue-white lights which flew off before he was given permission to fire on them.

ASSESSMENT

The immediate USAF explanation for the lights and radar returns was 'temperature inversions'. Contemporary weather records show temperature inversions over

the capital that night, but not such as to create radar returns. Witnesses have said that the blips were bright and clear, unlike those created by ground echoes. The USAF's Project Blue Book listed the cause of the events as 'unknown'.

CONTACT WITH VENUS

George Adamski's bizarre claim

TYPE: **Close encounter of the third kind**
PLACE: **Mojave Desert, California, USA**
DATE: **20 November 1952**

BACKGROUND

George Adamski was a burger-bar assistant who called himself a 'professor' and a 'philosopher'. He lived in Palomar Gardens, on the lower slopes of Mount Palomar, California. He was convinced

that the other planets of our Solar System were inhabited. Through giving lectures on UFOs and extra-terrestrials he heard rumors that flying saucers had been landing in the California desert.

On Thursday 20 November 1952, Adamski (then aged 62), his secretary Mrs Lucy McKinnis, and the proprietor of Palomar Gardens, Mrs Alice K. Wells, met with Mr and Mrs Al C. Bailey of Winslow, Arizona, and Dr and Mrs George H. Williamson of Prescott, Arizona, on the highway near Blythe, California, to go into the desert in the hope of seeing a UFO land.

THE EVENTS

After a light luncheon alfresco, the party scanned the sky. Then: 'Riding high, and without sound, there was a gigantic cigar-shaped silvery ship, without wings or appendages of any kind.' On a hunch Adamski asked to be driven down the road. Two of the party took him onto a dirt road, and then Adamski sent his

companions back to the original parking spot to watch. As they left, a number of aircraft roared into sight and tried to circle the huge craft. The ship turned its nose upward and shot out into space.

Soon he saw a flash in the sky and 'a beautiful craft appeared to be drifting through a saddle between two of the mountain peaks.' Then Adamski realized that a man was beckoning him from the opening of a ravine about 450 yards (410m) away. Only when he was within arm's length did he realize that he was looking at a visitor from another world.

'The beauty of his form surpassed anything I had ever seen,' he wrote later. The man was about 5ft 6in (1.5m) tall, weighed about 135lb (60kg), and appeared – in Earthly terms – to be about 28 years old. He had wavy, shoulder-length sandy hair. His skin was the color of a sun-tanned Caucasian's. He had an extremely high forehead, 'calm, grey-green eyes' that slanted slightly at the corners, high cheekbones, and a 'finely chiseled' nose. He seemed to be beard-

A 'mother ship' surrounded by smaller UFOs, in one of innumerable alleged UFO photographs produced by contactee George Adamski. He was once heard to remark bitterly: 'If it wasn't for FDR I'd never have had to get into the flying saucer business.' This comment makes sense in light of the rumor that Adamski had been a successful bootlegger during the Prohibition era and felt a special animosity toward Franklin D. Roosevelt for making the USA 'wet' again, so depriving Adamski of a sizable income. Flying saucer stories became Adamski's second, if belated, major money-spinning venture. His report of meeting a Venusian in the Mojave desert in 1952 was originally written as a work of fiction, but failed to find a publisher until remodeled by a ghost writer and touted as a true story.

less. The alien was wearing a single-piece, finely-woven chocolate-brown suit with no visible fasteners or pockets, with a broad waistband and a close-fitting high collar. His shoes were ox-blood red, with blunt toes.

Using a mixture of hand signals and telepathy, the alien said he was from the planet Venus. Venusians were on Earth because they were concerned that nuclear radiation would destroy the Earth. The Venusian refused to be photographed, lest he be recognized. Some of their craft had been shot down by 'men of this world'. The time would come when they would be able to land openly. Adamski was allowed to approach the saucer hovering nearby, but not to go inside it. Then the Venusian boarded his craft, and it glided silently away.

ASSESSMENT

Venus has an atmospheric pressure 94.5 times higher than our own. This alone would cause any Venusian not wearing massive pressurized body armor to explode the moment it set foot on Earth. Temperatures on Venus are commonly around 900°F (480°C) – five times hotter than boiling water. Venusian rain consists largely of hydrochloric and sulphuric acid, and the 'air' is almost entirely carbon dioxide. Life as we know it cannot exist on Venus. Four of the 'witnesses' to this encounter later recanted their testimony.

THE TUJUNGA CANYON ENCOUNTERS

One of the earliest abduction cases on record

TYPE: **Close encounter of the third kind**
PLACE: **Tujunga Canyons, California, USA**
DATE: **22 March 1953**

BACKGROUND

Sara Shaw and Jan Whitley (pseudonyms), both in their early twenties, were living as

companions in an isolated cabin in the Tujunga Canyons between the Los Angeles basin and the Mojave desert.

THE EVENTS

Sara was woken by a bright light outside sweeping back and forth across the house. She thought the light might be from motorcycles, and wondered if a biker gang they had seen earlier had returned to wreak havoc. Waking Jan, she saw the time was exactly 2:00am. She knelt on her bed to look out of the window, and felt giddy and confused. She glanced at the clock again, and realized that the time was 4:20am. Thoroughly frightened, the pair left the cabin at once and did not return for several days.

According to Sara Shaw's testimony under hypnosis in 1975, she and Jan Whitley had been taken out of their cabin and floated aboard a UFO. They were undressed, examined by machines and then by alien beings, who wore black body stockings and telepathically communicated a cure for cancer to Sara. Sara said she enjoyed the attention of the male aliens while she was naked. The women parted on good terms with the aliens and were floated back to the cabin.

ASSESSMENT

Jan Whitley produced no recall of events during the period of missing time, consciously or in trance. The 'cure for cancer' turned out to be common acetic acid (vinegar). D. Scott Rogo, who helped investigate the case, concluded that Sara was fantasizing a symbolic rape that indicated her dissatisfaction with her lesbian relationship with Jan. He notes that Sara later married a quadriplegic; after a divorce and counseling she entered a conventional marriage. The fantasy, said Rogo, 'was objectified into physical reality in the form of a genuine UFO sighting and abduction', and confirmed his belief that UFO events may be turned into physical reality by an unknown force that uses imagery or ideas already in the subject's mind, and in answer to the subject's psychological needs.

SHAPE-SHIFTERS IN THE AIR LANES

A planeload of passengers see a bizarre group of UFOs

TYPE: **Multiple daylight disks, multiple witnesses**
PLACE: **North Atlantic Ocean**
DATE: **29 June 1954**

BACKGROUND

Taking off from Idlewild (now John F. Kennedy) Airport, New York, the Boeing Stratocruiser *Centaurus* of British Overseas Airways Corporation was lumbering along at 230 knots (415km/h) at 19,000ft (5700m), en route to Newfoundland for a refueling stopover before crossing the Atlantic to England.

THE EVENTS

Over the sea off the coast of Labrador, Capt. James Howard saw off his port side a huge, apparently metallic, object emerge from a gap in the cloud above him. Circling this were six smaller objects. The larger object kept changing shape. Capt. Howard sketched some of its forms on his kneepad: they included a pear, a telephone handset, and a boomerang or delta-wing shape. Co-pilot Lee Boyd raised ground control and said tersely: 'We are not alone.' 'We know,' came the reply. 'What is it?' asked Boyd. 'We don't know, but we've scrambled a Sabre [jet fighter] from Goose Bay to investigate.'

The UFOs kept pace with the Stratocruiser at a distance of about three miles (5km) for 20 minutes, watched by the crew and 30 passengers. As the Sabre approached, the six smaller objects lined up and merged one by one into the larger one. Then this began to shrink. When the Sabre came over, the UFO vanished.

ASSESSMENT

When the plane landed to refuel, intelligence officers told the crew there had been other sightings in the area. So the authorities knew there was something there, even if they didn't know its nature.

OUT OF AFRICA

Two sightings in a French colony

TYPE: **Lights in the sky, multiple witnesses**
PLACE: **Ivory Coast, West Africa**
DATE: **18 September 1954**

BACKGROUND

Ivory Coast was a French colony until 1960. UFO sightings were rarely reported from European colonial possessions.

THE EVENTS

At about 8:30pm, a luminous red elliptical UFO was seen at Danae. It arrived at speed, halted, and hovered for five minutes above many witnesses before speeding away. At the same time over Soubre in the south-west of the country, another UFO performed the same maneuver against a clear sky. Among the witnesses was the French chief administrator of the town.

ASSESSMENT

News of the French wave of Fall 1954 (see below) had hardly begun to break. These sightings occurred too early to be ascribed to a form of psychological contagion among expatriates, and involved many African witnesses besides.

LANDINGS IN FRANCE

The wave of 1954

TYPE: **Close encounters of the second and third kind**
PLACE: **France**
DATE: **Fall, 1954**

BACKGROUND

At least 156 reports of UFOs that had been observed landing or stationary on the ground reached the French authorities between the middle of September and November 1954. A sample of these reports follows.

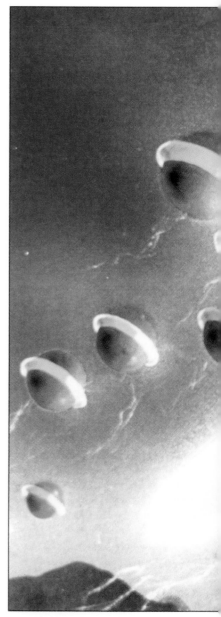

THE EVENTS

- 10 September – Quaroubles: At 10:30pm Marius Dewilde was disturbed by his dog howling. Outside, he saw two 3ft (1m) tall, armless entities 'shuffling along on very short legs'. From a 'shape' nearby a beam of white-green light shot out and paralyzed him. The entities entered the shape, which rose with a whistling noise and flew away eastward, glowing red. Ground mark-

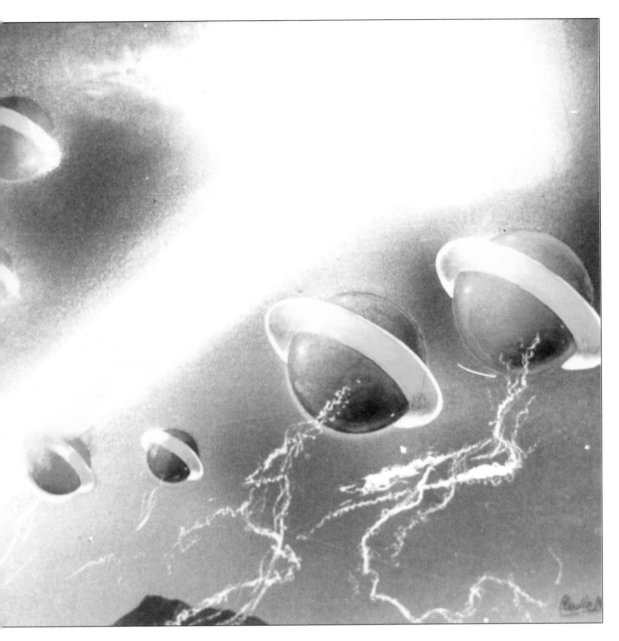

ings were later discovered that, an engineer calculated, would have taken a 30-tonne weight to make. Five other witnesses also saw the red light.

- 2 October – Croix d'Epine: 19-year-old mechanic Ernest Delatre was riding a motor scooter home when a brightly lit egg-shaped orange UFO, the size of a small bus, landed in the road. He saw dark shapes 'like potato bags' moving near it. As he approached the UFO

took off, changing color to blue. Two other witnesses in nearby villages also independently reported the UFO.

- 4 October – Poncey: Mme Fourneret and her son saw an elongated, 10ft (3m) wide luminous orange 'body' land about 20 yards (18m) from their house, and fled. Armed neighbors investigated soon after, and found a large, freshly-made hole that looked as if the earth had been sucked out of it. The earth

Artist's rendition of 30 or so Saturn-like globes seen by French headmaster M. Prigent and his family in October 1952 (see account on page 55).

itself was nowhere to be found.

- 20 October – Turquenstein: Jean Schoubrenner was driving near the village when a huge light glowed on the road ahead. About 20 yards (18m)

U F O

away from it, he felt paralyzed, and his car engine failed. He felt heat suffuse his body. The UFO flew away a few seconds later, and he and the car returned to normal.

ASSESSMENT

No sightings were made in any of the major population centers. Only 15 per cent of the landing reports were made by lone witnesses. Something more than a purely psychological phenomenon would appear to have been at work.

THE SIEGE AT THE SUTTON PLACE

Levitating, bullet-proof aliens attack a farm

TYPE: **Close encounter of the third kind**
PLACE: **Sutton Farm, Kelly, near Hopkinsville, Kentucky, USA**
DATE: **21-22 August 1955**

BACKGROUND

At the Sutton farm that night were eight adults and three children. Billy Ray Taylor and his wife June were visiting Elmer, the elder of the two Sutton boys. At about 7:00pm Billy Ray went out into the yard to fetch a drink from the well. He saw a gigantic object 'real bright, but with an exhaust all the colors of the rainbow' land in a dried-out gulch nearby. But when he told the Suttons what he had seen, no one bothered to go outside and look.

THE EVENTS

An hour later the dog began barking in the yard. Elmer and Billy Ray, suspecting intruders, picked up their guns and went to the kitchen door. Slowly approaching the house was a small 'shining' man with his hands held over his head. The men opened fire. The tiny figure somersaulted backwards from the impact of the shots, which hit it with a sound 'as if you had shot into a pail'. Then it fled.

Several more creatures approached the house from different angles, and were shot at. One was heard on the kitchen roof; Elmer and Billy Ray both fired at it, and it fell — then 'floated' another 40ft (12m) to settle on a fence. The two fired again, simultaneously. The thing fell and then scuttled off into the weeds behind the fence on all fours. Shooting had no terminal effect on any of the intruders, and they seemed more afraid of the lights from the Suttons' torches than of bullets. When hit by either they dropped on all fours and ran.

The creatures were all a little over 3ft (1m) tall when upright. They had round, egg-shaped heads, very large, yellow eyes spaced wide apart, and huge, elephant-like ears. Their long, thin arms ended in claw-like hands. They had slim, straight, silvery-colored bodies that seemed to be lit from the inside. This inner light intensified whenever they were shot at — or even shouted at.

The frightened family locked themselves into the house. Finally, after about three hours during which the intruders peered in through the windows from time to time, all eight adults and the three children ran for the two cars on the farm and drove to Hopkinsville, seven miles (11km) south on Route 41, to alert the police. Six officers including the local police chief returned to the farm with the family and searched the place, but found no sign of the visitors. They left at about 2:00am, and the family went to bed. Then the creatures returned, surrounding the house, and peering in the windows — and getting shot at some more. They withdrew at about 5:15am.

ASSESSMENT

June Taylor was the only one present not to see the creatures, because she was too terrified to look. Only Billy Ray saw the UFO, but a neighbor, living a quarter mile (0.4km) away, saw lights moving around the Sutton place about the time the UFO landed; he thought that the Suttons' pigs had gotten loose. Billy Ray Taylor and the Sutton family never retracted their story.

A DEVICE OF UNKNOWN ORIGIN

UFOs buzz USAF bases in eastern England

TYPE: **Radar-visual sighting**
PLACE: **Bentwaters and Lakenheath AFBs, near Ipswich, Suffolk, England**
DATE: **13 August 1956**

BACKGROUND

The Royal Air Force bases at Bentwaters and Lakenheath were both leased to the USAF. Any unknown aircraft coming in from the east over the North Sea was reckoned to be potentially hostile. On the night of 13-14 August several UFOs flying at fantastic speeds were picked up by up to six military radars simultaneously, from 9:30pm on. The final intrusion was the most dramatic.

THE EVENTS

At 10:55pm ground radar at Bentwaters picked up an unidentified target coming in from the sea at 2000-4000mph (3200-6450km/h), speeds well beyond the capacity of any conventional aircraft. The UFO flew directly over the base and disappeared from the screen 30 miles (48km) to the west. A control tower operator saw it pass over, and the pilot of a USAF C-47 at 4000ft (1200m) saw a fuzzy light flash from the plane to the ground. The UFO appeared on radar at Lakenheath, performing aerobatics. The base alerted the RAF, who scrambled a Venom NF2a fighter from RAF Waterbeach. The Venom soon made contact, but the UFO flipped over and came up behind the fighter, which then tried to shake it off – without success. A second Venom joined in, but the UFO dropped away. It was last seen on radar heading north at 600mph (970km/h).

ASSESSMENT

Despite its habitual skepticism, the Scientific Study of Unidentified Flying Objects (commonly known as the Condon Committee, which reported its findings in 1969) called this 'the most puzzling and unusual case in the radar-visual files'.

After conducting an in-depth examination of all the facts of the case the Committee reached the conclusion that 'the apparently rational, intelligent behavior of the UFO suggests a mechanical device of unknown origin as the most probable explanation.'

Neither did an exhaustive analysis of the technical aspects of the radar-visual data – conducted over a long period by Martin L. Shough – progress any further toward clearing up the Bentwaters mystery; on the contrary, these investigations served only to confirm the large number of anomalies.

'MORE BEAUTIFUL THAN ANY I HAVE EVER SEEN'

Antonio Villas Boas seduced by an alien

TYPE: **Close encounter of the third kind**
PLACE: **São Francisco de Salles, Minas Gerais, Brazil**
DATE: **15-16 October 1957**

BACKGROUND

Aged 23, Antonio Villas Boas was living with his parents, his brothers and sisters-in-law on a small farm. On the night of 15-16 October 1957, he was out alone, plowing the fields by the light of his tractor's headlamps.

THE EVENTS

At about 1:00am, Villas Boas saw a 'large red star' descending out of the sky toward the end of the field he was working. As the red light came down to about 150ft (45m) above him, he could see it was an egg-shaped object. Its brilliant glow drowned out the lights of his tractor as it landed no more than 50ft (15m) from where he was sitting. Purple lights were set in its rim. Three spurs were set at the front, lit up with red light. The upper, domed part of the machine was

Ella Louise Fortune, who worked as a nurse at the Mescalero Indian Reservation near Three Rivers, New Mexico, took this picture while driving along Highway 54 at about 1:30pm on 16 October 1957. The UFO was hovering motionless over Holloman Air Force Base. Opinions of the picture have been divided and ambiguous. Investigators for NICAP and US Air Force analysts suggested that the 'UFO' was in fact a cloud. An APRO consultant maintained that the object was emitting twice as much light as a cloud would in the prevailing conditions, but felt the object was 'not solid'.

spinning anti-clockwise, and as it slowed to land changed color from red to green. Antonio tried to make off on his tractor, but the engine died after a few yards. He started to struggle across the ploughed field on foot. Then he was grabbed by three creatures – no higher than his shoulder; he was 5ft 5in (1.5m) tall – and dragged to the waiting craft. He was taken up a flexible ladder into the machine, to a small, square, brightly lit room with metallic walls.

There were five small entities present: two kept a firm hold on him. They were wearing tight-fitting suits of thick, soft, unevenly striped gray material, and large,

Two of four photographs taken from the Brazilian Navy ship *Almirante Saldanha* by Almira Barauna off Trindade Island on 16 January 1958. The original photographs were numbered showing the sequence in which the pictures were taken. Ever since the USAF Project Blue Book investigator remarked that a UFO sighting over a barren island was unlikely 'as everyone knows Martians are extremely comfort-loving creatures', ufologists have debated the merits and demerits of this case and disputed the nature of the evidence – even down to the details of events aboard the ship and afterward.

The latest hypothesis comes from skeptic Steuart Campbell, who argues in his 1994 book *The UFO Mystery Solved* that the sighting and the photographs were genuine – but that the phenomenon was generated by a combination of a mirage of the planet Jupiter and wind and temperature inversions. Jupiter was in the position ringed in shot number four. Campbell's explanation has been criticized on two grounds: Jupiter is not bright enough to be visible in daylight, and it was anyway too high above the horizon to create a mirage.

broad helmets reinforced with bands of metal. Pipes led down from the helmets to their clothes, two going under each armpit and one down their backs. Thick-soled 'shoes' seemed to be integral to their suits, as did thick, unwieldy gloves. All Villas Boas could see of the creatures' faces through the helmets were their small, pale blue eyes.

He was then taken into another bright room, this time oval-shaped. The aliens attempted to converse, in 'slow barks and yelps, neither very clear nor very hoarse, some longer, some shorter, at times containing several different sounds all at once.' Failing to communicate, the aliens then stripped Villas Boas of his clothes. One of the beings rubbed a wet sponge-like thing over his skin, and then he was led through still another door. Over it were red 'letters' that he reproduced later for investigators. In this chamber, sparsely furnished with a few chairs and a

couch, the aliens used 'a sort of chalice', to take a blood sample from him, then left. A weird odor filled the room, which made him vomit.

He had been alone, naked, for half an hour when the door opened to reveal a nude woman, who was 'more beautiful than any I have ever seen before'. She stood shoulder-high to him. Her hair was parted in the middle, and reached halfway down her neck. It was smooth and fair, except for her pubic hair, which was bright red. She had a pointed chin, straight nose, high cheekbones, and large blue eyes. Her body, said Villas Boas, was 'slim, and her breasts stood up high and well separated. Her waistline was thin, her belly flat, her hips well developed, and her thighs were large.'

He continued: 'We ended up on the couch, where we lay together for the first time. It was a normal act and she reacted as any other woman would. Then we had some petting, followed by another act, but by now she had begun to deny herself to me, to end the matter.' Antonio became angry, as it dawned on him that 'all they wanted [was] a good stallion to improve their stock.' Before she left, she pointed to her stomach, and then at the sky, as if to say that she would bear their child on her home planet.

After this, Villas Boas was given back his clothes and taken on a guided tour of the alien craft, during which he tried, and failed, to purloin an instrument as a keep-sake. Then he was carried back to the ground. The UFO took off listing slightly to one side. It disappeared into the sky like a bullet. He had been aboard the craft for 4 hours, 15 minutes.

ASSESSMENT

In 1978 Villas Boas surfaced on TV in Brazil – no peasant farmer, but a happily married lawyer with four children. He changed just one item of his testimony: the woman had taken a sperm sample during their second act of intercourse. Unlike many who recall abduction by aliens, Villas Boas did not need hypnosis to give his detailed account. It was, therefore, objectively real; or real to him; or a fiction.

THE LIGHTS AT LEVELLAND

Multiple landings in Texas, USA

TYPE: **Lights in the sky, electromagnetic effects**
PLACE: **Levelland, Texas, USA**
DATE: **2-3 November 1957**

BACKGROUND

UFOs were seen within a 20 mile (30km) radius of Levelland, at Clovis, Canadian and Midland (Texas), and at Clovis (New Mexico), within a space of two and a half hours. In the USSR that night, Sputnik 2 was launched.

THE EVENTS

Just before 11:00pm, Levelland police took a report from farmhand Pedro Saucedo who, with a companion, had seen a yellow-and-white torpedo-shaped UFO, about 200ft (60m) long. As it moved toward their truck the lights and motor died. They jumped out and felt a blast of heat as the UFO rushed overhead, then the truck's lights came on again. At midnight, Jim Wheeler's car was affected by a 200ft (60m) egg-shaped UFO about four miles (6.5km) east of town. At 12:45am, a glowing red UFO affected a truck driven by Ronald Martin. At about 1:30am, Sheriff Weir Clem saw brilliant red oval lights flash across the road ahead of him.

ASSESSMENT

Ufologists have suggested the Levelland flap was engineered by government agencies to distract attention from the Soviet space program, which was then markedly more successful than the US effort. Similar effects on vehicles are reported in encounters with 'earthlights' or 'spook lights', but these tend to appear repeatedly in specific areas, and this did not happen at Levelland.

THE TRINDADE ISLAND PHOTOGRAPHS

A Brazilian navy ship's crew witness a fly-by

TYPE: **Close encounter of the first kind**
PLACE: **Trindade Island, South Atlantic Ocean**
DATE: **16 January 1958**

BACKGROUND

The training ship *Almirante Saldhana*, commanded by Capt. Carlos Alberto

UFO

Bacellar, had been surveying the waters around Trindade (750 miles [1210km] north-east of Rio de Janeiro) as part of the International Geophysical Year. Among the civilian technical team on board was photographer Almiro Barauna.

THE EVENTS

The standard account says that just after 12:00 noon, as the ship was preparing to get under way, two of the civilians noticed a bright light heading toward the island and shouted to Barauna to photograph it. Within 20 seconds, he snapped off six shots as the UFO approached, swung behind Mount Desegado, reappeared, then flew away. Two shots failed to catch the UFO altogether. Many of the 48 crew members on deck watched the spectacle. Capt. Bacellar, who had been below decks during the sighting, insisted the pictures were developed immediately, had a darkroom improvised, and took every precaution to ensure that Barauna could not tamper with the film.

ASSESSMENT

The photographs were published in the Brazilian press on 21 February. United Press International reported on 25 February that the Brazilian Navy had analysed them and that Brazil's president, Juscelino Kubitschek, had vouched for their authenticity. But local reports quoted a Navy spokesman as saying: 'No

Artist's impression of the UFO witnessed by the Rev. William Gill and dozens of others at the mission at Boianai, Papua New Guinea, in June 1959. Skeptic Donald Menzel's attempt to rubbish Gill's account was not up to the astronomer's usual high standard. He claimed that Gill was not wearing his eyeglasses at the time (he was), and that the entire event revolved around a sighting of Venus – although witnesses separately identified the planet, and the UFO was visible beneath cloud cover at times.

officer or sailor from the NE *Almirante Saldhana* witnessed the event'. Later, when Donald H. Menzel and Lyle G. Boyd made their own enquiries, the response was that 'the Navy has no connection with the case.' Then it transpired that Barauna had previously published UFO pictures that were admittedly fakes. Moreover, on close examination, the Trinidade photographs display an image different from and larger than that of the bright light reported by the witnesses. Ground Saucer Watch, however, declared the pictures *bona fide* after digital enhancement tests.

THE PASTOR AND HIS FLOCK

UFOs pay three long visits to a missionary

TYPE: **Close encounter of the third kind**
PLACE: **Boianai, Papua New Guinea**
DATE: **26-28 June 1959**

BACKGROUND

During 1959 there were 79 reports of UFO activity in Papua New Guinea; 61

events occurred in June and July. The most striking were the three episodes witnessed by missionary Rev. William Bruce Gill and a total of 37 others on three consecutive evenings.

THE EVENTS

At 6:45pm on 26 June, the Rev. Gill was outdoors. He noted Venus in the sky, visible among patches of low clouds. But above it he also saw 'this sparkling object'. It was very bright, and after a while descended toward the mission. Gill called two of the mission staff, who were soon joined by others to watch the UFO. It was circular, with a wide base from which four 'legs' projected. From time to time a shaft of blue light shone at an angle into the sky. Then, four men appeared on the upper deck of the UFO. Over the next 15 minutes they moved around on the UFO, although not all were always visible. By 7:10pm the clouds completely covered the sky. The UFO remained visible below them for another 10 minutes, then rose through the clouds. A little over an hour later, a UFO reappeared and hovered over the mission; before long, smaller UFOs were 'coming and going through the clouds'. Light from the objects was reflected onto the clouds as they weaved about. The UFOs came and went like this for nearly two more hours.

At dusk on 27 June, a nurse at the mission hospital saw a UFO and called Gill; about a dozen others also came to watch. Again, four figures appeared on the UFO's upper deck. One 'seemed to be looking down on us', so Gill waved to it. The figure waved back. Others on the ground waved too, and soon all four on the UFO were responding. Gill tried signaling with a torch, beckoning it to land, but got only waves in return before the figures re-entered the UFO. Shortly after this, at 6:30pm, 'a bit fed up' that the ufonauts made no attempt to land, Gill went off to have his dinner. UFOs were seen in three other local villages that evening.

From about 6:45pm until 11:20pm on 28 June the UFOs reappeared, sometimes as many as eight at a time. But they mostly stayed high in the sky, and no figures could be seen on the one that flew low over the mission.

ASSESSMENT

Papua New Guinea was under Australian administration in 1959. Royal Australian Air Force investigators concluded that at least three of the UFOs were planets, distorted by the atmosphere in the unsettled tropical weather. Skeptical ufologist Philip J. Klass found it amazing that anyone would go to dinner when faced with the prospect of making an extra-terrestrial contact. Jacques Vallée and J. Allen Hynek considered the case one of the strongest on record in view of the credibility of the Rev. Gill and the number of other witnesses.

SPEAKING WITH THE SPACE PEOPLE

....

Individuals who met with aliens in the Fifties

TYPE: **Contactees**
PLACE: **Brazil, South Africa, USA**
DATE: **1950-1960**

BACKGROUND

Contactee cases are not the same as close encounters of the third kind. Dr J. Allen Hynek noted 'contactees cases are characterized by a "favored" human intermediary, an almost always solitary "contact man" who somehow has the special attribute of being able to see UFOs and to communicate with their crews almost at will.'

The most famous contactee of the Fifties, and the first to publish such claims, was George Adamski. He went on to tell even more extraordinary tales than the one of his alleged meeting with a Venusian in November 1952 (see separate case above). Having captured public attention with this account, he published the sequel in 1955. *Inside The Spaceships* recounts how in the

months after his meeting in the desert he met other Venusians who were living in Los Angeles. He visited one of their 'mother ships', where he met similarly human-like natives of Mars and Saturn. The aliens also took him on a trip to view the far side of the Moon. Through the ship's viewing instruments he saw a pleasant Alpine scene: snowy mountains with timbered slopes, lakes and rivers, and a bustling city where vehicles floated through the streets. After a feast of vegetarian food, Adamski was shown similar scenes beamed from Venus. The natives, he was told, had a normal life-span of 1000 Earth years, thanks to their healthy diet and the protection that their planet's cloud cover gave them from the Sun's rays. The extraordinarily long lives of space people is a recurring theme in other contactees' accounts.

Adamski was certainly inventive and possibly capable of self-delusion. When confronted by photographs taken by the Soviet Luna 3 space probe of the far side of the Moon in October 1959, Adamski retorted that the Russians had retouched the pictures to deceive US space scientists. Later contactees seem to have suffered from a similar confusion between reality and fantasy. But their motives were probably more selfless than Adamski's; he reveled in fame, and appreciated the wealth his books brought. It seems astonishing that anyone believed him, but he created the context in which other contactees told their stories – and were believed in turn. A selection of those accounts follows.

THE EVENTS

• 4 July 1950 – Daniel Fry approached a landed saucer near White Sands Proving Grounds, New Mexico, and heard a voice say: 'Better not touch the hull, pal, it's still hot.' The voice came from an extra-terrestrial entity calling itself A-lan, at the time 900 miles (1450km) above the Earth's surface in a 'mother ship'. Fry was invited aboard the landed, remotely controled saucer and was given a ride to New York and back that took only half an hour. A-lan gave Fry the mission to publish the off-worlders' message that 'understanding is the key to peace and happiness'. A-lan said that his people were descended from an Earthly super-race who, having survived a nuclear conflagration, had migrated into space 30,000 years before. They had settled on Mars, then taken to living in space. Their mother ship had been their home for generations. Further communications with A-lan were purely by telepathy, although Fry produced a series of photographs and films of UFOs until at least the mid-Sixties. He is said to have taken a polygraph test on live television, but 'flunked it flat'.

- July 1952 – Truman Bethurum was asleep in a truck on Highway 91, 70 miles (110 km) west of Las Vegas, Nevada, and awoken by the voices of eight small beings with olive skins and dark hair, grouped around the cab. He saw a 300ft (90m) wide saucer hovering soundlessly a few feet above the ground. The aliens told him: 'Our homes are our castles in a faraway land.' He was taken aboard the UFO, where he met its beautiful captain, Aura Rhanes. She spoke perfect English, in rhyming couplets. She explained that her ship came from the planet Clarion, which was permanently hidden from Earth behind the Moon. She said that all the planets in the Solar System had an atmosphere like Earth's. Clarion was free

An alleged 'Venusian man' standing in front of his flying saucer. The photograph is one of many produced in the 1950s by contactee Howard Menger, who explained that the spacemen refused to have their pictures taken in good light, lest they be recognized as aliens during stays on Earth. One of Menger's tasks, he said, was to help the visiting Venusians integrate into Earthly society – cutting the men's shoulder-length hair, for instance and, on one famous occasion, bringing Venusian women a selection of terrestrial underwear. They rejected the bras on the grounds that they couldn't wear them and never had.

of disease, crime, and politicians, and appeared to have a matriarchal society. Over the next three months, she had 10 further meetings with Bethurum. Sometimes she materialized in his bedroom, which distressed his wife. Bethurum was promised a visit to Clarion, but it never happened. Bethurum set eyes on Aura Rhanes once more, in a restaurant in Glendale, Nevada, but when he spoke to her she claimed not to know him.

- 24 May 1952 – Orfeo Angelucci had his first message from aliens, who called themselves 'Space Brothers', through a video link from a UFO in a field near Los Angeles. They warned him that 'material advancement' was threatening humanity's evolution. The aliens maintained that they did not need spacecraft, but manifested flying saucers, which could travel at the speed of light, so that humanity could perceive them. 'The speed of light is the speed of truth,' they said, obscurely. In July 1952 Angelucci came upon a UFO parked under a freeway, and stepped in. It took off, and he was given a discourse on the Space Brothers' philosophy, which ended with a musical rendition of the Lord's Prayer and a white beam of light shining from above, in whose glow Angelucci 'knew the mystery of life'. In the course of many subsequent encounters and saucer rides, Angelucci visited the aliens' (unnamed) planet, met Jesus of Nazareth (who told him He was an alien, and that 'This is the beginning of the New Age'), and was informed that in a previous life he had been a Space Brother himself, named Neptune. Angelucci was told that unless humans learned to co-operate together, a catastrophe would strike the Earth in 1986.

- April 1953 – Dino Kraspedon was visited at his home in São Paulo, Brazil, by the captain of a flying saucer from Jupiter, whom he had first met in mountains near Paraná the previous November. Many further meetings took place; they discussed celestial mechanics, theology and UFO propulsion. Kraspedon was warned that a second sun would join the Solar System, and of the dangers of the nuclear age.

- 27 December 1954 – Elizabeth Klarer was alarmed when she briefly saw the attractive occupant of a 55ft (17m) wide

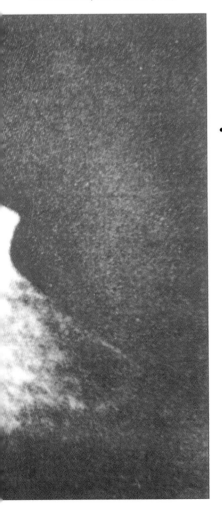

saucer that was hovering over a hill near her farmhouse in the Drakensberg mountains, South Africa. On 7 April 1956 (then aged 46) she visited the hill again and found the same handsome humanoid, dressed in a cream-colored suit, beside his UFO. It was love at second sight. 'Not afraid this time?' he asked in perfect English, and she replied: 'I have known your face within my heart all my life.' 'I am not from any place on this planet called Earth,' he whispered with his lips in her hair. His name was Akon and his home the planet Meton, near Alpha Centauri. Klarer took a trip with him in his craft, which was powered by 'natural forces', and discussed life on his planet and music in particular. When Klarer became pregnant by Akon, he took her to Meton, where their son Ayling was born. Metonites were vegetarian, and the planet was free from war, disease, politics and money. Klarer stayed there only four months because she had difficulty breathing the atmosphere. Her last contact with Akon was in 1963, when he visited her in South Africa with their son.

- 1956-57 – Howard Menger claimed his contact with the 'Space People' began when he was eight, in 1932, and involved a curvaceous blonde whom he met in a wood. In August 1956, a flurry of UFO sightings around his New Jersey home led to another series of contacts. Menger's Space People were from Venus, Mars and Saturn. They gave him a model of a 'free energy motor' (a perpetual motion machine), although this was never seen working. He also made a record of music he had learned from the aliens. Menger returned from the Moon with specimens of lunar potatoes which he handed to the US government and in whose custody they have since remained. He was much concerned with nutrition, and devoted 63 pages of his book about his contacts to dietary matters. Like Orfeo Angelucci, Menger was told he had been a space person living on Saturn in a former life. His second wife, Constance Weber, claimed to be a Venusian known as Marla.

ASSESSMENT

Dr Hynek's comment that contactees are frequently 'pseudo-religious fanatics... bringing us regular messages from the "space men" with singularly little content' is perhaps too harsh. Most seem to have had mundane, if incredible, relations with their contacts, and their claims about the cosmos raise a smile rather than ire. The planets from which these tall, blond, handsome voyagers claim to come are uninhabitable. And it is impossible that a planet (the alleged 'Clarion') could remain permanently out of sight and undetected 'behind the Sun' in the same orbit as Earth. Such a body would in any case be detectable by its effects on the orbits of other planets.

Three of these accounts are of special interest to those who try to gauge the reality of the contactee experience.

'Dino Kraspedon' was an alias for Aladino Felix. He made a series of strikingly accurate predictions (for example of the assassinations of Martin Luther King and Robert Kennedy) in the mid-Sixties; the last prophesied an outbreak of robberies, bombings and murders in Brazil. These indeed occurred. Police finally arrested the perpetrators on 22 August 1968. Their leader's name was Aladino Felix.

The first reports of Elizabeth Klarer's meeting with Akon were published within months of the event in *Flying Saucer Review*, where she maintained that her lover was a Venusian, was with another crew member, and was wearing a 'dark-brown' suit. She also made a point of saying: '...the tall, soft-spoken Venusian told me that the air I had been enjoying so much in the craft was Venusian air!' These statements contradict the account in her book *Beyond The Light Barrier*, published in 1977.

In the early Sixties Howard Menger recanted his contactee tales, claiming that the CIA had enlisted him in an experiment to test reactions to extra-terrestrial reports and contact and had given him faked films of UFO sightings. Then, in 1967, he retracted his earlier 'confession', and returned to his original theme – 'What most people don't want to hear, a message of love and understanding.'

CHAPTER 4

Abductions and Absurdities

STRANGE MESSAGES, STAR MAPS AND SWAMP GAS

When the Sixties opened things were not quite what they seemed in ufology. For while many ufologists were still looking askance at contactee reports and close encounters of the third kind, a whole new aspect of the UFO phenomenon had started to emerge – abductions by alien entities. Most researchers remained unaware of these cases until the middle of the

One of many UFOs photographed by mechanic Paul Villa in the Sixties. This shot was taken on 16 June 1963 near Albuquerque, New Mexico, USA. According to Villa, he received a telepathic invitation to meet the UFO. Five men and four women, between 7 and 9ft (2-2.7m) tall, 'all beautiful people, immaculately groomed, wearing tight-fitting one-piece uniforms' emerged from the craft. They said they were from Coma Berenices (a genuine star group). For some reason Villa did not take snaps of the off-worlders as well as their UFO. According to the USAF's Project Blue Book, Villa sincerely believed he had met extra-terrestrials, and faked his pictures to give his story credibility.

decade. For example, it was not until 1965 that a case history of Antonio Villas Boas's encounter (see Chapter Three) was widely published in English, and only in 1969 was his identity revealed, in Charles Bowen's landmark study *The Humanoids*. Indeed, those who knew about what became known as 'the AVB case' were so unfamiliar with the abduction scenario that at first they regarded it as 'too wild to print', and did so only after considerable heart-searching.

The story of Betty and Barney Hill's abduction on 19 September 1961 broke only in 1966, with the publication of John G. Fuller's *The Interrupted Journey*. It took both ufology and the general public by storm, for it seemed to be the first case of its kind. Serious ufologists were confounded. For instance, the leading authority on UFOs, Dr J. Allen Hynek, was not inclined to believe any claim of meeting visitors from outer space. He expressed grave doubts about even comparatively reassuring reports of contacts with aliens, like those of Adamski and Klarer, especially if they involved claims of repeated contact (as these did). But the Hills' encounter has since become one of the most celebrated in UFO history, and is still generating debate today.

The case is still 'live' partly because of the role that hypnosis played in establishing what the couple believed happened to them that night. Many dedicated ufologists, as well as out-and-out skeptics, argue that hypnosis has since been misused in UFO research. This was not so in the Hills' case – the hypnotist was entirely unbiased about UFOs as such, and concluded that their story was based on dreams, not objective reality. But the essential pattern of events described by the Hills has been repeated by hundreds of abductees since.

Ufologists continue to argue over the significance of this, and in retrospect the Betty and Barney Hill case can be seen as the thin end of a wedge that has since split ufology into two camps. There are those who are convinced that the Hills' and others' memories of abduction, mostly recalled under hypnosis, represent certain proof of extra-terrestrial intervention in human affairs. And there are those who don't necessarily reject the possibility that UFOs are extra-terrestrial, but who do think that hypnotic regression is at best unreliable and at worst dangerous and damaging – as when it is used by amateurs to extract very disturbing, but not necessarily accurate, memories from very young children.

UFO

WAVES OF THE FUTURE?

There was nothing steady about the UFO phenomenon during the Sixties. In Argentina sightings crested in 1962; Eastern Europe saw an upsurge of reports in 1966; in the USA and Europe that year, the number of reports nearly doubled over that of the previous year. In 1967, the volume of reports rose to 60 times that of 1960, and four times that of 1966. And then, through the rest of the decade, the reports tailed away.

The leap in reported UFO sightings in the West parallels the emergence of a specific youth culture, which culminated in the rock 'n' roll-drenched, psychedelic 'summer of love' in San Francisco in 1967. Yet, as Paul Devereux has pointed out in his seminal study *Earthlights*: 'many of the UFO sightings in 1967 were... by members of the public who were not part of the "psychedelic generation" – airline pilots, policemen, suburban housewives, radio reporters, and so on.' But, as Devereux also noted, in 1967 the 'sense

of a new pulse of life was everywhere being felt, [and] the possibilities of new beginnings took on clearer dimensions.' Suburban housewives and the like who were not ashamed to admit their familiarity with the Beatles' *Sgt. Pepper's Lonely Hearts Club Band*, or even Pink Floyd's *Saucerful of Secrets*, were less embarrassed than ever before to admit having seen a UFO.

But the same conditions did not apply on the other side of the Iron Curtain. Even if Czechoslovakia was moving toward the brief optimism of the 'Prague Spring' of 1968, there was no climactic 'summer of love'. In this period, East-West tensions became more marked, and most of the Soviet bloc was reacting against the American military effort in Viet Nam; while in the rest of the world – in Southern Africa, in the Middle East, in South America – Soviet resources were being poured into 'liberation' movements and other efforts to destabilize the status quo underwritten by the West.

The waves of 1966 and 1967 may thus tell us two things. First, the special cultural conditions in the West allowed something like the true level of UFO sightings there to emerge. And second, the Argentine wave of 1962 and the Eastern European wave of 1966 indicate that there was a genuine rise in the level of UFO activity around the world from the early to the mid-Sixties. It seemed especially greater than before in the West only because of a greater readiness to report it. Quite why these waves occurred remains an enigma.

ON THE BRINK OF INVASION

Among ufologists, the abduction debate overshadowed the close encounters of the third kind that cropped up regularly throughout the decade, although some of them were of such 'high strangeness' that, as the saying has it, they had to be true because no one could have made them up. Cases in point: Joe Simonton's gift of buckwheat cakes from aliens in 1961,

ABDUCTIONS AND ABSURDITIES

Gary Wilcox's encounter with entities claiming to be Martians – in 1964, when it was well known that Mars was incapable of supporting any but the most primitive life form – and Jerry Townsend's 1965 meeting with a comic-book 'space ship' and robots that might have come straight from a low-budget sci-fi movie.

One of the most alert ufologists, the French radio expert Aimé Michel, remarked many times on the absurdity of many UFO phenomena, from the shape and behavior of the craft to the looks, dress and utterances of alien entities. In the end he abandoned the subject, saying UFOs were 'above human comprehension'. Charles Bowen, one of Michel's long-standing associates, noted in *The Humanoids* that alien behavior often seemed pointless, like 'diversionary play to give people a giggle'. In *Challenge to Science* (1966), computer scientist Jacques Vallée dismissed the messages given by aliens as systematically misleading.

As analyst Martin Kottmeyer has noted, by the middle of the decade there seemed to be a consensus among writers on UFOs that the saucers and their occupants represented a threat to humanity. The least that UFOs were intent on, according to Jim and Coral Lorenzen, was reconnaissance of the Earth; and they were disturbed that in the years since 1947 the degree and kind of interaction between UFOs and humans had intensified. The phenomenon had altered from simple sightings of strange, inexplicable lights in the night sky or silvery, highly maneuverable disks seen in daylight to encounters with alien craft that, for instance, caused cars to fail. They wondered if the increase in failures in regional electricity supplies, like the New York blackout of 1965, was not also due to alien interference.

This apparent UFO, pictured over Leadville, Colorado, USA, on 4 June 1960, was declared a 'lens aberration' – in other words, a reflection – by USAF analysts.

And close encounters were on the increase. In these, the entities made cryptic, cold and aloof pronouncements, often refusing to discuss their origins, unlike the benign beings who spoke wisdom to George Adamski, Daniel Fry, Truman Bethurum and others in the Fifties. 'We are facing potential danger,' wrote the Lorenzens. 'The existence of a species of superior beings in the universe could cause the civilization of Earth to topple.'

George Fawcett produced a catalog of the horrible effects UFOs can have on witnesses, from electric shocks and radiation burns to temporary paralysis or – in six cases he cited – death. Jerome Clark cited one case in which UFOs had reportedly killed an entire village full of people, and others in which witnesses had had their memories erased. One of the most explicit forms of this paranoia appeared on the flyleaf of *Flying Saucers – Serious Business* by Frank Edwards – a notice that read, in part:

WARNING!
NEAR APPROACHES OF UNIDENTIFIED FLYING OBJECTS CAN BE HARMFUL TO HUMAN BEINGS.
DO NOT STAND UNDER A UFO THAT IS HOVERING AT LOW ALTITUDE.
DO NOT TOUCH OR ATTEMPT TO TOUCH A UFO THAT HAS LANDED.
DON'T TAKE CHANCES WITH UFOS.

Brad Steiger went further, accusing UFOs of beaming down hypnotic drugs into Earth's water supplies, and of preparing to launch a full-scale invasion of the USA: 'We must be prepared to establish peaceful communication or be prepared to accept annihilation.' Michael Campione called for government-funded safety measures to 'ensure national survival', and advocated setting aside areas of airports as UFO landing pads. The best defense against a hostile, nuclear-powered UFO was, he maintained, an ordinary flashlight, as he thought its beam would interfere with the UFO's power plant. Even J. Allen Hynek, usually so

moderate in his opinions, told *Playboy* magazine in 1967 of his concern that the Soviets might solve the UFO mystery before US experts did, which could have catastrophic consequences for the American way of life.

For UFO commentators in the Sixties, the air was thick with a sense of impending disaster. Virtually all the ufologists who had assessed the situation called urgently for resources to be put into internationally co-ordinated scientific efforts to solve the UFO enigma before matters got out of hand.

COVER-UP IN COLORADO?

The nearest any government came to answering this call was the study funded by the USAF and undertaken at the University of Colorado from October 1966 until June 1968. This was the outcome of a meeting in February 1966 of a USAF Scientific Advisory Board Ad Hoc Committee to review the work of the USAF's Project Blue Book, which had been collecting and, within its limited resources, investigating UFO reports since March 1952.

Composed of psychologists, engineers and astronomers under physicist Brian O'Brien, the committee concluded that 'analysis of new sightings may provide some additions to scientific knowledge of value to the Air Force. Moreover, some of the case records... that were listed as "identified" were sightings where the evidence collected was too meager or too indefinite to permit positive listing in the identified category. Because of this, the committee recommends that the present program be strengthened to provide opportunity for scientific investigation of selected sightings in more detail and depth than has been possible to date.' The committee proposed that: 'Contracts be negotiated with a few selected universities to provide scientific teams to investigate promptly and in depth certain selected sightings of UFOs.'

With pressure also coming from Congress to 'do something' about UFOs, the USAF awarded a $572,146 contract

71

to the University of Colorado to make impartial assessments of reports from the Blue Book files. The project was to be headed by the respected physicist Dr Edward U. Condon.

Then, in the spring of 1968, Dr David Saunders tried to discredit what was supposed to be the most elaborate and exhaustive study of UFOs ever undertaken. Disgusted at the way the work was being done, Saunders leaked a memo that the project's co-ordinator, Robert Low,

had written in August 1966 while negotiating the USAF contract. Low had told the USAF: 'Our study would be conducted almost exclusively by non-believers who... could and probably would add an impressive body of evidence that there is no reality to the observations. The trick would be, I think, to describe the project so that, to the public, it would appear a totally objective study but, to the scientific community, would present a group of non-believers trying their best

to be objective but having an almost zero expectation of finding a saucer.' Condon fired Saunders for insubordination, but the damage was done. Saunders' allegations cost Condon's final report dearly in credibility among believers in UFOs.

The Condon Report, as *The Scientific Study of Unidentified Flying Objects* is usually known, was eventually published on 9 January 1969. It was a massive, 1485-page dossier, and in deference to busy journalists Condon's summary of the report was printed first – and the summary was all that the media reported. The key finding: 'Careful consideration of the record... leads us to conclude that further extensive study of UFOs probably cannot be justified in the expectation that science will be advanced thereby.'

For those who bothered to read the rest of the report, Condon's summary was extraordinary, for it bore hardly any relation to what his colleagues had actually written. Of the 87 UFO sightings analysed, they declared about 25 per cent inexplicable. In a further 8 per cent, debunkers among them had striven desperately to find 'natural' explanations for otherwise unaccountable events. For example, one analysis ends implausibly: 'This unusual sighting should therefore be assigned to... some almost certainly natural phenomenon which is so rare that it apparently has never been reported before or since.' This kind of squirming, added to Low's shenanigans, led many ufologists to think the government was

A trio of UFOs photographed in Italy on 26 September 1960. The skeptic's doubts are immediately raised by the extraordinary blackness of the images compared to the bleached-out background, which suggests the images are pasted onto a window or a print before re-photographing. UFO believers counter this objection by saying the contrast may be caused by magnetic, gravitational or microwave emissions from the alien craft.

trying to hoodwink the people. The impression was confirmed when the USAF acted on Condon's conclusions and closed down Project Blue Book in December 1969.

Thus, as the Sixties drew to a close, another major theme of modern ufology was born. The belief in an organized and deliberate cover-up by government agencies of the truth about UFOs – which had previously been the refrain of a select few – entered the mainstream of the UFO debate. It was to take many forms in the years to come. Among those on the frontier of ufological research, the unacceptably shady aspects of the Condon Report inspired a new determination to uncover the facts. The decade that had opened with things being not quite as they seemed in ufology ended on the same note, but in a different key.

WATCHING THE SPACE RACE

TYPE: **Radar interference**
PLACE: **Cape Canaveral, Florida, USA**
DATE: **10 January 1961**

Just after the lift-off of the nationally televised test-launch of a Polaris rocket from Cape Canaveral a radar 'unknown' appeared on tracking scopes and approached the Polaris. The UFO's radar signature was so strong, and the object came so close to the US rocket, that automatic radar at the launch site locked onto the UFO instead of onto the test missile. After it had paced the Polaris for a few minutes, the UFO dropped away again and went out of radar range. Although this episode is recorded in full in the NASA log of the test-launch, no official explanation of the radar interference has been made public.

CRATERS IN KARELIA

TYPE: **Ground marking**
PLACE: **Karelia, Russia**
DATE: **February 1961**

BACKGROUND
Forester Vasili Bradski discovered a crater, 100ft (30m) long, 50ft (15m) wide and 10ft (3m) deep, beside a frozen lake. The crater had not been there when he had visited the spot two days previously and there was no trace of the tons of soil that must have been removed to make the hole. The thick ice covering the lake was broken near the crater.

THE EVENTS
A team of six investigators came from Leningrad and found crumbling black pellets, like buckwheat grains, on the lakeshore, and noted that the underside of the broken ice was green. Divers found two 330ft (100m) long scars on the floor of the lake, one near the shore, the other in the center of the lake. The case was studied at the University of Leningrad by Prof. Vsevolod Charmov. Water, soil and ice samples were normal, but nothing could explain the green stain. The black pellets showed an unusual metallic sheen, and would not dissolve in acid.

ASSESSMENT
The Soviet investigators speculated that something may have landed on the lakeside, skidded into the water and gouged the lake bed. The object had then apparently regained the air, since it was no longer in the lake. Chemists concluded that the pellets were not of natural origin. One of many interesting details in this unsolved case is the pellets' resemblance to buckwheat – traditionally, buckwheat cakes are left out as food for the fairies. There may thus be a connection between these ground markings and the events that occurred at Eagle River, Wisconsin, USA, two months later (see below). Whatever the reality may be, there has never been any obvious, mundane explanation of what Bradski found.

THREE MYSTERIOUS PANCAKES

A gift from olive-skinned aliens

TYPE: **Close encounter of the third kind**
PLACE: **Eagle River, Wisconsin, USA**
DATE: **18 April 1961**

BACKGROUND
In 1961 Joe Simonton, a 60-year-old chicken farmer, was living alone in his shack on the outskirts of Eagle River, Wisconsin. Sheriff Schroeder, who had known Simonton for 14 years, said he 'obviously believed the truth of what he was saying' about his unique close encounter with unidentified beings.

THE EVENTS
Simonton was eating breakfast at about 11:00am when he heard a noise like 'knobby tires on a wet pavement'. Through the window he saw a silver object coming down into his yard. It was 'brighter than chrome', about 12ft (3.5m) high and 30ft (9m) in diameter, shaped like two inverted bowls with exhaust pipes around its rim. Simonton went out and approached the craft as it settled, hovering just above the ground. A hatch opened, and inside he saw three clean-shaven men, each about 5ft (1.5m) tall, with black hair, who 'resembled Italians'. They were wearing black suits with turtleneck tops and knitted helmets. One handed Simonton a two-handled jug, indicating he needed something to drink. Simonton went inside, filled the jug with water, and returned to the craft, where another man was now frying food on a flameless grill. Simonton noticed that the interior of the ship was 'the color of wrought iron', and contained several instrument panels. He indicated he would like to have some food in return for his water, and was given three pancakes, each about 3 inches (7.5cm) across. One occupant then closed the hatch, and the

Analyses showed the pancakes had been made from hydrogenated oil shortening, starch, wheat bran, soybean hulls and buckwheat hulls. The US Department of Health, Education and Welfare's Food and Drug Laboratory considered them to be of Earthly origin. Only a lack of salt in the recipe was unusual.

The USAF sent Major Robert Friend, Dr J. Allen Hynek and another officer, from Sawyer AFB, to investigate. They concluded that Simonton had been eating pancakes for breakfast and had undergone a 'waking dream' so vivid that he was unable to tell it from reality. (Today this would be called a 'virtual-reality experience'.) Dr Jacques Vallée, however, has pointed out that salt-free food is traditional fairy fare, and that fairies in Celtic lore particularly like buckwheat cakes. The implication is that 'fairies' and 'aliens' are aspects of the same phenomenon.

HYPNOTIC READING

Betty and Barney Hill's classic account of abduction

TYPE: Close encounter of the fourth kind
PLACE: Indian Head, New Hampshire, USA
DATE: 19 September 1961

BACKGROUND

Betty and Barney Hill, aged 41 and 39 respectively, were a mixed-race couple (he was black, she was caucasian) living in Portsmouth, New Hampshire. Barney worked as a mail sorter in Boston, commuting the 120-mile (193km) round trip each day; Betty was a social worker for the State of New Hampshire. Both were very active in civil rights campaigning and were on their church's United Nations committee. In mid-September 1961 they drove to Canada for a short break from their hectic schedule. Then, weather reports spoke of a hurricane

Artist's impression of the encounter with a UFO by Betty and Barney Hill in New Hampshire on 19 September 1961, which hypnosis later seemed to show had included an abduction of the couple. Significantly, later accounts of 'alien abductions' closely follow the pattern of events described by the Hills.

ship rose gently to 20ft (6m) from the ground, then sped away south with a blast that bent some nearby pine trees. The whole encounter had lasted no longer than five minutes. Simonton reported the event to a friend who was a county judge and member of NICAP, and who sent NICAP and the USAF a pancake each to analyse. Simonton tried the third cookie himself, and said it tasted 'like cardboard'.

moving along the East Coast. They decided on an all-night drive home to avoid the impending storm. At 9:00pm they had dinner in Colebrook, and then continued their journey southbound on US Highway 3.

THE EVENTS

Near Lancaster, just west of the White Mountains, Betty noticed a bright light, near the moon, and getting brighter. Barney suggested it was a satellite gone off course. However, the light didn't go away, and they stopped the car to see it better. Looking through binoculars, Barney thought it was an aircraft (he was an 'avid plane-watcher') and suggested various types it might be. They drove on slowly, but now the light seemed to be closer, and circling them. Betty looked through the binoculars and said she could see a huge craft with a double row of windows. They stopped again. Barney took the binoculars and walked towards the light, which had dropped to tree height, until he was only 50ft (15m) from it. Through the binoculars he now saw an object 'like a big pancake' with a row of windows; 'at least a dozen' occupants, dressed in Nazi-style uniforms, were visible. Suddenly, irrationally convinced he was about to be captured, he fled back to the car in terror. Later, the couple heard two sets of beeping sounds as they drove home. They reached Portsmouth in daylight, having taken 7 hours to cover the last 190 miles (300km) of their trip.

Betty reported the sighting to Pease AFB, and began avidly to read all she could about UFOs; within a week she reported their experience to NICAP. From 29 September to 3 October she had a series of nightmares in which she saw a group of humanoids blocking US 3; she and Barney were then led aboard the UFO they had seen and they were medically examined. In late October, in a session with NICAP investigators, Barney realized that the journey from Colebrook had taken two hours longer than it should have done. There seemed to be 'missing time' after the UFO sighting.

Barney began to suffer from ulcers, high blood pressure, and exhaustion from his gruelling commuting, and developed a ring of warts around his groin. He had psychiatric treatment for a year from summer 1962, and eventually asked his therapist to arrange regressive hypnosis to settle the question of what had really happened on 19 September 1961. He began hypnosis with Dr Benjamin Simon of Boston in December 1963, and was soon joined by Betty.

Both told approximately the same story under hypnosis. They had been roadblocked by humanoids with large eyes, no nose, and slitted, lipless mouths. Once on board the UFO, each was given a medical examination. A long needle was inserted into Betty's navel: she was told this was a pregnancy test. Barney had a circular instrument applied to his groin. After her examination, Betty was shown a star map with no legend on it, and told she would not remember the experience. Throughout, the aliens communicated in a mixture of direct language and telepathy. Somehow the couple were returned to their car, and watched the UFO depart as a glowing orange ball.

ASSESSMENT

Dr Simon noted that Betty's account under hypnosis precisely matched the content of her dreams, and concluded that the Hills had had an imaginary experience caused by fear after a genuine close encounter with a UFO. He also noted that: 'Hypnosis is the pathway to the Truth as it is felt and understood by the patient. The Truth is what he believes to be the truth, and this may or may not be consonant with the ultimate non-personal truth.'

Betty Hill continued to believe in the reality of her abduction (Barney died in 1969 of a cerebral hemorrhage) and reported many UFO sightings and encounters after it. However, the Hills' individual accounts of their abduction differed in many details, and there is good reason to think Barney was echoing Betty's descriptions of her dreams.

Betty's story contained many inconsistencies: for instance, while the humanoids used colloquial English, they also asked: 'What are vegetables? What is yellow?' She was told that she was having a pregnancy test by the aliens, although she had some years previously had a hysterectomy. Doubts have also been raised about whether the Hills, first slowly trailing a UFO and later in a panic, really suffered 'missing time'.

Ohio schoolteacher Margaret Fish used beads on string to construct configurations of the stars shown in the map Betty Hill remembered being shown by the aliens, and found a pattern indicating that they had come from Zeta Reticuli, about 3.7 light years from Earth. Charles W. Atterberg of Florida did much the same thing – and found a totally different set of stars. Then, astronomers Carl Sagan and Steven Soter used computers to check the positions of the 15 stars that Margaret Fish had said matched Betty's map. This produced a configuration that bore 'little similarity' to the Hill star-map.

There is, however, little doubt that the Hills saw a UFO of some kind. Pease AFB confirmed that radar had shown an 'unknown' in the air at the time the Hills had their encounter. But whether or not their abduction was a physically real event has to remain an open question.

UFOS ACT IN SELF-DEFENSE

TYPE: **Radar-visual**
PLACE: **Rybinsk, Russia**
DATE: **Summer 1961**

During summer 1961 missile defences were being put in place around Moscow. At one base, a huge UFO was detected on radar, flying at an altitude of 60,000ft (18,000m), along with an escort of smaller UFOs. The Rybinsk base commander responded with a salvo of missiles. The escorting UFOs descended toward the base. Its electrical equipment failed, and the missiles exploded well before reaching their targets. When the smaller UFOs rejoined the 'mother ship', the missile base's power was restored.

PLAYING CHICKEN OVER KIEV

TYPE: **Daylight disk**
PLACE: **Kiev, Ukraine**
DATE: **August 1961**

A Soviet Air Force pilot flying over Kiev was approached by a UFO that seemed to be playing games with him. It flew around in ever-decreasing spirals, coming closer and closer and then flitting away. The pilot pursued the UFO, which then came to a stop in the sky and hovered. When he came close to it, it moved further away. This 'game' continued through several 'moves' for about 12 minutes, and then the UFO accelerated away at about 6000mph (9700km/h).

MARY CELESTE OF THE SKIES

TYPE: **Radar contact and ground markings**
PLACE: **Sverdlovsk (now Yekaterinburg) Russia**
DATE: **1961**

A report apparently acquired from the Moscow Aviation Institute discloses that

This shot is typical of much purported UFO evidence. Taken in the Sixties by Japanese General Nagata, the photo disappoints in its lack of detail, reference points to the landscape, and so on. But, in a sense, photographers of UFOs can't win: while vague, blurred shots like this one are easily brushed aside, brilliantly clear pictures are dismissed as 'too good to be true' – often with good reason.

sometime in 1961 an Antonov AN-2P mail transport aircraft took off from the industrial city of Sverdlovsk heading east for Kurgan and, about 100 miles (160km) into its flight, disappeared from air traffic control (ATC) radar screens while the pilot was on the radio. At the same time, ATC was tracking a UFO in the vicinity of the air transport. The plane could not be raised by radio, and heliborne troops were despatched to investigate. They easily found the aircraft, precisely where it had disappeared from the radar monitors. The plane was in a forest clearing, but had left no crash trail and was entirely undamaged – the mail cargo was intact, and even the engines started without difficulty when tested. The plane appeared to have been lowered gently into the clearing. But there was no sign of any of the seven crew members, and

none of them has reappeared since. The recovery team found a 100ft (30m) wide circle of scorched grass about 100 yards (90m) from the aircraft, which suggested that a circular craft may have landed there. The case resembles the claim by William S. English (see Chapter Five) that a B-52 'crashed' intact in Laos in 1970.

THE 1962 UFO CRASH IN NEW MEXICO

TYPE: **Crash/retrieval episode**
PLACE: **South of Alamogordo, Otero county, New Mexico, USA**
DATE: **1962**

Some sources place this event near Holloman Air Force Base, 8 miles (13km) southeast of Alamogordo; others place it 90 miles (145km) south of the city. On some unspecified date in 1962, a UFO was tracked on military radar across 'two south-western states'. Jet interceptors were scrambled, but as the UFO crossed into New Mexican airspace it began to lose altitude. The craft crashed on the desert sand at 90mph (145km/h); its flight pattern immediately beforehand indicated that any occupants were either dead or had lost control before the impact. The UFO was circular, 68ft (20m) in diameter and 13ft (4m) high. It was taken to 'a major military base in the south-west' so that its means of propulsion could be investigated. Two 42 inch (1m) long beings were found dead inside. They had pink-gray skin, oversized heads, large eyes, tiny noses, small mouths and holes for ears. They were wearing one-piece

suits. Next day the bodies were removed to 'a major medical university hospital' somewhere in the US.

WATCHING THE SPACE RACE - 2

TYPE: **Radar-visuals**
PLACE: **Earth orbit, over Australia**
DATE: **16 May 1962**

During the 15th orbit of the Mercury 9 space capsule, astronaut Gordon L. Cooper reported the approach of a green UFO with a red tail. Ground tracking stations in Australia picked up the object on radar. It was moving from east to west, the opposite direction to most artificial satellites. NASA said only that there was 'nothing abnormal' about the event.

THE PAUL VILLA PHOTOGRAPHS

A message for mankind

TYPE: **Close encounters of the third kind**
PLACE: **Environs of Albuquerque, New Mexico, USA**
DATE: **18 April and 16 June 1963**

Mechanic Paul Villa, then aged 49, claimed that the craft in the picture he took on 18 April 1963 contained three beings with whom he conversed. Two months later, he photographed a different UFO that, he said, held nine entities from Coma Berenices, who visited him for an hour and a half.

Villa lived in Los Lunas, New Mexico. He took many photographs of UFOs, and sent them with 'relevant' literature to politicians and 'plain folks' in the hope that they could use them to help 'prisoners, orphans, the sick, poor and elderly'. Villa believed UFOs were 'only a small part of God's huge armies' that would

invade Earth and 'redeem humanity from their present immoral fallen condition'.

Conventional analysis by Project Blue Book and computer tests by Ground Saucer Watch showed that Villa's photographs had been faked with small models. Investigators concluded that Villa believed he had had contact with aliens, and fabricated his pictures to convince others of the truth of his experiences.

THE SIEGE AT TRANCAS

Ufonauts attack a lonely Argentine ranch

TYPE: **Close encounters of the third kind**
PLACE: **Trancas, Tucuman, Argentina**
DATE: **21 October 1963**

BACKGROUND

Argentina was in political turmoil following election victories that kept power in the hands of the military and deeply angered the Peronist opposition. The isolated Santa Teresa ranch near Trancas was run by the Moreno family: a middle-aged couple and their three grown daughters, Yolié (21 at the time of the events, married with a baby son), Yolanda, and Argentina. The five were alone at the homestead with their maid, Dora Martina Guzman, aged 15. At about 7:00pm the electricity generator broke down. By 8:00pm all the family but Yolié had gone to bed. Around 9:30pm, Dora Martina knocked on Yolié's door: she was frightened by strange lights outside. Yolié fetched Yolanda, and the two went out to investigate. The sisters saw what seemed to be a small, brightly lit train on the railroad track 200 yards (180m) away to the east of the house. Closer inspection revealed two brilliantly shining disks joined by an illuminated tube. About 40 apparently human figures were moving about inside the tube. The two women surmised that guerrillas had derailed a train. They returned to the house, dressed warmly and went out again, now with Dora Martina, who brought the Colt .38 pistol that she kept for self-defense.

THE EVENTS

As the three rounded the south side of the house, they saw a pale green light near the main gate. Yolié's flashlight revealed a metallic, disk-shaped, domed object hanging in the air, rocking gently. It was 30ft (9m) across, with six windows. Suddenly a multi-colored band of light started to rotate inside the UFO's windows, and a white mist began to form around it. There was a distinct smell of sulfur. Then, a bolt of flame shot from the UFO and struck the trio to the ground. Three more disks lit up along the railroad track. The nearest UFO, now obscured in mist, projected a seemingly 'solid' light-beam – which slowly extended itself like a tube. This reached the house and began to probe it. From the rail track, double 'tubes' of these weird lights began to reach forward until – after some minutes – their ends came to rest just in front of various outbuildings. The beams were perfectly cylindrical, and measured about 10ft (3m) in width.

The girls rushed indoors, where their parents were now awake. The temperature inside had risen to well over 100°F (37°C), and the smell of sulfur was everywhere. Everyone's skin itched and burned as the frightened family watched the UFOs. The beam from the nearest turned toward Trancas, two miles away. It took at least 10 minutes to reach the outskirts of the village, then, incredibly, bent in a U-turn back toward the ranch house. The UFO then 'withdrew' the tube of light, rose up and joined the other five bright disks on the railroad. All six disks then rose and flew east toward the Sierra Medina mountains.

The episode lasted perhaps 45 minutes. When the disks had departed, the Morenos ventured out. They found the mist generated by the nearest UFO still in the air, smelling of sulfur. (Next day, visitors noted the smell of sulfur was still strong in the house.) Where the UFO had

hovered was a 3ft (1m) high conical pile of white spheres; there were similar spheres on the railroad track.

ASSESSMENT

Tests on the white balls (which were 0.5 inches [1.25cm] in diameter) at the University of Tucuman showed they consisted of 96.45 per cent calcium carbonate and 3.51 per cent potassium carbonate. Neighbors José Acosta and the entire Huanca family had seen the disks on the railroad track. The Morenos had no reason to lie. In due course it was proved that they had not. Military maneuvers were apparently the stimulus for their experience; excitement did the rest.

WATCHING THE SPACE RACE - 3

TYPE: **Radar tracking**
PLACE: **Earth orbit**
DATE: **18 April 1964**

Radars tracking the first unmanned space capsule launched in NASA's Gemini program picked up four 'unknowns' closing in on the capsule while it was still in its first orbit. The UFOs took up a formation around the capsule and stayed with it for an entire orbit, then dropped away 'in an orderly fashion' before disappearing from the radar scopes.

MEN FROM MARS

Unlikely claims and prophecy from two ufonauts

TYPE: **Close encounters of the third kind**
PLACE: **Newark Valley, Tioga County, New York State, USA**
DATE: **24 April 1964**

BACKGROUND

Some time before 10:00am, dairy farmer Gary T. Wilcox was spreading manure on

a field near his farmhouse when he noticed something shiny about 800 yards (720m) away, among some trees at the top of the hill where he was working. He took it to be the wing tank or some other detached part of a damaged aircraft, and drove his tractor up the hill to investigate.

THE EVENTS

When Wilcox dismounted, he saw a cigar-shaped object about 20ft (6m) long and 16ft (5m) wide, hovering just off the ground. He kicked it. It felt like metallic canvas. Then, out from under it, came two 4ft (1.2m) tall creatures wearing seamless clothes and hoods over their heads that hid their features. Each was holding a tray of soil. In English, they said: 'Do not be alarmed. We have talked to people before. We are from what you people refer to as the planet Mars.' They then engaged Wilcox in a long conversation about fertilizers, explaining that they hoped to solve problems with 'the rocky structure of Mars' by studying Earth's agricultural techniques. They also talked about space travel. They could come to Earth only every two years, and landed in daylight because their ship was less visible then. The two entities predicted the deaths of two Soviet cosmonauts and of US astronauts John Glenn and Virgil 'Gus' Grissom within the year. Finally, they asked for a bag of fertilizer. While Wilcox was walking to fetch it, the craft took off noiselessly and departed northward at high speed. Later that day Wilcox left a bag of fertilizer at the landing site. Next morning it had gone.

ASSESSMENT

Wilcox's encounter occurred at a time when space scientists believed that nothing more complex than bacteria might be able to survive on Mars. It now seems most likely that Mars cannot support any form of life. 'Gus' Grissom did die in a space accident, but not until January 1967, during a ground test of an Apollo craft. A 1968 investigation by psychiatrist Berthold Schwarz concluded that Wilcox was 'truthful... with no emotional illness', and that 'his experience was "real"', although interpreting it was 'a complicated and uncertain matter.' Wilcox had no other UFO experiences, before or since. Dr Jacques Vallée has pointed to similarities with the case of Mrs Rosa Lotti-Dainelli in Italy in November 1954; others have speculated that the UFO and its occupants were the same as those that were seen at Socorro the following day.

A 16mm movie still of 'an approaching UFO' taken by Daniel W. Fry in May 1964 near Merlin, Oregon. Fry claimed to have seen and ridden in UFOs since the 1950s. Today all his stories are taken with a pinch of salt.

THE LANDING AT SOCORRO

Patrolman sees humanoids and mystery craft

TYPE: **Close encounter of the third kind, ground markings**
PLACE: **Socorro, New Mexico, USA**
DATE: **24 April 1964**

BACKGROUND

About six hours after Wilcox's bizarre encounter in New York State, another close encounter took place in New Mexico. At roughly 5:45pm local time patrolman Lonnie Zamora, on duty in the Socorro Two police cruiser, gave chase to a speeding black Chevrolet. The pursuit continued south out of town; then Zamora heard a brief roar and saw flame in the sky to his right. He knew that there was a shack containing dynamite in the vicinity; he thought it had blown up. He abandoned his chase and swung off the highway onto a dirt road that led over a ridge and past the shack. The flame – blue and orange, smokeless, long and narrow – was now descending toward the ground.

THE EVENTS

Zamora drove slowly down the other side of the ridge. The noise had stopped and the flame had vanished. He suddenly noticed 'a shiny type object to [the] south' between 100 and 200 yards (90-180m) off the road and below him in a gully. 'It looked,' Zamora told FBI agent J. Arthur Byrnes Jr later the same day, 'like a car turned upside down...standing on [its] radiator or trunk.'

Next to the object were 'two people in white coveralls.... One of these persons seemed to turn and look straight at my car and seemed startled – seemed

UFO

to quickly jump somewhat.' They seemed 'normal in shape – but possibly they were small adults or large kids.' Zamora radioed Sgt. Sam Chavez in Socorro, and approached on foot to within 100ft (30m) of the object. He saw it was oval and smooth, with no windows or doors, on girder-like legs, and noted red insignia on its side, about 2.5ft (0.75m) wide. Then the roar began again, low frequency at first, rising rapidly and getting 'very loud'. The object emitted flame and kicked up dust. There was no sign of the 'persons' he had seen before.

Zamora thought the thing might explode, and ran back beyond his car to the top of the ridge. The roar stopped, and he looked back to see the UFO 'going away from me in a south-west direction... possibly 10 to 15ft (3-4.5m) above the ground, and it cleared the dynamite

shack by about three feet.' The UFO, now traveling very fast but no longer emitting either noise or flame, rose up and sped away. It 'just cleared' a mountain in the distance and disappeared.

ASSESSMENT

Sgt. Chavez, Zamora, FBI Agent Byrne (in Socorro on another case) and Deputy Sheriff James Lucky investigated the spot where the UFO had landed, and where the brush was still burning. They found four burn marks, and four V-shaped depressions, between 1 and 2 inches (2.5-5cm) deep and roughly 18 inches (0.45m) long, in the ground in an asymmetrical diamond pattern around the burns. These corresponded to the 'legs' Zamora had seen on the mystery craft. An engineer's analysis later declared that each would have been bearing a load of at least one

tonne to press so deeply into the dense desert earth. Five other, smaller marks nearby were labeled 'footprints'.

Dr J. Allen Hynek arrived in Socorro on 28 April to investigate on behalf of the USAF's Project Blue Book. At his instigation, the USAF checked – to no avail – if any aerospace company had been privately developing such a craft. The USAF did not, however, follow up Hynek's request to trace the car driver who told the manager of a gas station on US Highway 85 (since superseded by Interstate 25) that he had seen some kind of aircraft just south of town, in trouble and landing – and with a police car approaching it.

Some skeptics have suggested that the mayor of Socorro might have had reason to perform a hoax, and others have taken the view that although Zamora probably

At noon on 3 August 1965 highway traffic engineer Rex Heflin was driving near the Santa Ana freeway when he saw a UFO. He stopped and snapped three Polaroid shots of it. He reckoned it was 750ft (225m) away, at an altitude of 150ft (45m), and 30ft (9m) in diameter. Although Heflin did not report the sighting, on 20 September the Santa Ana *Register* published the photos. Three days later a Project Blue Book investigator interviewed Heflin, who said that the previous day he had handed his Polaroids to a person claiming to be an official from North American Air Defense Command (NORAD). NORAD denied any contact with Heflin, and the originals have not been seen since. Project Blue Book labeled the pictures a hoax. In 1967 the Condon Committee re-opened the case and declared that Heflin's photos were strong evidence for the existence of UFOs, but computer analysis of the pictures by Ground Saucer Watch in the late 1970s finally established that they were indeed fakes.

saw a real 'ball of plasma' he imagined the rest of the experience. The USAF initially thought a Lunar Exploration Module (LEM) – then at the development stage – was responsible, but no LEM resembles what Zamora saw. Project Blue Book finally classified the sighting as 'unidentified', while Hynek himself concluded that 'a real physical event' occurred in Socorro that day.

This case had an intriguing postscript two days later. At about 3:00am on 26 April 1964 a man called Orlando Gallego saw a UFO, identical to the one reported by Zamora, land at La Madera, New Mexico. Gallego and his family denied all knowledge of the Socorro sighting or of Zamora. Investigating police officers found evidence of burning around the alleged landing site, and four inexplicable dents in the ground.

ROBOTIC ATTACK

TYPE: **Close encounters of the third kind**
PLACE: **Cisco Grove, Placer County California, USA**
DATE: **4-5 September 1964**

BACKGROUND

Donald Schrum, Tim T and Vincent A (full names withheld) set up camp in this remote area to hunt with bows and arrows. Toward sunset, Schrum lost the others, lit a fire to signal his whereabouts to searchers and took refuge in a tree.

THE EVENTS

Seeing rotating lights moving through the air toward him, Schrum assumed they were on a rescue helicopter. But then he saw a flash, and a dark object fell to the ground nearby. He saw a dome with a flashing light on it. Two neckless entities with prominent eyes, about 5.5ft (1.7m) tall, dressed in silvery uniforms with hoods, then approached the tree. They were joined by a dark, stocky robot with glowing orange eyes. Its square, hinged jaw opened and emitted a white vapor that made Schrum pass out. When he came to, the humanoids were trying to climb the tree. At one point Schrum shot three arrows at the robot, which made a bright flash with each hit. A second robot appeared at dawn, and flashes passed between it and the first. Schrum blacked out again from an especially large discharge of vapor. (Some accounts say that the alien group at last backed away, and that Schrum passed out from the downblast as the UFO took off.) He came round eventually – hanging by his belt from the tree, and chilled to the bone – and managed to locate his friends. Vincent A said he too had seen an unusual light.

ASSESSMENT

USAF investigators said Schrum had been a victim of his own imagination or a prank. Schrum established that there were no military exercises in the area

that night. That he suffered considerably and has avoided publicity suggest that his experience was authentic. Whether it was real is another matter.

THE 1964 UFO CRASH IN KANSAS

TYPE: **Crash/retrieval**
PLACE: **Fort Riley, Kansas, USA**
DATE: **10 December 1964**

According to a witness known only as 'AK', who was a PFC in the 1st Infantry Division at Fort Riley, a disk-shaped UFO, 35-48ft (11-15m) in diameter and 12-18ft (3.5-5.5m) in height, crashed shortly before 2:00am in Camp Forsyte, a remote training area of the base complex. The craft had a fin-like protrusion, a smooth surface like aluminum, and a black band of squares jutting out about 10 inches (25cm) around its rim. 'AK' said he was unaware of any occupants. 'AK' was one of several soldiers guarding the UFO while a Huey helicopter scoured the area with a searchlight for over two hours. A Major General at the scene told 'AK' that he would have his '---- shot off' if he talked about the incident. Some aspects of the case were later confirmed by a witness known only as 'Ron'.

THE SECOND RAID ON WASHINGTON

Radiation, races with jets and cover-up in the capital

TYPE: **Multiple sightings, vehicle effects, radar-visual evidence**
PLACE: **Environs of Washington, DC, USA**
DATE: **21 December 1964- 11 January 1965**

THE EVENTS

The famous 'flap' of midwinter 1964-65 over Washington, DC lasted for almost two months, but three events stand out in particular from all the rest.

The first occurred on 21 December, when Horace Burns of Grottoes, Virginia, was driving between Staunton and Waynesboro on US 250. His car stalled as a huge cone-shaped UFO glided across the road and landed in a nearby field. The UFO was domed, and gave out a blue glow. After a few minutes, it took off again and disappeared from view. Tests by Prof. Ernest Gehman and engineers from the Du Pont Corporation revealed a high radiation count where the UFO had landed. The USAF investigation, after three weeks of rain and snow and disruptive visits to the field by sightseers, found no such traces, and declared the sighting a 'mirage'. But less than a month later,

two motorists driving in opposite directions along US 60 near Williamsburg, Virginia, reported sighting an almost precisely similar UFO.

Late in December three UFOs were tracked by local radar traveling at an apparent speed of 4800mph (7700km/h). The USAF maintained that these anomalous blips were not UFOs, but had been caused by 'faulty equipment'.

Then on 11 January, six Army Signal Corps engineers in the Munitions Building, in downtown Washington, watched as disk-shaped UFOs zig-zagged across the city sky toward the Capitol, pursued by two delta-wing jet interceptors. The UFOs rapidly outpaced the jets and disappeared from sight. Newspaper reporters tried to follow up the story

with the US Department of Defense, but they were told by both civilian and military officials that the chase incident 'never happened'.

ASSESSMENT

The 1964-65 flap attracted far less publicity than the first over Washington in summer 1952 – and continues to do so. The official response to the later events was, if not swift, uniformly stifling. These facts would seem to indicate either that a kind of contagion had overtaken the citizens of Washington, and official channels were determined to keep it under control; or that since 1952 the USAF and other interested parties (such as the CIA) had learned a great deal about effective methods of debunking.

THE ARCHER
AND THE AGENTS

TYPE: **Close encounter of
the third kind**
PLACE: **Augusta archery range,
Augusta County, Virginia,
USA**
DATE: **19 January 1965**

At about 6:15pm engineering draftsman William Blackburn was chopping wood near the snow-covered Augusta range's clubhouse when he saw a pyramid- or conical-shaped object descending from the sky to the south. It then hovered at an estimated altitude of 3000ft (900m); Blackburn judged its diameter at over 200ft (60m). As he watched, a smaller UFO, about 60ft (18m) in diameter, landed within 50ft (15m) of him. Its surface was polished to a mirror-like finish. On top was a 'bubble' that made Blackburn feel 'quite strange' when he looked at it. An opening appeared in the UFO's side 'like someone took a slice of pie from it', and three humanoids floated out of it: their feet never touched the ground. They approached to within 35ft (11m) of Blackburn and made various unintelligible sounds. They were about 3ft (1m) tall, but otherwise like ordinary humans. Blackburn, frozen in amazement, made no response, and the beings floated back to the craft. Both UFOs then departed swiftly. They left no traces in the snow. Shortly after Blackburn's story was published in his local paper, *The Waynesboro News-Virginian*, a car with federal government license plates appeared in town: residents said it stuck out like a sore thumb. Blackburn was apparently 'sternly warned' by government agents, from an agency he declined to name, that he should say no more about his experience.

Artist's impression of lavender grower Maurice Masse's encounter with a UFO and its occupants near Valensole, France, in July 1965.

THE LAVENDER
FIELDS ENCOUNTER

Mysterious entities
paralyse a French farmer

TYPE: **Close encounter of
the third kind**
PLACE: **Valensole, France**
DATE: **1 July 1965**

BACKGROUND

Maurice Masse was 41 years old in 1965, a lavender farmer working land just over a mile from the house where he lived with his wife and two children. On 1 July he set out for work at 5:00am. At 5:45am, prior to starting his tractor, he heard a whistling sound that he took to be from a military helicopter. He was used to helicopters landing on his fields during exercises, and would often chat to the pilots.

THE EVENTS

Masse walked around the stones and saw a 'machine' among the lavender bushes about 100 yards (90m) away. It was shaped like a Rugby football with a cupola on top, and was 10-12ft (3-3.5m) wide and about 8ft (2.5m) high. It stood on six legs connected to a central pylon – looking, he said, 'like an enormous spider'. Beside the object were two figures the size of small boys, bending over a lavender bush. Masse had recently had his plants vandalized, and now he thought he had caught the culprits. He approached them cautiously. As he got closer he saw that they were not human: they were about 3ft (1m) tall, white-skinned, with heads three times the size of a human in relation to their bodies, with large ears, high fleshy cheekbones, big, oblique, lidless eyes, no chins, and round holes for mouths. They were wearing gray-green one-piece suits but no headgear; their heads were hairless. They noticed Masse when he was still 25ft (8m) from them. In obvious alarm, one took a small cylinder from its belt and pointed it at Masse who found himself rooted to the spot, unable

to move. The two creatures looked at him for a while, making guttural sounds to each other. He had no sense of hostility from them. The pair then returned to their craft, entering it through a sliding door. The whistling sound started again, and the craft hovered briefly while its legs began to rotate; then it flew off at high speed toward the west. After only 65ft (20m) or so it vanished from sight. Masse did not recover his ability to move for a further quarter hour. When he did, he immediately checked the place where the UFO had stood and found several markings in the earth, and a 1ft (0.3m) deep hole where the central pylon of the craft had rested. The ground around it was mushy. Later that day, he found the soil had rapidly hardened to the consistency of cement.

ASSESSMENT

Something physical certainly seems to have afflicted Masse's lavender field, for the vegetation near the landing site quickly died off, and lavender would not grow there again. Plants in a westerly strip 300ft (90m) long and up to 10ft (3m) wide had been damaged by intense heat. Masse himself collapsed three days after the incident and for some time slept habitually for 14-15 hours a day. When Masse was shown a picture of a model of the craft Lonnie Zamora had seen at Socorro in 1964, he at first thought someone else must have photographed 'his' UFO. When told about Zamora's experience, he sighed: 'You see then that I was not dreaming and that I'm not mad.' Danish folklorist Age Skjelborg examined the case in some detail. Among other findings he proposed that Masse's experience was a waking dream that had been triggered by fears about government plans to introduce new technology to the area – thus jeopardizing his livelihood – and informed by accounts from migrant workers of similar UFO encounters that had been reported in Italy in 1954. This argument is plausible as far as it goes, but it still does not account for the physical effects on the site afterwards.

UFO

THE GREEN TRIANGLE

TYPE: **Lights in the sky**
PLACE: **Ogre observatory, Latvia**
DATE: **26 July 1965**

Astronomers Robert and Esmerelda Vitolniek and Yan Melderis reported seeing a starlike triangular green UFO. On closer inspection through the observatory's telescope the UFO was made up of three individual green balls in triangular formation around a larger, central green light. The central sphere was estimated to be 300ft (90m) in diameter, and its height 60 miles (100km), but they were unable to offer any explanation for their sighting.

TRUCKER'S NIGHTMARE

TYPE: **Close encounter of the second kind**
PLACE: **Highway 15 south of Abilene, Kansas, USA**
DATE: **4 August 1965**

Trucker Don Tenopir from Nebraska was heading north toward Abilene with a load of grain. At about 1:30am a UFO swooped over his truck and landed on the pavement ahead of him. A car, coming the other way, swerved around the object and screeched to a halt. Tenopir jammed on his brakes. His lights failed, though the rig's GMC diesel kept on running. The UFO moved ahead, and the truck's headlights came back on. Tenopir could now see the object: a domed disk about 15ft (4m) in diameter, hovering a couple of feet off the ground. There were square windows around the top. 'Scared to death', Tenopir stayed in his cab, but the car driver got out and approached him. Before they could speak, the UFO threw out blue sparks from its base and took off noisily. Both drivers fled. Tenopir reported the incident to the police in Abilene, but he received no follow-up from city, state, government or military authorities. The case bears an interesting resemblance to the encounter in Hampshire, England, that occurred in November 1967 (see below).

THE EXETER INCIDENTS

Police and citizens versus the Air Force

TYPE: **Lights in the sky, close encounter of the first kind, multiple witnesses**
PLACE: **Exeter, New Hampshire, USA**
DATE: **September 1965**

BACKGROUND

Fall 1965 saw a flurry of UFO sightings in and around Exeter, New Hampshire. Among the witnesses were:
- A Mrs Jalbert, who with her four sons repeatedly saw a silvery object with bright flashing lights hovering near power lines by their home; occasionally an aircraft would pursue it.
- Two young people who saw a UFO emerge from the sea at Hampton Beach; afterwards, flying at very low altitude, it pursued their car.
- A Mrs Blodgett, who saw a blinding ball of light, rotating at high speed, hovering over treetops 100ft (30m) away.
- Author John G. Fuller who, while investigating the Exeter flap, one night saw a high-flying orange-red disk being pursued by a jet fighter.
- The most dramatic of the events, and those that were most ineptly handled by USAF investigators, took place on 3 September and were witnessed by teenager Norman Muscarello and by police patrolmen Eugene Bertrand and David Hunt.

THE EVENTS

At around 1:30am patrolman Bertrand checked a parked car. The driver was clearly distraught and told him that she had been followed for 12 miles (19km) by a huge, silent UFO, which had eventually left at enormous speed. Incredulous, Bertrand did not take the woman's name

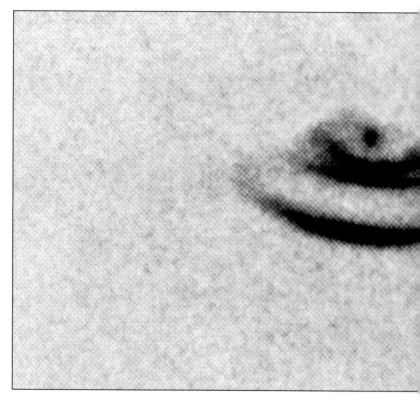

or details but, when he checked in to the police station shortly after, found 18-year-old Muscarello had just come in to report a similar encounter on Route 150. The pair returned to the spot where they found that the phenomeon was still active. Bertrand reported: 'A group of five red lights came from behind a group of trees near us. They were extremely bright and flashed on one at a time. The lights started to move around over the field. At one time, they came so close I fell to the ground and started to draw my gun. The lights were so bright, I was unable to make out any form. There was no sound or vibration but the farm animals were upset and making a lot of noise.... Mr Muscarello and I ran to the car. [At 2:55am] I radioed Patrolman David Hunt who arrived in a few minutes. He also observed the lights....'

Hunt's account confirms Bertrand's. After the lights disappeared, police took a call from a man in a phone booth, saying a UFO was flying right at him. The line then went dead. The caller was never traced.

ASSESSMENT

Investigators from Pease AFB noted that five B-47 bombers were airborne at the time of the sightings, but dismissed any connection between them and the reported incidents. On 27 October the Pentagon issued a statement ascribing the sightings to aircraft taking part in a Strategic Air Command exercise and to distortions of stars and planets caused by temperature inversions. A month later, the police had an unsolicited letter from USAF Project Blue Book suggesting that the sightings had been caused by a high-altitude USAF exercise code-named 'Big Blast'. This, however, had ended at 2:00am. When the officers pointed out this and other discrepancies in the letter, the Pentagon's response was to reclassify the sightings as 'unknown'. Philip Klass proposed that they were corona discharges from high-tension power lines, near which many local witnesses had seen UFOs. Robert Sheaffer noted that the UFOs were seen in exactly the same positions as certain bright planets that were easily visible on this especially clear night. Kim Hansen suggested that the UFOs might be natural phenomena, like the lights seen at Hessdalen, Norway, and Marfa, Texas. Nevertheless, the three principal witnesses remained unconvinced by all these explanations, which they regarded as post facto rationalizations of a UFO experience that, to them, was unarguably real.

This photograph of the 'Warminster Thing', taken by Gordon Faulkner on 29 August 1965 from the town center and highly publicized in the tabloid press, sparked years of interest in UFOs around this quiet Wiltshire town. Then, in 1994, one Richard Hooton confessed that he and Faulkner had faked the picture with a button and a cotton reel. Faulkner, however, declared he was 'mystified' as he had never known anyone named Hooton, and stood by his picture.

BEINGS LIKE BEER CANS

TYPE: **Close encounter of the third kind**
PLACE: **Long Prairie, Minnesota, USA**
DATE: **23 October 1965**

Most bizarre of all the perceived occupants of UFOs have been the so-called robot figures, and possibly the weirdest of all was reported by Jerry Townsend, a radio station employee from Minnesota. In the evening of 23 October 1965 he was driving toward Long Prairie when his car's electrical systems went dead. In front of him on the road was a V-2-style 'spaceship', between 30 and 35ft (9-10.5m) tall, and resting on the tips of three fins, that might have been, as one commentator put it, 'culled straight from the pulp era of science fiction.' Undaunted, Townsend got out of the car and saw, coming from beneath the rocket, three ludicrous objects walking towards him. They were no more than 6 inches (15cm) tall, reeling like drunken sailors on two fins, and shaped like beer cans. Whenever they halted, a third, rear fin descended to keep them upright. In due course they tottered back to their anti-quated 'rocket', and it took off. Take-off was also witnessed by two hunters, who were some distance from the scene.

THE WARMINSTER SAGA

TYPE: **Lights in the sky, daylight disk**
PLACE: **Warminster, Wiltshire, UK**
DATE: **1965 onward**

Hundreds of UFO sightings were reported from Warminster in the Sixties and Seventies following the publication in 1965 by a tabloid newspaper of a UFO allegedly seen flying near the town. 'Skywatching' on nearby hills became something of a social event for many

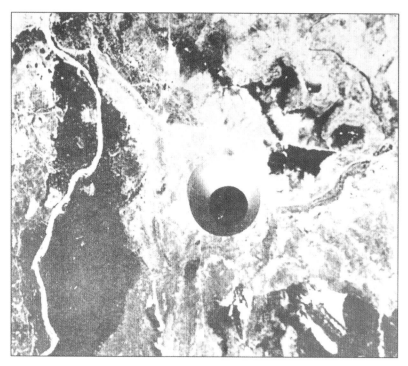

This striking and unusual UFO photo has a curious history. Inake Oses of Venezuela maintained that on 13 February 1966 he had been surveying an area some 50 miles (80 km) south of Calobozo from an aircraft flying at about 8000 ft (2450m), spotted the UFO, and told the pilot to give chase. The UFO paused over a mining area, then shot off southward at fantastic speed. In due course Oses confessed he had faked the picture – along with the renowned 'Avensa Airliner' UFO picture – as revenge against 'UFO buffs' who had mocked him for not believing in 'flying saucers'.

people, not all of whom were reliable witnesses, and a local journalist published several colorful accounts of the sightings. British researchers Barry Gooding and Paul Devereux analysed the Warminster phenomena and found genuine anomalies. Devereux noted tectonic faults beside Cley Hill, a major viewpoint for UFOs in the district and concluded that the Warminster UFOs were 'earthlights'.

THE SWAMP GAS FIASCO

Dr Hynek's most famous diagnosis

TYPE: **Lights in the sky**
PLACE: **Hillsdale and Dexter, Michigan, USA**
DATE: **20-21 March 1966**

BACKGROUND

These cases are most important for the effect they had on their most celebrated investigator. Early 1966 saw a rash of UFO reports in Michigan, involving over

100 witnesses. Dr J. Allen Hynek, consultant astronomer to the USAF's Project Blue Book, was sent to investigate the two sightings described below.

THE EVENTS

Civil defense director William Van Horn, with an assistant dean of Hillsdale College and no fewer than 87 co-eds, watched a glowing, football-shaped UFO for over four hours as it maneuvered near the campus, looped around an airport beacon, and finally disappeared over a nearby swamp. Van Horn had the UFO in sight through binoculars and was certain it was some kind of craft. It vanished as police arrived to investigate, then reappeared when they had left.

Near Dexter the next day, two police officers and three further independent witnesses all saw a large glowing object rise from a swamp on some farmland. The UFO hovered for a while at an estimated altitude of 1000ft (300m) and then flew off into the distance. One witness described it as a domed disk showing various lights, with a 'quilted' surface and antennae on its underside.

ASSESSMENT

Hynek believed the Hillsdale and Dexter sightings were of swamp gas, and announced this conclusion to the press. The media misreported Hynek as claiming that this was the cause of all the Michigan sightings. Press cartoonists lampooned him, and Michigan was briefly dubbed 'the Swamp Gas State'. Shortly afterward, Hynek's pronouncements on UFOs became less critical of the extra-terestrial hypothesis, and he called for 'a scientific effort on a much larger scale than any heretofore... for a frontal attack on this problem.' The Hillsdale and Dexter sightings may, nonetheless, be explicable in terms of the Earthlights Hypothesis.

BLACKOUT AT NHA TRANG

TYPE: **Light in the sky, electromagnetic effects, multiple witnesses**
PLACE: **US forces base, Nha Trang, South Viet Nam**
DATE: **June 1966**

At about 9:45pm, Nha Trang was busy. Apart from the usual activity on the base, eight bulldozers were at work, soldiers were watching an outdoor movie, and two Douglas A-1E Skyraider attack planes were preparing for take-off on the nearby airstrip. In the bay a Shell oil tanker lay at anchor. Suddenly the northern sky was lit up. First reactions were that it was an enemy flare, but the brilliant light then started to move and approached the base. As it came towards the observers it varied its speed, before it stopped dead and started to hover over the base at a height of about 300-500ft (90-150m), illuminating the entire valley. At this point all the engines and power failed on the base, on the anchored tanker in the bay and on some diesels. After about four minutes in this position, the UFO shot straight up and disappeared from sight within three seconds. After the object had gone, full power was restored at the base as quickly and as unaccountably as it had gone off in the first place.

BENDING LIGHT BEAMS

Type: Close encounter of the second kind, electromagnetic effects, ground markings
Place: Bealiba, Victoria, Australia
Date: 4 April 1966

Ronald Sullivan was driving on a long, straight stretch of road nine miles east of Bealiba in the Australian state of Victoria during the night of 4 April 1966 when his headlight beams suddenly and inexplicably bent part of the way along their length towards the right – as if they had been solid but malleable pieces of pipe. In astonishment and great alarm, Sullivan screeched his car to a stop, and was then treated to a brilliant display of colored lights coming from a field by the road. After that, an object rose up from the field and vanished. Before reporting the incident to police, Sullivan had his lights checked: they were in perfect order. When police investigated the site they found a circular depression about 5ft (1.5m) across and 5 inches (12.5cm) at its deepest in the field. Sullivan reported that he 'did not believe in UFOs'.

UFO photographed by barber Ralph Ditter at his house in Roseville, a suburb of Zanesville, Ohio, on 13 November 1966. For years, Ditter exhibited this and another UFO picture taken at the same time in his barber shop. The Condon Committee examined both exhaustively, and concluded they were faked. Ditter failed to respond to requests for 'clarification' of the differences between his account of the sighting and the apparent facts.

One of a series of photos taken in the Huaylas Valley near Yungay, Peru, in March 1967 by Augusto Arrando, on a hiking expedition in the mountains some 10,000ft (3050 m) above sea level. J. Richard Greenwell made strenuous attempts to locate Arrando, but failed to meet the man in person. Hope of authenticating the photos probably vanished forever when Yungay and most of its 20,000 inhabitants were buried by a gigantic avalanche in May 1970.

THE EASTERN EUROPEAN WAVE

TYPE: **Various reports**
PLACE: **USSR, Poland, Czechoslovakia**
DATE: **1966**

A flood of UFO sightings were made in these three countries during 1966. Here is a small sample of the cases involving witnesses of high professional standing who, because of the oppressive nature of Eastern bloc society at the time, had a great deal to lose by creating hoaxes. At this time the official Soviet line on the subject was that UFO witnesses were 'idiots or incorrigible liars' (*Pravda*, 9 January 1961) and that the objects were 'an invention of the US Secretary of State for Defense, Robert McNamara, in order to spread alarm through the world' (Radio Moscow, 1965).

In April 1966, Soviet Air Force Major Baidukov was flying in the region of Odessa in the Crimea when his airborne radar detected a UFO as it descended from an altitude of over 30 miles (50km) to a little over 10 miles (16km). Ground radar confirmed the signal, and the UFO was visible to Baidukov himself.

On 17 June, V.G. Krylov and a team of geophysicists working at Blista in the northern Caucasus watched a UFO resembling a small red disk for 45 minutes as it too descended from an altitude of about 30 miles (50km) to a little over 10 miles (16km).

In October, 45 witnesses including the director of the Hydromagnetic School at Kerson, V.I. Duginov, saw a flying disk – its diameter when it was viewed from about 10 miles (16km) appeared to be three times greater than that of the Sun.

THE MOUNT CLEMENS HOAX

Seeing is believing

TYPE: **Alleged daylight disk**
PLACE: **Mount St Clemens, Michigan, USA**
DATE: **9 January 1967**

Teenage brothers Dan and Grant Jaroslaw said that from Mount Clemens they saw a dark gray UFO hover over Lake St Clair and then take off at speed toward the south-east, and they produced four photographs of the object. These pictures were reproduced in numerous newspapers and UFO magazines, and analysed by USAF Project Blue Book, which had its reservations. Officially, the verdict was 'insufficient data for evaluation', as the USAF did not see the original negatives, but Blue Book's consultant Dr J. Allen Hynek was later reported as saying: 'Analysis so far does not show any indication of a possible hoax.' The pictures entered the pantheon of 'genuine' evidence. In 1976, however, the brothers wrote to Dr Hynek confessing that they had faked the pictures as a joke which then got out of hand. The UFO was a model suspended from a thread. The episode illustrates the willingness of UFO 'believers' to accept all photographic evidence at face value and the long life that a well-constructed hoax can enjoy even among those who are usually on their guard against fakes.

THE ANDREASSON ABDUCTION

A flight to a crystal city

TYPE: **Close encounter of the fourth kind**
PLACE: **South Ashburnham, Massachusetts, USA**
DATE: **25 January 1967**

BACKGROUND

In the foggy evening of 25 January 1967, Betty Andreasson was at home with her seven children and her parents, who were there to help out while her husband was in hospital recovering from a car accident. At about 7:00pm the house lights failed. Betty saw a pink light glowing through the kitchen window. Her father saw small creatures, 'just like Hallowe'en freaks', in the yard; one of them looked at him 'and I felt kind of queer.' The lights then came back on. Betty's family were frozen in a kind of catatonic trance, but she saw four 4ft (1.2m) tall entities enter the house through the closed door. The beings were typical 'Grays', wearing skintight blue uniforms. Betty remembered nothing further about this event until she underwent hypnotic regression in early 1977.

THE EVENTS

Under hypnosis, Betty recalled that the leader of the Grays informed her telepathically that the aliens needed 'food for their minds' and that his name was Quazgaa. She gave him a copy of the Christian Bible; in return he gave her a 'thin blue book'. The aliens asked her to follow them 'so that she could help the world'. Betty reluctantly agreed, and was led outside to an oval craft. Aboard it, she was given a painful physical examination: a long needle was thrust into her navel, and a probe into her nose.

Next she was put on a chair, hoses were attached to her nose and mouth, and a transparent, airtight cover was placed over her and the chair. Gray fluid filled this 'container', and Betty felt a pleasant pulsating sensation. The fluid was then drained away, and two aliens led Betty down a dark tunnel and out of the craft to a lifeless landscape, where everything, even the air, was colored red. Walking between square buildings, she was alarmed to see lemur-like creatures without heads but with eyes on stalks climbing over them. The party passed through a circular membrane into a new setting imbued with green.

At the end of their path was a pyramid and a display of airborne crystals, giving out an intense light. But blocking the way was a 15ft (4.5m) tall bird. Radiating intense heat, this vanished: in its place was a fire. Out of its ashes crawled a fat worm. Betty then heard a powerful voice (which she believed came from God) telling her she had been chosen for 'a mission', whose details would be forthcoming at a later time. The party then returned to the craft through the colored realms, Betty was sealed up again, and she eventually found herself being led out of the UFO into her back yard again. Quazgaa told her that 'secrets' had been 'locked' in her mind. It was still night; inside the house, the family was still in suspended animation. The aliens led them to their beds, and left. The encounter had lasted an estimated 3 hours 40 minutes.

ASSESSMENT

Betty Andreasson is a devout, fundamentalist Christian and many aspects of her unique account reflect religious and other symbolic images. The case investigator, Raymond Fowler, suggested that these were deliberately used by the aliens to win her confidence. But Dr Alvin Lawson believes many of these features support his hypothesis that abductions are dramatizations of memories of being born. Unfortunately, the book 'Quazgaa' gave Mrs Andreasson disappeared shortly after her experience, and she had no recall of the 'secrets' implanted in her mind. But her father and eldest daughter, Becky, were aware of aliens entering the house despite their paralytic state. Voice-stress and psychiatric tests showed Betty Andreasson to be sane and reliable.

'EVIDENCE' FOR THE UMMO CONTACTS

The classic Spanish contact case

TYPE: **Daylight disk, photographs, multiple witnesses**
PLACE: **San José de Valderas, Madrid, Spain**
DATE: **1 June 1967**

The object appeared at sundown and maneuvered around the area for about a quarter of an hour. Witnesses estimated its diameter at about 40ft (12m) Its distinctive feature was the astronomical sign for Uranus on its underside. The UFO then flew along the line of the Extremadura Highway, where it was seen by further witnesses as a ball of light, and landed near a restaurant in the Santa Monica district. Landing marks and small metal rods were later found at the site. When broken, these rods issued a liquid that rapidly evaporated and were found to contain green polyvinyl fluoride strips engraved with the Uranus symbol. At the time this material was made exclusively for NASA by Dupont de Nemours and was not commercially available. Two sets of photos of the sightings were given to Madrid newspapers by anonymous or untraceable witnesses. When digitally enhanced by GSW, the 'spacecraft' were shown to be models hanging on thread.

The insignia on the UFOs was a trademark of the Ummo contactee case that had intrigued a group of ufologists in Spain since 1961. Besides occasional photographic evidence, there was an enormous amount of written material presented to interested parties by an anonymous intermediary, which included impressive physics, math and philosophy, purportedly from inhabitants of the planet Ummo circling the star Wolf 424. Some Ummites were allegedly living on Earth.

Several interpretations of the Ummo material have been made, from a secret military intelligence experiment in mind control by CIA or KGB, to 'samizdat literature saying things that could not be said openly in Francoist Spain.' In 1993 Spanish ufologist Louis R. Gonzales published a long analysis that concluded the Ummo affair was the work of lone hoaxer Jordan Pena. If this is true, Pena must have taken quick advantage of genuine multi-witness UFO sightings in Madrid when faking his photos. The true origin of that UFO (and of the mysterious vinyl strips) has never been established.

THE CALGARY PHOTOGRAPHS

Can experts be fooled?

TYPE: **Daylight disks**
PLACE: **South-west of Calgary, Alberta, Canada**
DATE: **3 July 1967**

Warren Smith and two companions were traveling back from a hunting trip. At about 5:30pm they saw a UFO flying toward them in a westerly direction, losing height as it approached. When it came within a range of about 2000ft (600m), Smith photographed it. The object, still descending, flew out of sight among some trees, then rose above them. Smith took a second photo. The UFO hovered momentarily, dropped a small object, and sped away to the south.

To this day, there has been no final verdict on whether these pictures are genuine or fake. They were analysed scientifically both by Dr J. Allen Hynek and the Defense Photographic Interpretation Center of the Royal Canadian Air Force, who judged that the photos showed an unidentified doughnut-shaped craft, 40-50ft (12-15m) in diameter and 11-14ft (3.5-4m) thick. Ground Saucer Watch (GSW) tested the first of the photographs and declared that it was indeed genuine, but denounced the second as 'the crudest attempt at a hoax we have ever seen.' However, the second print they analysed had not been taken from the original negative, and GSW suggested in fairness that this was a possible reason for the discrepancy between this and the first photograph.

FOUR VISITS TO KISLOVODSK

TYPE: **Daylight disks**
PLACE: **Kislovodsk, Caucasus, Russia**
DATE: **18 July, 18 August, 4 September, 18 October 1967**

The most detailed of this series of sightings occurred on 18 August 1967, when astronomer Anatoli Sazanov and 11 other members of the astrophysical station near Kislovodsk saw a yellow, crescent-shaped but asymmetrical UFO, accompanied by a

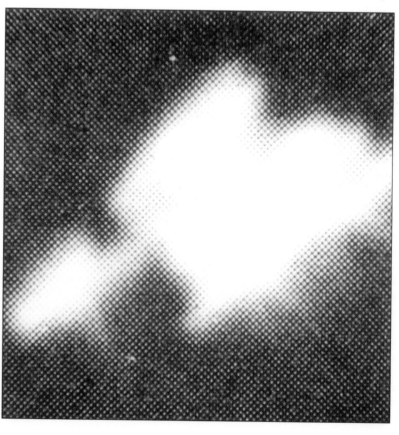

This UFO was photographed by Robert Burke early in the morning of 24 November 1967 at St Leonard's-on-Sea, Sussex, England. The bright, blue-white light remained over the sea for about an hour, growing and diminishing in intensity.

luminous point. They estimated the UFO's length as at least 150m (400ft) and its speed as 18,000km/h (11,250mph). Other members of the station and local inhabitants witnessed the same object on the other dates. The staff of Kazan Observatory confirmed the accuracy of these reports.

FLYING CROSS

Strange maneuvers over England's west country

TYPE: Close encounter of
        the first kind
PLACE: Moigne Downs, Dorset,
        England
DATE: 26 October 1967

BACKGROUND

On the night of 24 October, two police motor patrol officers in Devon pursued a vast illuminated flying cross for 12 miles (20km) along the border of Dartmoor. The UFO was also sighted in other parts of the country at different times that same night. Two days later, retired Royal Air Force intelligence officer J.B.W. 'Angus' Brooks was taking his German Shepherd and Dalmatian dogs for a morning walk across Moigne Downs near the south Dorset coast. At 11:25am, while sheltering in a hollow from the roaring Force 8 wind, he noticed a thin contrail in the south-western sky.

THE EVENTS

Brooks rapidly realized that the 'contrail' was actually a craft of some kind, flying headlong toward him. It decelerated very fast, and stopped, hovering silently, at about 250ft (75m) above the ground, 400 yards (350m) from where he was lying. It consisted of a central disk, 25ft (8m) in diameter and 12ft (3.5m) thick, with one girder-like 'fuselage' pointing forward and three protruding behind, parallel to one another. These were each about 75ft (22m) long, 7ft (2m) high and 8ft (2.5m) wide. As the craft came to a halt, the two

outer rear fuselages swung through 90° to form a cross with the disk at the center, then the whole object rotated 90° clockwise. Brooks watched the UFO hanging in the air like this for 22 minutes, although his German Shepherd dog, extremely agitated, kept pawing him. Brooks noted that the craft had no windows, and was made of translucent material that changed color to match the sky. The fuselages had nose cones and groove fins. Finally front and rear fuselages swung to line up with one of those on one side, and the UFO flew off, single fuselage forward, continuing north-east.

ASSESSMENT

British Ministry of Defence investigators suggested that Brooks had fallen asleep while sheltering from the wind. As he dozed off cell debris in his eye – possibly from his recent corneal transplant operation – had created images that, in his following dream, he developed to match the flying cross seen in previous days and widely reported. Brooks responded: 'The fact that the gale was howling and my Alsatian dog was painfully clawing me to leave the spot was hardly conducive to "dropping off".' The Ministry also said: 'Our radar cover is such that we are also quite satisfied that there is no clandestine aerial activity over the United Kingdom under terrestrial control.' This statement begs several interesting questions. Besides, the UK has little radar cover below 5000ft (1500m) beyond the immediate airspace around large city airports.

COVERED UP OVERNIGHT

TYPE: Close encounter of
        the second kind,
        multiple witnesses
PLACE: Avon and Sopley,
        Hampshire, UK
DATE: 6 November 1967

Sometime between 1:00am and 2:00am, Carl Farlow was driving a truck loaded with domestic cookers on the A338 trunk

road between the villages of Sopley and Avon in Hampshire, England. He was approaching a junction near a bridge over the river Avon when his wagon's lights died. Its diesel engine (which of course does not depend on an electrical ignition system) kept running and, assuming a simple short circuit of some kind, he pulled up to look into the cause of the sudden malfunction.

Before he could climb down from the cab, he was astonished to see a bizarre egg-shaped object move from right to left across the road in front of him at about 25ft (7.5m) from the ground. It was magenta-colored, with a white base, and was perhaps 80ft (24m) long – big enough to overhang both sides of the road as it passed across, exuding a smell 'like a drill boring through wood' and making a sound 'like a refrigerator'. As it crossed the road it accelerated gradually, and after a few seconds it disappeared altogether from sight.

Farlow then realized that a Jaguar sedan, which had been coming in the opposite direction, was stranded on the other side of the UFO's path. Its driver, who was a veterinarian, approached Farlow, explained that his vehicle was out of action and his lady passenger hysterical, and suggested they call the police. A call from a nearby phone booth – which was working, though its lights too were dead – brought the police to the scene shortly afterward. Their preliminary inspection of the site showed that the surface of the road seemed to have melted – almost inconceivable in an English winter. The vet's passenger was taken to hospital to be treated for shock, while the two men were questioned first by police and later by an official from the Ministry of Defence.

Next day, Farlow returned to his truck. A bulldozer was leveling the road, the phone booth was being repainted, and other people seemed to be investigating the area with instruments. A week or so later, on the same route, Farlow saw that some 70 yards of that particular stretch of road had been resurfaced.

THE SCHIRMER ABDUCTION

Key evidence from hypnotic regression

TYPE: **Close encounter of the fourth kind**
PLACE: **Ashland, Nebraska, USA**
DATE: **3 December 1967**

BACKGROUND

Early in the morning Patrolman Herbert Schirmer was at the junction of Highways 3 and 63 near Ashland when he saw a football-shaped UFO on the ground, displaying red lights and standing on a tripod. After the sighting, Schirmer realized he seemed to have 'lost' a period of about 20 minutes, and he had an inexplicable red weal on his neck. The Condon Committee asked Dr Leo Sprinkle to regress the police officer hypnotically; he was also regressed five months later by Dr Loring G. Williams, on 8 June 1968.

THE EVENTS

According to Schirmer's testimony under hypnosis, entities about 4ft (1.5m) tall emerged from the landed UFO and surrounded his patrol car. Terrified, he tried to draw his revolver, but was prevented from doing so by a telepathically-conveyed command. One of the aliens held a 'box-like thing' that covered the car with green light or gas. An entity touched his neck and hurt him. The aliens questioned him about the nearby electricity plant and water reservoir. When he admitted he was 'the watchman of this town' he was taken aboard the UFO where he was told the craft was operated by 'reversible electromagnetism' and drew energy from earthly power lines and water sources. The aliens came from a nearby galaxy and had several bases on Earth. Schirmer asked if the aliens kidnapped people. They replied that they 'had a program known as "breeding analysis" and some humans had been used in these experiments.'

ASSESSMENT

This appears to be the first overt reference in an abduction case to a genetic program conducted by aliens, although there were strong hints in the Villas Boas and Hill cases. There are several explanations for this and other details given by the aliens to Schirmer. He may have been subjected to leading questions by his hypnotist. He may, more or less unconsciously, have mixed together material from reading about UFOs and in particular the Hill case, as similar details occur in other cases, ufological writings and in science fiction. Or the regression may have worked perfectly, and he was recalling events exactly as they occurred.

THE ABDUCTION THAT WASN'T

TYPE: **Teleportation**
PLACE: **Near Chascomus, Argentina**
DATE: **May 1968**

A Dr Gerardo Vidal and his wife, of Chascomus, were driving at night with another couple in separate cars to dinner in Maipu (or Mar del Plata) near Buenos Aires, when a dense fog enveloped the Vidals' vehicle. They did not emerge from the cloud, and friends and relatives searched the area without finding any trace of them or their car. Two days later, Dr Vidal phoned his family to say that he was alive and well. He and his wife had driven out of the fog to find themselves on a dusty road in broad daylight. Their watches had stopped, they had pains in their necks, and the surface of their car had apparently been scorched. They drove on to the nearest city, which turned out to be Mexico City, 4000 miles (6450km) from home, where they took shelter at the Argentine embassy. On their return, Señora Vidal spent some time in hospital being treated for shock; the car was sent to the USA for tests. Dr Vidal would say only that he had been told to say nothing.

This account is included in this catalogue because it has been repeated in numerous reputable UFO books as fact – even though no UFO has ever been mentioned in connection with it! The verdict on the case was definitively stated by Dr Jacques Vallée in his 1990 book *Confrontations*: 'This event is described in detail in a dozen books. When I visited Argentina [this] was one of the first cases I enquired about. My Argentine friends laughed. They had spent years looking for the Vidals. They kept finding people who knew people who knew the Vidals.... But they never found the Vidals.

'There are no Vidals. The incident never happened.'

A TALL BLUE MAN

TYPE: **Close encounter of the third kind**
PLACE: **Villa Carlos Paz, Cordoba, Argentina**
DATE: **13 June 1968**

At about 12:40am Maria Eliada Pretzel, aged 19, said goodnight to her fiancé and to some guests leaving the family's Motel La Cuesta in Villa Carlos La Paz, on Highway 20 about 500 miles (800km) west of Buenos Aires. Her father was out for the evening. She turned off the motel lights, then noticed a light in the lobby. There, she was confronted by a fair-haired man, over 6ft (2m) tall, dressed in a skin-tight suit that had shiny sky-blue scales. In his left hand he carried a sky-blue sphere, which was moving about.

 UFO captured by the camera near Kanab, Utah, USA, on 21 March 1968. The craft bears a distinct resemblance to the flying saucers that George Adamski claimed to have filmed in the early Fifties – an indication either that such objects are real, or that hoaxers are remarkably lacking in imagination.

Constantly smiling, he moved his right hand, on which he wore a huge ring, up and down in front of her. Light came from his fingertips, and Maria felt increasingly lethargic, though she felt 'goodness and kindness' emanating from the creature. At the same time he was mumbling in a tongue that to Maria sounded 'like Chinese'. Maria was petrified, but after a few minutes the entity walked slowly to the side door and let himself out. Maria fainted, and was found at about 12:50am by her father. A few moments before, as he was returning home, he had seen an object, apparently on the highway about 50 yards (45m) away, that was shining two brilliant red light beams at the motel. After a few seconds both the lights and the object vanished. Señor Pretzel ran home, where he found Maria in a state of collapse. She took some days to recover from her harrowing experience. The police promised to investigate the matter, but they never reported their findings.

CAN UFOS KILL?

TYPE: **Close encounter of the third kind**
PLACE: **Pilar De Goiás, Brazil**
DATE: **13 August 1967**

At about 4:00pm Inácio de Souza and his wife Louiza returned home to the ranch where 41-year-old, illiterate Inácio worked as a hand, about 150 miles (240km) from Brasilia. The establishment was large enough to have a landing strip, and here de Souza saw three people – wearing skin-tight yellow clothes, according to his wife – apparently playing. The three noticed de Souza at the same time, and began to approach. Then he noticed a strange aircraft – 'like an upturned washbasin' – on the runway. Frightened, he unslung the .44 carbine he was carrying and fired at the figure that was nearest to him. The response was a green beam of light from the craft. It hit de Souza on the head and shoulders. The three trespassers then ran to the craft and got into it; the craft then took off vertically, humming as it went into the daylight sky. De Souza developed symptoms from nausea to tremors, and was flown 180 miles (290km) to Goiâna to see a doctor. He was diagnosed as having leukemia, and the examining doctor dismissed his story about the UFO and the aliens as an hallucination. De Souza, who had reportedly been entirely robust until his encounter, died on 11 October 1967.

HOW DID LADY DIE?

TYPE: **Animal mutilation**
PLACE: **Alamosa County,
Colorado, USA**
DATE: **15 September 1967**

Lady, a three-year-old Appaloosa saddle pony, was found dead and strangely mutilated after she had been missing for two days. She had been skinned to the bone in places, and a cut had been made around her neck with surgical precision. Her carcase contained no blood, and her vital organs were missing. On the ground over about 5000 square yards (1500sq. m) around her remains there were 15 circular impressions that looked like exhaust marks from some sort of internal combustion engine. There were no footprints anywhere near the site of the incident. Tests for the cause of death proved inconclusive, although two bullets were found in Lady's body. The case was the first of many animal mutilations (ascribed variously to ufonauts, natural causes, and secret biological warfare projects) to receive heavy publicity during the period. Lady's unexplained death occurred during a rash of UFO sightings, and there was a further outbreak of mysterious animal mutilations in Pennsylvania, USA shortly afterward.

DISGUSTING OCTOPODS

TYPE: **Close encounter of
the third kind**
PLACE: **Serra De Almos, Spain**
DATE: **16 August 1968**

An unnamed chicken farmer was feeding his birds at around 6:00am when he saw lights like reflections from car headlamps. On investigation he was confronted by a dome-shaped object hovering about 3ft (1m) above the ground and emitting an intense light. He approached, and saw two 'octopus-like' entities run to the far side of the object. They were about 3ft (1m) tall, with four or five legs, light-colored and 'thoroughly disgusting' to behold. The UFO took off as soon as the creatures were inside it.

THE STRANGE CASE OF DR X

The UFO that healed a doctor

TYPE: **Close encounter of
the second kind**
PLACE: **Southern France**
DATE: **1 November 1968**

BACKGROUND

Dr X's name and whereabouts have always been withheld to protect his privacy. At about 4:00am the crying of his 14-month-old son woke him up. When the doctor went to investigate, the child was pointing excitedly out of the window. The sky looked stormy, and Dr X saw flashes of light over the valley, which he took to be lightning. He calmed his son.

THE EVENTS

Dr X then opened the window to look over the landscape outside. He saw two disk-shaped UFOs, white above and red beneath, each shining a light beam downwards. Both had antennae on top. They were approaching the house. As they did, they merged into one object, identical to the original two. The beam of light rotated and shone directly at the doctor,

and then there was a loud bang. The UFO vanished, to be replaced by a cloudy shape like an after-image; this soon dispersed. Disturbed, Dr X immediately wrote an account of the episode, and then woke his wife to tell her about it. At this point he realized that a constant pain in his leg, from a combat wound sustained years before in Algeria, had gone, and so had bruises from an accident he had had three days previously while chopping wood. After Dr X went back to bed, his wife heard him talking in his sleep. She noted a particularly weird utterance: 'Contact will be re-established by falling down the stairs on 2 November.'

Dr X, not surprisingly, slept through till the following afternoon. When he awoke he remembered nothing of the events in the night, even when his wife showed him his own notes. Then, later, he fell down the stairs, and his memory of the previous night was restored. The pain from his leg injury never returned, but he did suffer from cramp and pains around the navel. Most odd, a strange triangular discoloration appeared on his stomach and on that of his son. These marks have disappeared and reappeared over the following years: they were photographed last in 1986.

ASSESSMENT

Any judgment of this case has to be tentative without greater knowledge of the participants' identities and their background. The difficulty is compounded by reports that in the years since 1968 the family in the case has experienced numerous other paranormal phenomena that range across the board from telepathy to levitation. Knowing the location of the events might make it possible to assess whether the family had been subject to local but natural geophysical effects, which although unexplained have been known to leave recurrent physical after-effects and to render those exposed to them highly sensitive to extrasensory perception thereafter. If that were so, the details of the UFO(s) could be put down to the work of the imagination under tension. As things stand at the moment, however, given the lack of available information, the case remains both insoluble and extremely strange.

Forestry worker Duane Martin (left) tests the remains of Snippy the Appaloosa pony for radiation. The horse's owner, Mrs Berle Lewis (center) and teacher Mrs Leona Wellington look on. Snippy's death in September 1967 was the first publicized example of the animal mutilation mystery that has recurred on many occasions and plagued rural American States ever since.

THE DA SILVA ABDUCTION

TYPE: **Close encounter of the fourth kind**
PLACE: **Bebedouro, north of Belo Horizonte, Minas Gerais, Brazil**
DATE: **4 May 1969**

Jose Antonio da Silva was on a fishing trip north of Belo Horizonte, when at 3:00pm he was paralysed by a burst of light and borne off to an upright, cylindrical craft with a 'saucer' at top and bottom, by two 4ft (1.2m) tall creatures in dull silver suits and masks. Once inside, he was tied up and given a helmet to wear. The machine then took off and after an 'interminable' period, landed. Da Silva was blindfolded and taken to a brilliantly lit room, in which he saw the bodies of four other humans. Then he was interrogated by about 15 tiny creatures. They were stockily built, with long red beards and hair, big noses, large ears and no teeth. They took his fishing gear, ID card, and banknotes. They asked him to be 'their guide among men'. When he refused, he was returned to Earth. He woke to find himself near Victoria, Espirito Santo, 200 miles (320km) from where he had been fishing. He had been missing four and a half days.

WATCHING THE SPACE RACE-4

TYPE: **Radar visual**
PLACE: **Trajectory to the Moon**
DATE: **14-15 November 1969**

During the Apollo 12 mission, watchers through optical telescopes in Europe saw two flashing UFOs accompanying the spacecraft on its outbound voyage. Those on board the NASA craft – Charles 'Pete' Conrad, Dick Gordon and Alan Bean – also caught sight of their unknown escort. NASA later said the UFOs were 'nothing which could be termed abnormal in the space environment.'

CHAPTER 5

A New Ufology

THE PHENOMENA BECOME MORE COMPLEX AND NEW THEORIES EMERGE

From the modern-day perspective, the Seventies appear to be a unique decade in ufology. The oddities of the UFO experience multiplied, but for once, by and large, the commentary and analysis of ufologists actually reflected what was happening in the field, and not what was going on in the commentators' imaginations. In part this may have been simply because none of the dire predictions that had been made in the Sixties about UFOs ever came to pass – the invasions or knock-out attacks, the mass druggings or mass landings, the collapse of the American Way or the Soviet success in solving the enigma.

Most of those who had bruited them about faded into the background of ufology, their places at the frontier of research and speculation taken by a new generation. These were men and women

UFO photographed on 27 October 1979 at Motonau, New Zealand. Two former New Zealand Air Force photographic analysts called the picture 'inscrutable'. It was one of a series taken in the early morning, and only one frame on the film contained the UFO image. No one saw or heard the object in the sky at the time, so what was it? A split-second fly-by by the aliens, or a lens flare?

who had no preconceptions about UFOs, who were neither shocked nor infatuated by the Extra-Terrestrial Hypothesis (ETH), but who recognized a genuine mystery when they encountered one. Whether the solution lay in outer space or the human mind was irrelevant: the answer to the enigma would be found only by looking at the facts of UFO cases.

RICH AND STRANGE

There were fewer contactee claims and more tales of abductions in the Seventies, but otherwise the pattern of UFO experiences remained little changed from the rich blossoming of strangeness in the Sixties. But the details of many reports showed a marked increase in weirdness.

To take a few random cases: the 'brain-like' entities that confronted John Hodges and Peter Rodriguez in August 1971; the wild claims of Swiss contactee Eduard 'Billy' Meier, among them that he had photographed the eye of God; the surreal encounters between Dr Herbert Hopkins's family and men (and one woman) in black in September 1976; and the sinister implications of Franck Fontaine's abduction at Cergy-Pontoise, France, in November 1979.

Investigators and analysts such as Jerome Clark, Jacques Vallée, John Keel, J. Allen Hynek (now that he was released from his obligations as an Air Force consultant), D. Scott Rogo, Alvin Lawson,

Jenny Randles and John Rimmer – complemented by the skeptical commentaries of Philip J. Klass, James Oberg and others – had little compunction in stating the obvious about these kinds of data or the nature of what had gone before.

In *The Invisible College*, Jacques Vallée commented that UFOs seemed to pose no threat to humanity, but: 'The primary impact of UFOs appears to be on human belief.' Then he asked rhetorically: 'Could it be that someone is playing a fantastic trick on us?' Dr Hynek remarked that UFOs 'appear to be playing games with us' in *The Hynek UFO Report*. D. Scott Rogo considered that the abduction scenario seemed designed to make victims look like 'total fools'. Even old-timers like APRO founders Jim and Coral Lorenzen concluded that 'someone is putting us on! UFO encounters are in some sense a charade.' African ufologist Cynthia Hind looked at things from the other end of the telescope (as it were) and wondered if aliens were here, not to play pranks, but to be entertained. John Keel even went as far as to ask: 'If there is a universal mind, must it be sane?'

Some of these, and other writers, noted that the absurdity of the phenomenon implied a deep indifference to human affairs. It is surprising that none saw the obvious parallel with some kinds of agonized religious experience, in which the believer is at the mercy of some incomprehensible and uncaring god – a state that Shakespeare epitomized in *King Lear*: 'As flies to wanton boys, are we to the gods; they kill us for their sport.' But perhaps even today the thought that the UFO experience may be a new or substitute religion in the making, is too shocking or too strange to contemplate.

MEN IN BLACK

However they might regard the phenomenon as a whole, the new generation of ufologists has had to interpret some very odd testimony. One of the most baffling cases of the decade involved Dr Herbert Hopkins, a physician and hypnotherapist who had investigated an abduction in Maine, and was – as was his son's family – subjected to one of the most unnerving possible side-effects of a UFO encounter – a visit from mysterious 'Men In Black'.

Men In Black (MIB) typically resemble humorless G-men from a Forties or Fifties Hollywood B-movie. They may produce ID and claim to be from a government department or, occasionally, a UFO research group. To reinforce their authority, they often relate intimate personal details of their unwilling host's life – as if to say 'We know all about you.' And they almost always know of UFO experiences before the witnesses have discussed them with anyone else, and menace witnesses with horrible consequences if they talk. They threaten in movie-speak: 'If you want your wife to stay as pretty as she is, you'd better....'

One of the earliest MIB appearances was reported as part of the Maury Island hoax (see Chapter Two); they made a dramatic claim to a permanent place in UFO history in 1953 when Albert K. Bender claimed that three mysterious visitors had advised him, in a manner he could not refuse, to refrain from publishing his conclusions about the true nature of UFOs – and to close down his UFO research organization and its journal as well. Terrified, Bender retired comprehensively from ufology in consequence.

The sinister characters Bender describes have, with minor variations,

appeared to many other UFO witnesses to warn them off making a report. Typically, they dress in black, pristine but dated suits and hats, with white shirts, and travel in threes – the trio very rarely includes a woman. They are often described as tanned and, when not wearing wrap-around sunglasses, as having oriental features and slanted eyes. An especially weird aspect of the MIB is their transport. Their car is usually a Cadillac or some other prestige model which looks brand-new but has been out of production for years, even decades. The vehicles' license plates, if checked, invariably turn out to have unissued numbers. Some claim that MIB represent part of the alleged government cover-up of UFO events and official knowledge of them, although this disregards the fact that no MIB have yet followed through on their threats. Dr Hopkins's MIB displayed most of these features, and they are a fine illustration of the characteristic Seventies' escalation of UFO phenomena in general.

A FRESH EYE

The 'new ufologists' of the Seventies were as prepared to accept a psychological solution to the UFO enigma as they were to accept objective proof of the ETH. One major research advance tended to support the former point of view. Another was at least able to show whether something physically real was involved in photographs of UFOs.

In the Seventies, Ground Saucer Watch (GSW) took a NASA computer program designed to enhance pictures taken in space and adapted it to analyse UFO photos. By 1979 they had digitally 'interrogated' some 700 still and movie pictures, and found a mere 38 that appeared to be of *bona fide* UFOs. Although GSW did not regard these results as any proof whatever of the extra-terrestrial origin of the objects, the work was often seized on by proponents of the ETH to support their own belief.

If GSW unintentionally strengthened the argument for the ETH, Dr Alvin Lawson discovered that people who have

no knowledge of or interest in UFOs will create essentially the same details of an abduction story as those that are reported by 'real' abductees.

This potentially devastating piece of research was conducted in 1977 by Lawson, Dr W.C. McCall and ufologist John DeHerrerra at Anaheim Memorial Hospital, near Los Angeles. The trio recruited 16 volunteers who, in Lawson's words, 'knew little and cared less' about UFOs. They were given the bare bones of a typical abduction story: seeing a UFO land, being taken aboard and seeing the inside of the spacecraft, and being 'examined' by the aliens. The subjects of the experiment were simply asked, at each stage, what they saw or felt happening. And in detail after elaborate detail, the volunteers poured out images and experiences that were uncannily similar to those described by 'real' UFO abductees.

NO SIMPLE SOLUTION

Lawson noted that the alien figures described by both genuine claimants and the creators of fictional abductions matched the archetypes that psychologist C.G. Jung suggested were part of everyone's unconscious imagery. It would be easy to conclude that people claiming to have been abducted by UFOs were simply calling on imagery that is buried deep in everyone's unconscious mind. But, in answer to his own question, 'Do these similarities prove that close encounter cases are illusory?', Lawson gave four reasons why abduction reports might still be genuine.

First, many abductions and close encounter reports involve multiple witnesses; that they all would have identical hallucinations seemed highly unlikely. Second, the physical scars that many abductees can show to be a result of their experiences 'suggest that something happened'. Third, close encounter witnesses recognize how unlikely the events are that unfold during their experience, and yet they remain convinced of their reality; fourth, psychologists can identify the 'trigger' that triggers most hallucinations in the human mind, but there is no consistent factor in abduction or encounter cases that enables the investigators to pinpoint an unmistakably imaginary experience.

'I myself feel certain,' Lawson wrote, 'that accounts given by witnesses reflect what their senses have reported – that is, they do actually perceive humanoids… and so on. But if [the perceived entities are] already in the collective unconscious, they are already… in the mind of the witness before his close encounter.' The real mystery, Lawson suggested, was not what the witness saw but what stimulated those archetypal images to arise from the witness's unconscious in the first place. Neither he nor his experiment, he said, could answer that question.

Nor could anyone else answer it, except perhaps the most recalcitrant

Truck driver Lars Thörn, aged 25, took this picture with a 16mm Minolta camera at 7.55pm on 6 May 1971, 3 miles (5km) north-east of the shooting range near Skillingaryd, Sweden. Thörn said he was riding on a moped with his four-year-old son when he saw 'something shining above the hills'. He left his moped, clambered 65ft (20m) up a slope for a better view. The UFO 'stopped and hung still in the air with a sort of wobbling movement', and Thörn took two photographs. When he first saw the UFO it was flying no faster than 'a sports plane'. When it flew off, 'the speed was comparable with that of a jet fighter'. From the pictures, the size of the UFO was variously estimated at between 85ft (26m) and 20ft (6m). The negatives showed no variation in grain, indicating that the image had not been pasted in, and the light angles and intensity between the UFO and the background were found to be consistent. The photo was shown to be a fake: the UFO is a pair of glued-together hubcaps.

skeptics, and even they had some difficulty in explaining why the UFO phenomenon kept getting stranger throughout this period.

But for a few years at least, most of the new generation who tried to come to terms with all aspects of the UFO experience did their best to look at it dispassionately, coolly and clearly, and came fresh to the problem without any preconceptions or prejudices. The fresh light that they have cast on ufology has been timely and sometimes most revealing.

THE SKIERS' STORY

Attacked by an alien light beam

TYPE: **Close encounter of the third kind**
PLACE: **Imjärvi, Finland**
DATE: **7 January 1970**

BACKGROUND

Woodman Aarno Heinonen and farmer Esko Viljo, both Finnish competition cross-country skiers, were out in the forest near Imjärvi; at about 4:45pm they decided to rest in a clearing and watch the stars emerge in the sunset.

This picture was taken by Woody Akins at Charlotte, South Carolina, USA, in January 1971. It may show some species of unusual natural phenomenon – a UFO indeed, if not one of the 'alien flying saucer' variety.

THE EVENTS

The pair heard a buzzing sound and saw a very bright light in the sky approaching from the north. It swung round the glade and descended toward them from the south. They could now see it was surrounded by a luminous red-gray mist. When the cloud descended to about 50ft (15m) above the ground they saw at its center a disk about 10ft (3m) in diameter. The disk hovered at this height, still buzzing. Then, said Heinonen: 'The huge disk began to descend along with the red-gray fog, which became more thin and transparent. It stopped at a height of 3-4 metres (10-13ft), so near I could have touched it with my ski-stick. We saw it had a dome on the upper side. Along the lower edge was a kind of raised part on which were three spheres or domes spaced equidistantly. From the center of the bottom projected a tube approximately 25cm (10in) in diameter, from which there suddenly came an intense beam of light.

'Suddenly I felt as if somebody had pulled me backwards. In the same second I caught sight of the creature. It was standing in the middle of the light beam with a black box in its hands. It was about 90cm (3ft) tall, with very thin arms and legs. Its face was like pale wax. The nose was a hook rather than a nose. The ears were very small and narrowed toward the head.' The creature wore 'some kind of overall in a light green material' and 'a conical helmet shining like metal.'

The entity pointed the black box at Heinonen, and a blinding, pulsating yellow light shone at him. A red mist came down over the area, and red, green and purple sparks showered around the skiers 'like tapers, about 10cm (4in) long' that 'floated out in long curves'. The mist became thicker and thicker, until, said Viljo: 'Suddenly the beam melted, flew up like a flickering flame, and was sucked into the gap in the craft. After that it was as if the fog curtain was torn to pieces. The air above us was empty!'

After a few minutes Heinonen found that he could not use his right leg, which had been nearest the strange light beam. Viljo half carried, half dragged his friend to his home, about 2 miles (3km) away. Over the following months Heinonen suffered severe memory losses, continuing pain, exhaustion, and headaches. For two months his urine was 'like black coffee'. Viljo suffered facial swellings, headaches and eye troubles.

ASSESSMENT

Investigators, including local doctors and Matt Tuuri, Professor of Electrophysics at Helsinki University, agreed that the men had had a genuinely strange experience. Professor Tuuri noted that X-rays would cause the reported symptoms, and that the cause of the incident seemed to be 'an abnormal electrical phenomenon.' No more than usual levels of radiation were found at the site, but at the same time as the skiers' encounter, two neighbors had also seen unexplained brights lights around Imjärvi.

Any verdict on the case is complicated by Heinonen's claims to have had 23 further UFO sightings between this occasion and August 1972. He claims that on two occasions he met an 'extremely beautiful' spacewoman, who told him that three different species of alien had visited Imjärvi. When he tried to photograph her, he said, both she and his camera vanished. Even if all Heinonen's experiences are psychic or hallucinatory, the question of what caused them remains.

A SAGA OF STRANGENESS

The bizarre consequences of a military mission

TYPE: **Close encounter of the second kind, cover-up**
PLACE: **Laos, England and USA**
DATE: **1970-1980**

BACKGROUND

In May 1970 William S. English was serving as an officer with US Army Special Forces in Viet Nam. According to his testimony, his A-team was 'tasked' with locating a B-52 bomber that had crashed in dense jungle in Laos, and if possible to rescue the crew. The consequences of this mission were to have repercussions over several years.

THE EVENTS

English and his A-team located the B-52 by helicopter. It was lying among the trees 'as if pressed down by a giant hand' – there was no damage at all to either the aircraft or the vegetation around it. All the crew were on board, in their seats, but hideously mutilated – although there was no blood anywhere. The team took dog tags, code books etc, blew up the aircraft, and left. Some weeks later all members of the A-team except English were wiped out in an ambush.

English left the Army in 1973. By 1976 he was working as an intelligence analyst at RAF Chicksands, a USAF/National Security Agency electronic listening post, in England. Late in June 1976 he was given a 625-page document to assess. Named *Grudge/Blue Book Report #13*, it detailed captured alien craft (including their armaments), autopsies performed on alien bodies, and close-encounter reports. Among the close-encounter reports were photographs English had taken of the dead crew of the downed B-52 in Laos, and testimony to the effect that the bomber had crashed after having been attacked by a UFO. Seeing his own photographs helped convince English that the report was genuine.

A few weeks after this, English was summarily dismissed from his post (either because of his positive rating of the *Grudge/Blue Book Report #13* document or because he had not been intended to see it) by the base commander at RAF Chicksands and deported the very same day to the USA. In about 1980, in Tucson, Arizona, he was approached by one Colonel Robert Black, who had dismissed him from Chicksands. Black also had been released from the USAF for reasons connected with *Grudge/Blue Book Report #13*, but told English he had evidence that a large UFO was buried somewhere near White Sands Missile Range, and invited him to join an expedition to find it. English, Black, and a former USAF sergeant equipped a 4x4 van and infiltrated it into the range. One evening English was about 1000yds (900m) from the vehicle when helicopters came into view and rocketed the van, destroying it and killing his companions. English escaped to Tucson on foot, and then went 'underground', eventually settling in Virginia for some years.

ASSESSMENT

The story of the crashed but intact B-52 echoes the Sverdlovsk case of 1961 (see Chapter Four). However, there is no record of a B-52 crashing anywhere in South-East Asia during 1970. The existence of *Grudge/Blue Book Report #13* is denied by the USAF, although it is certainly possible that English was given the dossier he describes to test his ability to detect disinformation (a test he failed). Colonel Robert Black was not the commander of RAF Chicksands in 1976, or at any other time; two retired USAF colonels of that name are still alive today. White Sands Missile Range authorities categorically deny having armed helicopters let alone having rocketed any intruders' vehicles. Either there has been a cover-up of enormous proportions in this case, or at least parts of it are fabrications. English stands by his story.

A LEAP IN TIME

Teleportation in Australia

TYPE: **Close encounter of the second kind**
PLACE: **North of Calliope River, Queensland, Australia**
DATE: **12 August 1971**

BACKGROUND

A Finnish couple, Ben and Helen K, were driving the winding road from Gladstone to Rockhampton through fog at night. They were short of gas; passing a closed service station at about 11:35pm, they noticed a green light at treetop level.

THE EVENTS

Ben and Helen suddenly felt they had been driving in a straight line for a long time, and realized they had been repeating the same words over and over. They noticed a circle of lights above them to the left just before they passed a sign to Port Alma, 25 miles (40km) north of the Calliope River. The next thing they knew, they were at a railroad crossing just outside Rockhampton. They checked in to an open gas station, and found they had somehow traveled nearly 80 miles (130km) in 40 minutes: yet they had no memory of that time even passing.

ASSESSMENT

Police dismissed the event as 'somnambulism' (i.e., the witnesses fell asleep at the wheel). But there is a genuine mystery. The couple met another driver at the gas station who had passed them earlier on the road and could not understand how they made such good time, and without passing him. Attempts at hypnotic regression failed to reveal any fresh information.

DOWN IN DAPPLE GREY LANE

Bizarre brain-like entities herald an abduction

TYPE: **Close encounter of the third kind**
PLACE: **Dapple Grey Lane, South Los Angeles, California, USA**
DATE: **August 1971**

BACKGROUND

John Hodges and Peter Rodriguez had been visiting a mutual friend in Dapple Grey Lane. At 2:00am the pair left; getting into Hodges' car, they saw two brain-like objects on the road, about as high as a man's waist and apparently alive.

THE EVENTS

Hodges drove around the 'brains', took Rodriguez home, and then headed for his own apartment. He arrived there two hours later than he expected. Under regressive hypnosis in 1978, he maintained that he encountered the 'brains' again outside his apartment. He was projected from his car into a machine-filled 'control room'. Here he was confronted by humanoids who warned him of the danger of nuclear war. Hodges said that during the hypnosis sessions he was abducted

again, and was told he had been given a brain implant in order to heighten his psychic awareness, and that the human race was the product of millions of years of genetic experimentation.

ASSESSMENT

All abductions revealed under regressive hypnosis need to be treated with caution. This one is interesting because it combines the standard abduction account and the recurrent 'message for humanity' scenario.

CLOSE INSPECTION

Five lights dazzle a French farmer

TYPE: **Close encounter of the first kind**
PLACE: **Lot-et-Garonne, Bordeaux, France**
DATE: **14 November 1971**

BACKGROUND

By the lights from his tractor, farmer Angelo Cellot was plowing one of his fields late into the night, despite an overcast sky and drizzling rain.

THE EVENTS

At about 1:50am Cellot thought he saw the distant light of another tractor. Then he realized the light was in the air and moving toward him. Now thinking it came from a helicopter, he carried on working. The light, with another red light in front of it, followed him up the field and hovered directly above. Then five extremely powerful beams blazed down from it. He was unable to make out the nature of the object behind them. When the UFO began to descend toward him, Cellot fled, leaving the tractor with its lights on and its engine running. Almost immediately the UFO rose and flew slowly away to the north. Only now did Cellot realize that it had made no noise whatever. Thoroughly shaken, he then drove home.

ASSESSMENT

Was this an unidentified natural phenomenon, a secret reconnaissance drone, an alien spacecraft or the hallucination of an exhausted man? This case is inconclusive because so little of the UFO was seen. Interestingly, there was no electromagnetic interference with the tractor.

SHOOT FIRST

Questions remain about a South African UFO

TYPE: **Close encounter of the second kind**
PLACE: **Fort Beaufort, Cape Province, South Africa**
DATE: **26 June 1972**

BACKGROUND

At 9:00am on this sunny winter day, farmer Bernie Smit was in his fields. One

of his laborers, Boer de Klerk, ran up to tell him that he had seen a shiny spherical object with a bright 'star' atop it hovering over some nearby trees.

THE EVENTS

According to de Klerk, the UFO was about 3ft (1m) wide, and red when he first saw it. It moved among some bushes leaving a gray-white trail, and when it emerged it was green. Suddenly it turned yellow-white. Smit got his .303 rifle and fired about eight shots at the UFO. The ball then slipped behind some trees, apparently unscathed. At about 10:00am two police officers arrived, and more shots were fired at the UFO, which was now black, but turned to gray. Smit hit the 'star', and the UFO stopped changing color. Smit and the officers tried to approach the UFO, but it dodged away behind trees and bushes. Eventually it disappeared into impenetrable bush. Later, marks on the ground consistent

with those made by a 'hard, heavy, spherical object' were found.

ASSESSMENT

The first of a flood of UFO events in South Africa, this object's size, color and behavior suggest ball lightning or plasma.

SOLID LIGHT SHOW

Another five lights in France

TYPE: **Close encounter of the second kind, multiple witnesses**
PLACE: **Taizé, Cluny, Saone-et-Loire, France**
DATE: **11 August 1972**

BACKGROUND

Taizé is a Protestant monastery about 6 miles (10km) north of Cluny. On this occasion, late at night, about 35 people had gathered in an open-air theater for a discussion. It was overcast with light rain.

THE EVENTS

At about 2:00am, one of the group alerted the rest to a 'star' descending on the opposite side of the valley behind them. Everyone heard a whistling sound as it came down, and soon saw a dark object 'bigger than a bus' hovering against the hill. Next, the UFO 'lit up' with two orange and five yellow lights. Slowly, the yellow lights began to extend seemingly solid beams toward the ground. One end of the UFO emitted sparks that turned into three small disks that gyrated around the larger object. At about 3:00am, four of the witnesses decided to take a closer look. As they made their way across the fields, a mass of red particles surrounded them. When the four had reached about mid-way between the UFO and the monastery, they came across a dark mass on the ground, around which a red light darted haphazardly. Beams from their flashlights were literally bent up and away from it. Unnerved, they decided to back off. As they were on their way, the lights on the UFO suddenly went out, and the three minor disks vanished into it. One of the four shone his flashlight at the UFO, and its largest light flashed back, giving out an intense heat. The UFO then moved away and flew off toward Cluny. It was lost to sight by 4:40am.

ASSESSMENT

The UFO siege at Trancas, Argentina, on 21 October 1963, and the sighting at Bealiba, Australia, on 4 April 1966 (see Chapter Four) featured similar bizarre light effects. Whether the religious

UFO photographed on 29 May 1973 at Pinetown, Natal, South Africa. Although not regarded as a 'hot spot' for UFOs, South Africa does have a high proportion of sightings and even alleged contacts for the size of its population.

UFO

atmosphere of the Taizé monastery contributed to the sighting is a moot point, but brilliant lights seen under an overcast sky, far from any road, are unlikely to have come from an astronomical object or a conventional vehicle.

THE PIEDMONT FLAP

A contagion of sightings

TYPE: **Lights in the sky**
PLACE: **Piedmont, Missouri, USA**
DATE: **February–April 1973**

BACKGROUND

The first sightings in Piedmont were given national media exposure; over the next three months, over 200 citizens reported anomalous lights in the night sky.

THE EVENTS

On 12 April, pilot Kenneth Pingle saw a circular UFO heading toward his plane; when he gave chase, it reversed direction and flew away. The Piedmont UFOs came in various colors, although the most common were red, green and white. Most were described as round; some reportedly were domed disks, and some had portholes. Three alleged landing sites were found, including one where treetops had been broken off and the trees swirled counterclockwise. UFOs were seen entering and leaving nearby Clearwater Lake, and one couple reported seeing an alien figure dressed in something resembling a wetsuit. Metallic-looking daylight disks were also reported.

ASSESSMENT

The Piedmont flap appears to have been mild mass hysteria generated by early media reports and unusual weather conditions. All the events were carefully investigated by the International UFO Bureau, Dr J. Allen Hynek and others. Most of the lights seem to have been stars, distorted by excess moisture in the atmosphere; many others were seen near power lines and may have been plasmas.

Others were identified as sunlight from below the horizon reflecting off high-flying aircraft. Nothing unusual was found at the 'landing sites'. The figure in the wetsuit was probably a man in a wetsuit. The case shows how easy it is to misconstrue natural or man-made objects.

PROBED BY BLUE LIGHTS

The curious case of a UFO 'mugging'

TYPE: **Close encounter of the second kind**
PLACE: **Catanduva, São Paulo, Brazil**
DATE: **22 May 1973**

BACKGROUND

Librarian Onilson Papero, aged 41, was driving through rain just outside Catanduva at 3:00am, when his radio started to play up.

THE EVENTS

Driving up a hill, Papero saw a blue circle of light about 8in (20cm) in diameter inside his car. When it passed in front of him, he could see the car engine through it. Next a blue beam of light shone on him from the hilltop, and came toward him. He pulled off the road to avoid a collision, and got out of the car, which was suddenly very stuffy. He now saw that the light was coming from a gray, elliptical craft about 25ft (8m) thick and 35ft (11m) wide. A tube began to extend from it, and Papero ran – only to be held back by an invisible force that felt like 'a rubber lasso'. A blue beam of light probed his car, making it transparent. Papero then fainted.

Two men passing in a car came upon Papero an hour later, and sped on to fetch the police from Catanduva. Returning to the scene, they found Papero's briefcase open and its contents hurled about inside the car. Papero, still lying on the shoulder, came round when they

moved him; the key to the briefcase was still in his pocket, and nothing was missing from it. Papero was taken to hospital for observation. Two days after his experience, patches of skin on his back and stomach itched and then turned blue; later, they turned yellow, and then disappeared. No cause for the rashes could be found. Papero was assessed as mentally sound and normal.

ASSESSMENT

Perhaps no significance should be attached to the episode with the brief-case: a passing villain may have broken into it and found nothing valuable. Blue light beams feature in many UFO reports, especially abductions, but this seems to be the only example of 'X-ray vision'.

A DROP TO DRINK

A UFO connects with Japanese water

TYPE: **Close encounter of the third kind**
PLACE: **Tomakomai, Hokkaido, Japan**
DATE: **22 May 1973**

BACKGROUND

Student Masaaki Kudou had taken a summer job as a security guard at a Tomakomai timber yard near the sea. After a routine patrol by car one still, starry night he parked where he could overlook the site and the bay beyond.

THE EVENTS

What at first seemed a shooting star suddenly stopped in its tracks, vanished, reappeared, and began to gyrate slowly down over the bay. It stopped about 70ft (21m) above the water, and lowered a transparent tube toward the water with a soft *min-min-min* sound. When the tube reached the water, it began to glow. The tube was withdrawn, and the UFO moved to hover over Kudou's car. Everything around the car was lit up like day. Kudou was afraid the UFO would attack or even kill him. Leaning over to watch through his windshield, Kudou saw that the UFO was perfectly smooth and glowing white, with windows around it. Through one he could see the shape of a humanoid figure; two smaller figures were visible through another. Three or four more UFOs now

joined the first, and with them a large, brown cylinder. The spheres maneuvered and vanished into the cylinder, which then sped away to the north. Kudou, who felt as if he had been bound hand and foot, regained his senses. His car radio was making a meaningless din, and he had a severe headache. The events had lasted about 12 minutes.

ASSESSMENT

Reports of UFOs apparently taking on water are not uncommon, although no one can explain why the machines of reputedly 'technologically superior' aliens should need to refuel like steam locomotives. Nevertheless, there is no obvious explanation for the events in this case.

THE PASCAGOULA AFFAIR

The abduction of Charles Hickson and Calvin Parker

TYPE: **Close encounter of the fourth kind**
PLACE: **Pascagoula, Jackson County, Mississippi, USA**
DATE: **11 October 1973**

BACKGROUND

Charles E. Hickson, aged 45, and Calvin R. Parker Jr, aged 19, were spending the evening fishing off the pier of the abandoned Shaupeter shipyard on the Pascagoula River. At about 9:00pm Hickson turned to get fresh bait, and heard a 'zipping sound'.

THE EVENTS

Hickson saw an egg-shaped blue-gray craft hovering close to the ground nearby. An opening appeared in the UFO and three 5ft (1.5m) creatures floated out of it. Each had gray, wrinkled skin, pincers for hands, small cone-shaped ears and a small pointed nose. The entities gathered up the two fishermen – at this point Parker fainted – and floated them into the craft. Hickson then found himself in a

An apparent UFO caught on film near Ajaccio, Corsica, in late February 1974. While taking a picture of the sunset, the photographer saw a 'silent luminous mass' move across the sky. Was it a cloud, or was it a UFO?

brightly-lit room with no visible light source. Parker was taken to an adjoining chamber. Hickson was suspended so that he could move only his eyes, and a free-floating object resembling a gigantic eye moved back and forth above his body, as if examining it. After 20 minutes or so, the pair were floated back to the pier. Hickson landed on his feet. Parker then regained consciousness. The UFO was gone 'in less than a second'.

ASSESSMENT

The two men first attempted to tell their story to the *Pascagoula Mississippi Press*, but the newspaper office was closed. At 11:00pm they reported their experience to the sheriff's office. The interview was taped, and afterward the pair were left alone while, unknown to them, the recording continued. Hickson and Parker continued to discuss the sighting in agitated tones. Next day they were medically examined at Keesler AFB at Biloxi: no trace of radiation or other problems were found.

On 30 October, in New Orleans, Hickson took a polygraph test that convinced the operator that he was telling the truth. At this point Hickson's story began to come apart. (Parker, meanwhile, had been hospitalized with a nervous breakdown.) His accounts of the size of the UFO and the time of its arrival changed from interview to interview, as did his description of the aliens' features. A month after the incident, he claimed to have had a serious eye injury from the brightness of the lights in the UFO – although no injury had been detected by USAF doctors. Philip Klass discovered that the New Orleans polygraph operator was both inexperienced and unqualified. No one on the busy nearby US Route 90 saw anything unusual at the time of the encounter. And Hickson was in serious financial difficulty, having filed for bankruptcy on 6 July, and needed funds. The Pascagoula abduction looks like a fisherman's tale indeed.

THE POLICE CHIEF AND THE ALIEN

An alleged ufonaut is captured on film

TYPE: **Close encounter of the third kind**
PLACE: **Falkville, Alabama, USA**
DATE: **17 October 1973**

BACKGROUND

When Falkville police chief Jeff Greenhaw received a phone call from a woman saying a 'spaceship' had landed in a field near town, he grabbed a Polaroid camera and raced to the scene.

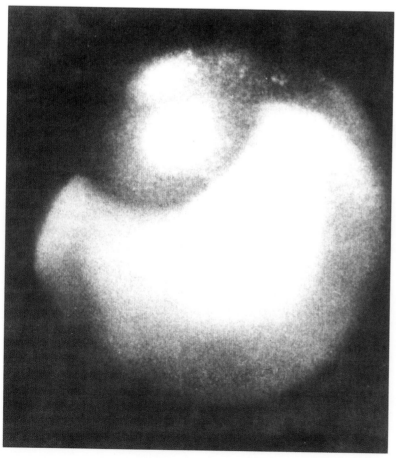

Charles Fernandez, aged 16, photographed this UFO at about 6:15pm on 19 November 1974. He was about to leave the family home at Uzès, near Nîmes, in southern France, when he noticed a brightly shining ball of light about 115ft (35m) away. He estimated that the globe was no larger than 8ft (2.5m) across. Despite a strong wind (the mistral from the north-east) the object was motionless. After watching the light for some 15 minutes, Fernandez went outside, approached to within 80ft (25m) of the UFO, and photographed it. Shortly afterward, a bright cylinder about 3ft (1m) long emerged from beneath the ball of light, and then both rocketed into the sky. Those attracted by the Earthlights Hypothesis will be intrigued to know that the UFO at times seemed transparent, and appeared near a 15,000-volt power line and directly above an underground stream.

THE EVENTS

Arriving at around 10:00pm, Greenhaw found no sign of the UFO, but he did see a creature that looked like a man wrapped in aluminum foil walking toward him with a mechanical gait, and with an antenna on its head. Greenhaw took four shots with the Polaroid, and turned on the spotlight on his patrol car. The creature immediately fled. Greenhaw went in hot pursuit, but even in his car he couldn't begin to keep up: 'He was running faster than any human I ever saw,' he said.

ASSESSMENT

Other residents also saw UFOs in the locality at the time of Greenhaw's encounter. However, the publicity the case attracted did him no good. He was asked to resign his job. It is just possible that he was hoaxed by a prankster. But the unanswered question remains: what human could outrun a car traveling at up to 35mph (55km/h)?

CAPTAIN COYNE'S ENCOUNTER

A helicopter crew evades an onrushing UFO

TYPE: **Close encounter of the second kind**
PLACE: **Near Mansfield, Ohio, USA**
DATE: **18 October 1973**

BACKGROUND

Captain Lawrence J. Coyne was in command of US Army Reserve Bell UH-1 ('Huey') helicopter 68-15444 on a return flight at night from Cleveland to Columbus, Ohio. Co-pilot First Sgt. A.D. Jezzi was at the controls. Also on board were crew chief Staff Sgt. Robert Yancsek and the flight medic, Staff Sgt. John Healey. The Huey was flying at 2500ft (750m) on a heading of 30°, and it was seven miles (11km) from Mansfield when the alarm was raised.

THE EVENTS

Just after 11:00pm, Yanacsek reported that a red light was pacing the aircraft to the east. Moments later he yelled that it had turned and was on a collision course with the Huey, flying at perhaps 600 knots (1000km/h). Coyne, thinking it was a military jet, took the controls and went into a power dive to 1700ft (510m). The crew felt the Huey drop, and then an astonished Coyne saw the altimeter register a climb of 1000ft (300m) per minute to 3500ft (1000m), although the collective pitch control remained fully 'down'. He also saw the object was not a jet: it stopped and hovered over the chopper. A beam of green light swung from the UFO and lit up the Huey's interior. Then the object slowly continued on westward until it had passed Mansfield airport, seven miles (11km) away, when it accelerated sharply and then turned onto a north-west heading. Attempts to raise Mansfield by radio failed: both UHF and VHF channels were dead until about 10 minutes after the encounter.

ASSESSMENT

Philip Klass contended that the reserve soldiers had been taken in by an Orionid fireball. J. Allen Hynek retorted: 'Klass's theory is untenable,' and showed exactly why the UFO did not behave anything like a meteor. The case remains a classic – and a fertile ground for controversy.

RAPED BY AN ALIEN

A horrific encounter in rural England

TYPE: **Close encounter of the fourth kind**
PLACE: **Langford Budville, Somerset, England**
DATE: **16 October 1973**

BACKGROUND

Mrs A (name withheld), aged 43, was driving down a country lane at about 11:00pm when the lights and engine of her car failed. She got out to see what had gone wrong.

THE EVENTS

Mrs A felt something touch her, and turned to see a 'robot-like' figure, about 6ft (2m) tall. She fainted. When she recovered consciousness, she was standing with the robot next to a domed craft, 20ft (6m) across and 40ft (12m) high. She fainted again. She came round to find herself strapped naked onto a metallic table in a freezing cold, colorless room whose walls glowed strangely. Three tall humanoid figures made a physical examination: nail and blood samples were taken and a device was put over her vagina; she felt a sucking sensation, as if ova were being extracted. Two aliens then left the room. The third raped her. Mrs A wanted to scream, but her throat was sore. She fainted a third time. She regained her senses in her car, which now worked perfectly. Three hours had passed.

ASSESSMENT

Possible interpretations of this case are legion, from fantasy to covering up a shame-ridden illicit liaison to an account of the literal truth. The degree of violence used, the clear, conscious recall of the victim, and her immediately informing both her husband and the police make it distinct from most incidents of its kind.

THE BEIT BRIDGE ENCOUNTER

An extraordinary case of vehicle interference

TYPE: **Close encounter of the second kind**
PLACE: **Salisbury, Rhodesia (now Harare, Zimbabwe) to Durban, South Africa**
Date: **31 May 1974**

BACKGROUND

Peter, aged 24, and his wife Frances, aged 21 (pseudonyms), were driving a Peugeot

404 sedan south from what was then Salisbury to Durban. The route took them over the border with South Africa at Beit Bridge, on the Limpopo river. Two sets of strange events occurred between 2:30am and 7:30am.

THE EVENTS

About 20 miles (32km) south of Umvuma in Rhodesia (now Zimbabwe), Frances noticed a light pacing the car to its left. The headlights faded, and the couple felt extremely cold and wrapped themselves in blankets. Realizing he was driving well over the speed limit, Peter took his foot off the gas – and nothing happened. The headlights died completely, and Peter had no control at all over the car, which raced down the road at about 90mph (145km/h). When Fort Victoria came in sight, the UFO veered away, and the car returned to normal. The couple stopped for gas, and surprised the attendant by remarking how cold it was. Just outside Fort Victoria, the UFO reappeared, and once more Peter lost control of the car. Even odder, the road became entirely straight and empty and passed through lush tropical growth. (It is in fact notoriously bendy, and busy at night, and traverses arid landscape.) On reaching the border at Beit Bridge, 180 miles (290km) from Fort Victoria, the couple's watches were an hour slow, and they had used only 22 cents' worth of gas. Regressive hypnosis suggested the car had been in the control of a humanoid 'beamed' into the back seat of the car from the UFO, which came from a distant galaxy. The humanoid claimed it could take on any shape, from a duck to a normal human.

ASSESSMENT

Frances was asleep for much of the second part of the journey, so Peter is the only witness – and was the only one to be hypnotized. UFOs that pace travelers over very long distances often turn out to be misidentified or distorted stars or planets. These skeptical explanations do not explain how the car used so little gas or the couple's slow watches, or

suggest a plausible reason why Peter should wish to hoax anyone – including his wife.

THE ELK HUNTER'S EXPERIENCE

The predator becomes the prey

TYPE: **Close encounter of the fourth kind**
PLACE: **Medicine Bow National Park, Wyoming, USA**
DATE: **25 October 1974**

BACKGROUND

At about 4:00pm, 40-year-old Carl Higdon left Riverton, Wyoming, in his pick-up to hunt elk in a remote corner of Medicine Bow National Park. In the forest, he came on five elk, raised his rifle, and fired at one.

THE EVENTS

Higdon was astounded that he could actually see the magnum round he had fired travel through the air and fall to the ground about 65ft (20m) away. He picked the bullet up and found it completely crushed. He then heard someone approaching: a tall, yellow-skinned being with bristling straw-colored hair, dressed in black. The entity asked Higdon if he was hungry (who, taken aback, said 'Yes') and gave him some pills to eat. Higdon was then taken to a 'cubicle' in which were two more black-suited creatures and the five elk he had been about to shoot. Higdon felt the cubicle accelerate and soon found himself in another realm, where lights on a tower were so bright that he complained. 'You're not any good for what we need,' said one of the entities. 'We'll take you back.' Shortly after that, Higdon found himself dumped back in the forest. Not knowing where he was, he wandered until he found his pick-up – although he did not recognize it, and it was five miles (8km) from where he had left it. He used the CB radio to summon

help. When he was found, he did not recognize his wife among the rescuers. His amnesia disappeared within 24 hours, and he began to recall more and more details of his strange journey.

ASSESSMENT

A psycho-social interpretation of this event might be that Higdon had doubts about the ethics of hunting. Firing a genuinely dud round from his rifle symbolically confirmed them and triggered an altered state of consciousness, which dramatized an internal conflict between his doubts and notions of 'masculinity'. Followers of the extra-terrestrial and related theories noted that Higdon had had a vasectomy, and was therefore no use to the aliens in their alleged breeding program. Higdon speculated along these lines himself.

CONTACT FROM THE PLEIADES

A Swiss farmer creates a saga single-handed

TYPE: **Contactee, close encounters of the third kind**
PLACE: **Hinwel, Canton of Zurich, Switzerland**
DATE: **January 1975-April 1978**

BACKGROUND

Just after 2:00pm on 28 January, farmer Eduard 'Billy' Meier was walking near his home when he observed a silvery, disk-shaped craft in the sky. He happened to have a camera about him, so he took several photographs of what he saw. Then the UFO swooped down and landed about 100 yards (90m) away. Meier ran toward it, but an invisible force halted him in his tracks after about 50 yards (45m). A figure emerged from the disk, which was about 25ft (8m) in diameter, and approached him. When it and its vehicle departed an hour and three quarters afterwards, Meier knew he had met a cosmonaut from the Pleiades, a star cluster in the constellation of Taurus, 430 light years from Earth.

THE EVENTS

In all, between January 1975 and April 1978, Meier met five Pleiadians – Semjase, Ptaah, Quetzal, Plaja and Asket – in 105 encounters, took over 600 photographs of their five types of flying disks, and wrote 3000 pages of notes on their conversations and general wisdom. According to Meier, the Pleiadians look like terrestrial Scandinavians, though their lifespan stretches to the equivalent of 1000 of our years. They came from a planet named Erra 'in the system of Taygeta' in the Pleiades, and before that came from a planet in the constellation of Lyra, from which they had emigrated millions of years before. They reached Earth thousands of years ago, as part of a continuing program of space exploration, in ships capable of traveling faster than light through 'hyperspace'. Their general message for mankind was that we should concentrate on the arts of peace and cultivating the life of the spirit – otherwise, Earth was 'an insane society rushing headlong to [its] own destruction.' The Pleiadians communicated with Meier both through telepathy and by speaking Swiss.

ASSESSMENT

By astronomical standards, the Pleiades are young: a mere 150 million years old. Its 500-odd stars are ferociously hot and burn out rapidly. In contrast, our Sun, a relatively cool, slow-burning yellow

This photograph, taken in February 1975 by Lance Willet of Nanaimo, British Columbia, Canada, is one of a number in which a UFO was caught by accident while the photographer was concentrating on an everyday subject. The object is clearly not a small model hung, or thrown, close to the camera – but there is little to indicate that it is not a bird or an aircraft.

dwarf, is some 4.49 billion years old, and it was 2.5 billion years old before conditions on Earth were able to support even the most primitive forms of life. The chances that any planet in the Pleiades is habitable are about zero. The Lyrans' preposterous claim is surprising in the light of their statement that they are '3000 years ahead of us' in civilization and intelligence – although the excruciating banality of their 'philosophical' utterances might make one think otherwise. Ground Saucer Watch's report on their computer analysis of the Meier photographs called them 'hoaxes, both crude and grandiose.'

THE DISK AT AKITA

A Japanese airport receives a visitor

TYPE: **Daylight disk, multiple witnesses**
PLACE: **Akita Airport, Northern Honshu, Japan**
DATE: **17 October 1975**

BACKGROUND

Japanese media reacted quickly to the UFO sighting at Akita airport, for Masaki Machida, a journalist at the local TV

station, was the first to notice the object and began filing his report at once.

THE EVENTS

The UFO was first seen descending from the east. At an altitude of about 5000ft (1500m) it began to hover, about 5 miles (8km) from the airport. Some 50 witnesses reported seeing a bright golden disk with white lights. The airport control tower warned incoming and outgoing aircraft to watch out for the UFO. After about five minutes, the disk flew on westward, out to sea.

ASSESSMENT

Captain Masarus Saito, a Toa Airlines pilot whose plane was passing nearby at the time, described the UFO as resembling two plates put together face-to-face. It is clear from this event that the classic 'flying saucer' was still alive and well in the Seventies.

THE NORAD FLAP

UFOs descend on Northern US military bases

TYPE: **Lights in the sky, multiple witnesses**
PLACE: **Military bases, USA**
DATE: **27 October- 11 November 1975**

BACKGROUND

It has long been noted that UFOs are strangely interested in military installations. The so-called 'NORAD flap', during which UFOs haunted bases of the North American Air Defense Command in the northern USA, is a fine example.

THE EVENTS

At around 8:00pm on 27 October, a whirring UFO showing a white strobe and reddish orange lights came within 1000ft (300m) of a nuclear weapons store at Loring AFB, Maine. During the 90 minutes of the UFO's visit, it was tracked on

radar as it flew over and around the base. On 29 October, radar detected an 'unknown' heading once more toward the weapons store. A helicopter failed to make visual contact with the UFO. The following night, a UFO was seen on three separate occasions but a helicopter sent to intercept it failed to make contact.

Also on 30 and 31 October, UFOs flew in formation over a weapons store at Wurtsmith AFB, Michigan. An aircraft sent to intercept them likewise failed to make contact.

On four consecutive nights (7-10 November), a number of UFOs reconnoitered Malmstrom AFB, Montana, ICBM launch sites (silos) in the State, and also visited Minot AFB, North Dakota. On 8 November, two F-106 jets from Great Falls AFB, Montana, went in pursuit of seven UFOs flying at between 9500ft (2850m) and 15,500ft (4650m). But the UFOs accelerated and decelerated rapidly from as little as 3.5mph (5.6km/h) to 170mph (275km/h), and while doing so they became invisible.

ASSESSMENT

A secret NORAD memo admitted that when the flap ended on 11 November, Air Guard helicopters, Strategic Air Command helicopters and NORAD F-106s had all 'failed to produce positive ID.' William H. Spaulding, however, suggested that the UFOs were Special Forces helicopters and other aircraft, equipped with silencing and stealth technology. He noted that the F-106 fighters from Great Falls were instructed to fly no lower than 12,000ft (3600m) and at moderate speed – the F-106 was capable of Mach 2, (about 1500mph [2400km/h]). Spaulding went on to say that the 'entire November flap represents a contrived military exercise, possibly involving both US and Canadian Special Forces, to covertly test detection capability and response.... The whole "crisis"... reeks of a military mission [in which] a few individuals [know] the facts and the operators within the military system are kept in the dark.'

MEN IN BLACK IN MAINE

The strange aftermath of an abduction

TYPE: **Close encounter of the fourth kind, Men In Black**
PLACE: **Tripp Pond, Androscoggin County, Maine, USA**
DATE: **27 October 1975- 24 September 1976**

BACKGROUND

On 27 October 1975, David Stephens, aged 21, and his 18-year-old friend 'Paul' had a long encounter with UFOs, including a period of missing time after which each realized that the other had bizarrely orange eyes. The first Man In Black (MIB) arrived the morning after, at the trailer that David and Paul shared.

THE EVENTS

Stephens was alone when a stockily-built man sporting a crew cut, dark glasses and dark suit called at the trailer, checked that Stephens had seen a UFO, said 'Better keep your mouth shut if you know what's good for you,' and hurriedly left. In due course Stephens underwent hypnotic regression with Dr Herbert Hopkins, which revealed a standard abduction scenario that occurred during the period of missing time. The 'examination' was non-invasive, and was carried out with a box-like device.

Nearly a year later, on 11 September 1976, Dr Hopkins was alone at home when a UFO investigator phoned to ask if he might visit him. The caller arrived at the door within seconds. Dressed almost entirely in black, he was entirely hairless and wearing lipstick. The MIB invited Dr Hopkins to watch while a coin vanished in the palm of his hand. They discussed UFOs, then the MIB's speech became slow and slurred. 'My energy is running low,' he finally said, 'must go now,' and fumbled his way to the door.

On 24 September, Dr Hopkins's son John and his daughter-in-law Maureen received a visit at their home from a man and a woman who were both wearing old-fashioned clothes and who seemed to have trouble walking properly. They asked John and Maureen a number of banal personal questions (for example: 'What do you talk about?'). Meanwhile, the man kept 'pawing and fondling' the woman in a startlingly intimate manner, and from time to time asked John if he was doing it correctly! When John left the room, the man asked Maureen 'how she was made', and if she had any photographs of herself naked. Soon, the strange pair announced they had to leave – and did, without saying goodbye, but not before it became apparent that they could walk only in dead-straight lines.

ASSESSMENT

There are few investigators who take MIB at face value. Dr Hopkins did not register how bizarre his visitor's behavior was until after he (or it) had left – and he was then extremely disturbed. This suggests a certain dream-like quality to the events, and suggests in turn that MIB (like many abductions) may not be physical entities but rather exist in some shadowy realm between solid and psychic reality.

A PROBLEM FOR THE SCIENTISTS

A landing in Minnesota leaves puzzling traces

TYPE: **Close encounter of the second kind**
PLACE: **Medford, Minnesota, USA**
DATE: **2 November 1975**

BACKGROUND

Late one Sunday evening, Jerry Kay and his wife were leaving his mother Helen's

UFO photographed by Shuichi Watanabe on 6 September 1976 at Sapporo City, Hokkaido, Japan. A provocative juxtaposition of images.

house in Medford; his sister Jane was busy doing her homework.

THE EVENTS

All members of the family saw a huge orange light descend from the sky and slowly alight on a nearby football field. Jerry was reminded of 'a huge pyrotechnic display being dropped by parachute.' Helen said it was unlike any airplane or helicopter she had seen.

ASSESSMENT

Samples of soil from the landing site were analysed in great detail by the Space Technology Laboratory at the University of Kansas, Lawrence. Although these samples showed a level of thermo-luminescence that was 10 times higher than that of control samples taken from near the site, they remained indistinguishable from lumps of unaffected soil when viewed under a microscope. Dr Edward Zellner, the University's Professor of Geology, Physics and Astronomy, called these variations 'unusual' and 'an anomaly', but he also commented that: 'Like so much of the other data [that] have been obtained on the UFO phenomenon, the results... are inconclusive.'

FIRE IN THE SKY

The Travis Walton abduction

TYPE: **Close encounter of the fourth kind**
PLACE: **Apache-Sitgreaves National Forest, near Snowflake, Arizona, USA**
DATE: **5 November 1975**

BACKGROUND

A woodcutting crew were leaving their worksite 155 miles (240km) north-west of Phoenix, Arizona, by truck in darkness at about 6:00pm.

THE EVENTS

A UFO, 20ft (6m) wide and 8ft (2.5m) high, with a dome on top, and glowing 'milky-yellow' landed and barred the logging road. One of the team, Travis Walton, got out of the truck and walked toward the UFO. A beam of bright green-blue light shot out from its base and hurled Walton into the air. His terrified buddies drove off, then returned after seeing a flash of light shoot up above the trees. They found the UFO gone and no sign of Walton. A full-scale search over

the next two days also failed to find him. Six days later, Walton phoned his sister from a booth in Heber, 12 miles (20km) from the spot where he had vanished.

Walton maintained that he had woken up inside the UFO in a room with three 5ft (1.5m) tall aliens. Walton tried to attack them, and they left the room. Walton ran out after them, and down a passage into what seemed to be the UFO's control room. He was led from there by a helmeted human out of the craft and into another, where he saw other human beings. A mask was put over his face, and he passed out. He awoke to see a UFO blasting into the sky above him, and walked to the nearest phone booth to call his sister.

ASSESSMENT

The case was one of the most controversial of the Seventies. Skeptics maintained that the abduction was a hoax. As Mike Rogers, head of the woodcutting crew, was behind on his contract schedule, he was in danger of losing money and of being unable to pay the crew until the following spring, when the work could be completed. He supposedly devised the abduction story to cut the contract short and get paid off. Polygraph tests on Walton proved unreliable and are disputed. Walton also had a prior interest in UFOs. His family were renowned practical jokers, and his mother allegedly showed no concern while he was missing. Yet the witnesses have stuck to their story for two decades.

Another 'accidental' UFO photograph. This was taken at Plymouth Zoo, Devon, England, in 1972 by Wilfred Power. It is occasionally argued that such pictures are the work of the 'cosmic joker', a kind of wrinkle in the Universe that causes UFOs, ghosts, lake monsters and the like to be photographed by chance but also causes cameras to jam when witnesses attempt to get hard proof of the anomalous objects' existence.

LIBERTY'S LOSS

Three women abducted in Kentucky

TYPE: **Close encounter of the fourth kind**
PLACE: **Stanford, Kentucky, USA**
DATE: **6 January 1975**

BACKGROUND

Mona Stafford, Louise Smith and Elaine Thomas had been out celebrating Mona's birthday in Lancaster. At about 11:30pm they were near Stanford, driving home to Liberty on the narrow, winding Route 78. A red UFO, perhaps 100ft (30m) across, appeared in the eastern sky with a bluish-white dome lit with a 'blinding' light.

THE EVENTS

The UFO shot out blue light beams; one of which lit up the car. Louise, the driver, pulled up. Mona tried to get out, but became paralysed. The light hurt their eyes. Louise drove on, and as they approached a gateway in a stone wall, the car went out of her control, traveling at 85mph (140km/h) down a long, straight, empty road entirely unlike the real Route 78 and the trio felt a burning heat. Normality returned, and they arrived at Louise's trailer home at 1:25am, 90 minutes later than expected. Over the next few days all three suffered symptoms of burning and weight loss.

All three women passed polygraph tests. Under regressive hypnosis, Mona Stafford gave a detailed description of an abduction in which her body was covered with a painful liquid, and a tube was thrust into her stomach.

ASSESSMENT

The events are similar to the Beit Bridge encounter of 31 May 1974, described

above. However, such extreme physical effects are uncommon in abductions.

THE SILENT WITNESS

A weird experience in New South Wales

TYPE: **Close encounter of the second kind**
PLACE: **Nemingha, near Tamworth, New South Wales, Australia**
DATE: **22 March 1976**

BACKGROUND

At about 5:45am a couple driving to Murrundi, New South Wales, stopped to consult the map. At that moment a small white car came towards them, and the couple stepped onto the road, hoping to ask directions.

THE EVENTS

A bright yellow-green light suddenly came from above, blotting out the approaching car, then went out again. The car drifted to the wrong side of the road, and was then enveloped in white haze. The car pulled up, its lights out. A woman got out and wiped the windshield with a cloth. She then threw the cloth on the ground, and it burst into flames. She drove away before the startled couple could react. They noted as the car passed that it was covered in a 'thick white substance not unlike white paint' all over except at the place on the windshield where it had been wiped.

ASSESSMENT

This seems to be the only case on record in which a UFO event was reported only by third parties. All attempts to trace the central witness ended in failure; if she could be found – if, indeed, she exists – her testimony would probably provide valuable data for comparison of the objective and subjective sides of the close encounter phenomenon.

PHANTOMS CHASE PHANTOMS

Jets pursue UFOs over Teheran

TYPE: **Radar Visual**
PLACE: **Teheran, Iran**
DATE: **19 September 1976**

BACKGROUND

Teheran residents reported seeing UFOs at about 12:30am. At about 1:30am an F-4 Phantom was scrambled from the Imperial Iranian Air Force (IIAF) base at Shahroki, about 130 miles (209km) southwest of the capital.

THE EVENTS

According to a report made the US military attaché in Iran, the F-4 was within 25 miles (40km) of the UFO when the jet's communications systems failed. When the jet turned away, the systems came back to life. A second F-4 took off at 1:40am, and its radar return from the UFO showed it to be the size of a Boeing 707 airliner. The UFO showed flashing colored strobe lights in a rectangular pattern. When the F-4 came within 25 miles (40km) of the UFO, the object sped away, thereafter maintaining the distance between the two. A second object then came from the UFO at high speed toward the F-4. The pilot tried to fire an AIM-9 missile, but his weapons-control panel went off and his radios failed. The second UFO rejoined the first, then another small object streaked from it at the ground. It came to rest and lit up the surrounding area. The F-4 descended to observe the area, then flew to Mehrabad airport. As it came in to land, another, cylindrical UFO passed over it and was seen by Mehrabad controlers.

ASSESSMENT

Only the second F-4 had had any electronics failures, and had a history of such faults. Philip J. Klass discovered that the IIAF aircrew had no night-flying experi-ence and were scrambled from a deep sleep, and so were easily confused. He put the events down to radar and radio malfunction due to bad maintenance, aircrew errors (pursuing a star) and meteors (the Aquarid and Southern Piscid showers were at their peak that night). The cylindrical UFO that passed over Mehrabad airport remains unexplained.

THE MOROCCAN ENIGMA

Shape-shifting UFO baffles US State Department

TYPE: **Lights in sky, multiple witnesses**
PLACE: **Agadir to Fez, Morocco, North Africa**
DATE: **19 September 1976**

BACKGROUND

Nearly four hours after the encounter over Teheran, this UFO was seen flying roughly parallel to the Atlantic coast over Morocco, north Africa.

THE EVENTS

For an hour from about 1:00am local time a bright UFO trailing sparks in its wake flew slowly at an estimated altitude of 3300ft (1000m) from across Morocco from the south to the north. Reports came from Agadir, Kalaa Sraghna, Essaouira, Casablanca, Rabat and Fez. The UFO looked like a disk at a distance, resolving into a cylindrical shape when it was viewed at closer quarters.

ASSESSMENT

The US Embassy in Morocco requested evaluation and response from the US State Department in Washington, DC. Secretary of State Henry Kissinger had the matter investigated, and although he was later able to advise the Ambassador that both meteors and a satellite re-entry had been ruled out as possibilities, his final judgment on the matter was unsatisfactorily inconclusive: 'It is difficult,'

Kissinger wrote, 'to offer any definitive explanation as to the cause or origin of the UFOs.'

UFO PANIC IN CHINA

A Chinese cinema crowd in uproar

TYPE: **Lights in the sky, multiple witnesses**
PLACE: **Zhang Po, Fujian, China**
DATE: **7 July 1977**

BACKGROUND

A crowd of 3000 people had gathered to enjoy an outdoor showing of a Romanian movie, *Alert on the Danube Delta*.

THE EVENTS

At about 8:30pm two huge orange UFOs suddenly swept out of the sky and over the heads of the crowd, humming and coming so close that people could feel their heat. Within seconds they had ascended and disappeared into the night.

ASSESSMENT

Two children were killed and 200 people injured in the ensuing chaos which, given the brevity of the sighting, would support its physical reality. The temptation to ascribe the sighting to fireballs can be dismissed, as the objects rose again into the sky after 'buzzing' the crowd.

UFO PANIC IN USSR

Panic in a Soviet town

TYPE: **Lights in the sky, multiple witnesses**
PLACE: **Petrozavodsk, Karelskaya (now Karelian, Russia)**
DATE: **20 September 1977**

BACKGROUND

This report of an unusual jellyfish-like UFO was issued by TASS, the official Soviet news agency.

THE EVENTS

At 4:00am, a huge star-like light appeared suddenly, spread out into a shape like a jellyfish, and moved slowly over the city of Petrozavodsk and then hovered for about 12 minutes. Thin rays of light shone down from it. The UFO then moved on east across Lake Onega, changing to a red semi-circular light within a gray cloud. It was seen as far away as Helsinki, Finland. In Petrozavodsk, panic and baseless rumors swept the city after the sighting.

ASSESSMENT

James Oberg concluded that the UFO may well have been a secret satellite that had been launched from the nearby Soviet space center at Plesetsk. But the launch of such satellites must have been a common occurrence in the Cold War, and so it seems reasonable to assume that the people of Petrozavodsk would have seen such things before and not have been alarmed by them.

ONE ALIEN DOWN

The invasion of Fort Dix

TYPE: **Close encounter of the third kind, alien retrieval**
PLACE: **Fort Dix/McGuire Air Force Base, New Jersey, USA**
DATE: **18 January 1978**

BACKGROUND

This report, investigated by Leonard Stringfield and Richard Hall, comes from a USAF security policeman known only as 'Blue Beret'.

THE EVENTS

A security patrol in McGuire saw UFOs hovering over the army base at Fort Dix. At least one UFO landed on a disused runway at McGuire. Aliens came out and one was shot dead by security police. USAF Blue Berets then cordoned off the area, and the body was crated and loaded on a flight from Wright-Patterson AFB.

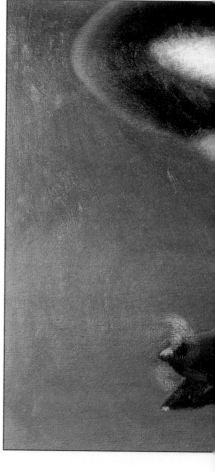

ASSESSMENT

This report suffers from the same lack of evidence as other crash/retrieval reports. The witness's anonymity does not help.

'LIKE A BIG BLUE LAMPSHADE'

Three big rigs meet a UFO on Interstate 70

TYPE: **Close encounter of the second kind**
PLACE: **Indianapolis, Indiana, USA**
DATE: **29 March 1978**

BACKGROUND

Around 9:30pm three truckers traveling in convoy were chatting together on their

Artist's impression of the encounter between Frederich Valentich, flying a Cessna 102, and something that was 'not an aircraft', over Bass Strait, Australia, in October 1978.

CBs when a bright blue light enveloped all three rigs for about five seconds.

THE EVENTS

None of the three were able to see beyond the hoods of their trucks. All exterior sounds ceased. The CB radios failed and the trucks' engines began to falter. Then the blue light – described by another driver in a car nearby as the shape of 'a big bright blue lampshade over the three trucks' – went out, and things suddenly returned to normal. The last trucker in the line shouted into his CB transmitter: 'Hey, UFO, if you have your ears on, I want to go with you!' The blue light came on again, for about 15 seconds, and displayed the same effects as before; the trucks slowed down to about 5mph (8km/h). When the light went out, normality returned.

ASSESSMENT

This case is unusual for having three principal witnesses as well as independent observers. Diesel engines – that do not need electrical sparks – were affected.

'IT'S COMING FOR ME RIGHT NOW'

The disappearance of Frederick Valentich

TYPE: **Close encounter of the second kind**
PLACE: **Bass Strait, Australia**
DATE: **21 October 1978**

BACKGROUND

Frederick Valentich, aged 20, took off in a rented Cessna 182 from Moorabbin Airport, Melbourne, at 6:19pm to make a 300 mile (480km) round trip to King Island in the Bass Strait. He had intended to collect crayfish for the officers of the local Air Training Corps, and expected to be back at Moorabbin by 10:00pm the same evening.

THE EVENTS

At 7:06pm, Melbourne ground control received a message from Valentich on the radio asking if there were any aircraft in his vicinity below 5000ft (1500m) altitude. Negative, said Melbourne. Valentich said an aircraft with four bright lights had just passed over, 1000ft (300m) above him. He was unable to tell the type. Then he said it was approaching him from the east, and: 'It's not an aircraft.... It has a long shape... coming for me right now....' Then the thing vanished. But Valentich's engine was rough-idling and coughing, and suddenly he said: 'Unknown aircraft now on top of me.' 'Acknowledge,' said Melbourne. There was a 17-second burst of 'metallic' noise, and after that no more from the Cessna. A search began at 7:28pm and although it went on for a week, no trace of Valentich or the aircraft was ever found.

ASSESSMENT

Here is a genuine mystery. This was Valentich's first solo night flight. Possibly inexperience led him to turn the aircraft on its back, causing the engine to die. He filed only a one-way flight plan, despite his stated intention to be back that night. This has led skeptics to suspect a hoax and a deliberate disappearance, though, as far as can be ascertained, Valentich had no motive for either. Which still leaves the possibility that Valentich collided with, or was captured by, a UFO.

THE KUWAIT FLAP

A UFO stops the oil flowing

TYPE: **Close encounter of the second kind**
PLACE: **Umm Al-Aish, northern Kuwait**
DATE: **10 November 1978**

BACKGROUND

Kuwait had never had a UFO sighting in its whole history until November 1978. The most dramatic of the rash of sightings all over the country that month is detailed here.

THE EVENTS

Seven technicians, among them an expatriate American citizen, working at the Kuwaiti Oil Company pumping station Gathering Center No 24 at Umm Al-Aish, watched as a cylindrical UFO with a dome and flashing red lights landed silently nearby. The oil pumps stopped working, then resumed normal operation when after seven minutes the UFO took off. The witnesses estimated its size as 'bigger than a jumbo jet', but the craft left no traces on the ground where it had landed. For the exact duration of the sighting, Kuwait's international telecommunications links ceased to function.

ASSESSMENT

No official verdict was given, but within two weeks of the sighting the government established a national investigative committee consisting of civil aviation experts, scientists and officials from the Ministry of the Interior.

THE NEW ZEALAND SPECTACULAR

A series of sightings captured on film

TYPE: **Radar-visual**
PLACE: **Kaikoura, between Wellington and Christchurch, New Zealand**
DATE: **30-31 December 1978**

BACKGROUND

On 21 December, the crew of an Argosy cargo plane flying from Blenheim (south of Wellington, South Island) to Dunedin made radar-visual contacts with UFOs. Media interest led Australian TV reporter Quentin Fogarty and a camera crew to follow the same route, also in an Argosy, on the night of 30-31 December.

THE EVENTS

The plane took off from Wellington at 11:46pm. At 12:10am, the captain and co-pilot saw lights off the Kaikoura Peninsula, which Wellington radar had also picked up as intermittent blips. At 12:22am, another radar-visual contact was made, and the UFO was filmed. There were other brief contacts before the Argosy landed just after 1:00am at

A UFO photographed by chance by Tsutomu Nakayama in Hawaii on 25 April 1974. Other photographs of the scene do not show the object, and Mr Nakayama himself was unaware of it in the sky when he took the shot. It may be a bird, a balloon, or just a blemish on the film.

Christchurch. At 2:16am the plane took off for the return flight to Blenheim. As the aircraft came above the cloud cover, a bright UFO showed ahead and to the right. Christchurch radar picked up a 'huge' object in a corresponding position about 20 miles (30km) from the plane. Film taken at this time showed an oval object with rings of light. During the flight the UFO approached to within 10 miles (16km) of the plane. Off Kaikoura, Wellington radar reported several objects near the plane; one of these, a flashing UFO, was filmed changing color from yellow-white to dull orange-red. The aircraft landed at 3:10am.

ASSESSMENT

Apart from UFOs, the New Zealand film has been analysed as showing Venus, Jupiter, temperature inversions, the brilliant lights from Japanese squid-fishing boats, and birds. The reliability of the radar returns has also been questioned. The Royal New Zealand Air Force was sufficiently impressed by the report to put a jet fighter on standby to intercept any further UFOs, but the case continues to generate controversy between skeptics and supporters.

UFO IN RETREAT

Aliens escape a pugnacious Chinese trucker

TYPE: **Close encounter of the third kind**
PLACE: **Lanxi, Zhejiang, China**
DATE: **13 October 1979**

BACKGROUND

Truck driver Wang Jian Min came upon a parked car at about 4:00am. The driver recounted seeing a UFO land on the road ahead, but he was too disturbed to approach it.

THE EVENTS

Wang drove on, the car following, to where a domed UFO was straddling the crest of a hill. Beside it were two aliens in silver-colored suits and helmets with lamps attached. Wang climbed from his truck, picked up a crowbar then and approached. The UFO and the entities disappeared as he came close.

ASSESSMENT

If the modern phase of the UFO phenomenon started in a specific context – post-war USA – this case shows that it had become global in scope, without changing its details, over two decades. Some ufologists argue that this demonstrates UFOs' objective nature.

WHO HOAXED WHOM?

Strange complications in a French abduction case

TYPE: **Close encounter of the third kind**
PLACE: **Cergy, Pontoise, Ile de France, France**
DATE: **26 November 1979**

BACKGROUND

Franck Fontaine, Jean-Pierre Prévost and Salomon N'Diaye made a precarious living selling jeans in street markets. They stayed overnight at Prévost's apartment in Cergy-Pontoise 25 miles (40km) from Paris to make an early start. At about 3:30am, they push-started their battered Ford Taunus, and were about to leave Fontaine to keep it running while the others fetched their wares.

THE EVENTS

Fontaine called his friends' attention to a white, elongated, luminous object descending beyond a nearby building. Saloman fetched his camera. He and Prévost went inside, and while looking for the UFO from the apartment window Prévost saw that the car had run down the road and stopped. On getting outside again, he and Salomon saw a sphere of fog surrounding the car. Around this three or four small spheres were floating in the air. They entered a cylinder that flew away at high speed. When the pair reached the car, Fontaine had vanished. They reported the events to the police, who questioned them for several days.

Seven days almost to the minute after disappearing, at 4:20am on 3 December, Fontaine returned to the flat, confused, angry and apparently unaware that any time had passed. He had passed out when the fog descended on the car, and woke up in a nearby cabbage field. During subsequent investigations by police and ufologists, two things occurred. One was the emergence of Prévost as a UFO 'cult' leader, who decided that the abduction was intended to put him in contact with aliens. Later he published a book about the affair and started a magazine. The other was Fontaine's gradual recollection of having being taken to a kind of laboratory. Two small luminous spheres spoke to him about the future of humanity. Then, in June 1983, Prévost confessed that the whole affair had been a hoax.

ASSESSMENT

There were problems with Prévost's 'confession': no one knew where Fontaine had been during his seven day absence; one witness at Cergy-Pontoise saw not one but two people in the car just before the abduction, and the first police officers on the scene saw fog around the car. If it was a hoax, why (and how) did the trio lay on such elaborate effects?

According to Jacques Vallée, they did not: the French Ministry of Defense was responsible for the abduction. An Air Force contact explained off the record that Fontaine had then been kept 'under an altered state of high suggestibility', i.e., drugged. Vallée concluded that the exercise was a social and psychological test, possibly with the aim of founding a UFO 'religion' that could be controled by the experimenters. At some point, the program was dropped. If this is true, it confirms suspicions that, whatever the reality behind UFOs, government agencies have deliberately manipulated it for their own ends.

CHAPTER 6

Natural or Unnatural?

RIFTS DEVELOP AMONG RESEARCHERS

AS SIGHTINGS AND ENCOUNTERS MULTIPLY

The cool air of objectivity that refreshed so much of ufology during the Seventies boiled up in the course of the Eighties to become a storm of paranoia and recrimination.

First came a revival of interest in the stories of crashed saucers (originally promoted in 1950 by Frank Scully, who was the unwitting victim of a hoax), following the publication of Charles Berlitz and William L. Moore's *The Roswell Incident* in 1980. Leonard Stringfield then made a specialty of garnering accounts, usually from witnesses who conveniently or inconveniently insisted on anonymity, of 'crash-retrieval' cases. Stringfield soon had over two dozen alleged crashes on his files, and other reports from people who claimed to have seen or, in one case, assisted at the autopsies of dead aliens removed from such crashes.

Stories like these led in turn to a revival of the belief that the US and quite

Artist's impression of the alleged abduction of Linda Cortile from her Manhattan apartment in November 1989. The episode has been hailed as the 'UFO case of the century' by those who believe it genuine, and dubbed 'the case that's tearing ufology apart' by those observing the scorn poured on it by moderate ufologists and skeptics alike.

probably other governments too were aware of far more about UFOs than they had ever admitted. In one notorious case, the US government actually exploited this belief and fed a mass of disinformation to one physicist, in order to let him carry on thinking that the secret military experiments that he had inadvertently tapped into were of alien, not Earthly, origin.

CONFUSION OR COVER-UP?

The discovery that this exercise had occurred confirmed some in their conviction that many apparent UFO phenomena were of military origin, and that by encouraging belief in UFOs governments were able to shield their own clandestine activities from too close inspection. William H. Spaulding was chief among the proponents of this idea, which he called the 'Federal Hypothesis'. He based his conclusions on a mass of previously top-secret UFO-related papers released to the public through actions brought under the Freedom of Information Act (FOIA). Spaulding became convinced that there were no 'UFOs' as such, and certainly no flying saucers from outer space.

Others – notably Timothy Good in the UK and John Lear and Bill Cooper in the USA – went much further, and in the opposite direction, as a result of scrutinizing documents released under FOIA provisions. They maintained that the US government had actually contacted aliens,

and had concluded a deal whereby off-worlders would be allowed a free hand in abductions and animal experiments in return for technological information. Few mainstream ufologists accepted this proposition, not least because such evidence of it as existed was so flimsy. What seemed to be proof, in the shape of the 'Majestic 12' documents, which purported to be presidential briefing papers on continuing contact with aliens, turned out to be faked. But a real mystery still remains – who faked them, and why?

However, the Eighties did see at least two plausible instances of possible government and military deceit in handling actual UFO events, as opposed to mere documents. One was the Huffman, Texas, close encounter of 1980, after which the two women and boy involved suffered what seemed to be radiation sickness – showing symptoms far more severe than any known from similar cases before. The US Government denied all knowledge of the incident, despite the fact that military-type helicopters had been present at the scene of the encounter.

The other was the UFO landing, or crash, in Rendlesham Forest, England, shortly afterward, which was apparently witnessed by scores of US servicemen. Initial denials by the USAF and the British Ministry of Defence were followed by extraordinary documentation, from official sources, of the event. Ironically, and

UFO

some would say deliberately, this sudden new openness served only to confuse investigators as to the truth of what happened. It is still possible to interpret the evidence in several ways.

BEST-SELLING ALIENS

The major concern of UFO believers in the Eighties, however, was undoubtedly alien abductions. Budd Hopkins published his seminal *Missing Time* in 1982, but it was Whitley Strieber's *Communion* that became an international best-seller in 1987 and made the abduction scenario common knowledge in every household. Strieber later concluded that his experience was not due to aliens, but Budd Hopkins developed the theory that abductions were part of a program of alien genetic sampling or even systematic manipulation of the human race. The proposition provoked a storm of controversy that still rages, and not merely between ufologists and skeptics. Hopkins' and others' reliance on gathering their evidence through hypnosis attracted enormous criticism.

Those untouched, or unimpressed, by all these claims of conspiracy pursued other lines of enquiry into the phenomenon. In 1982, Paul Devereux in the UK published *Earthlights*, a study that showed an extraordinary correlation between geological stresses and faults and UFO sightings. Devereux did not claim to explain the mechanism that produced anomalous lights or how they in turn affected mental processes (scientific research into this is still continuing today in Japan and the USA). But he produced fascinating data that linked the earthlights with medieval dragon sightings, mysterious or magical ancient sites, and altered states of consciousness as well as UFOs. Here were the makings of a theory that might account for many UFO experiences.

Meanwhile other ufologists explored the possibility that UFOs might be some species of psychic phenomenon. Lt. Col. Thomas A. Bearden in the USA proposed that UFOs were material objects – but ones that an individual's unconscious and

the collective unconscious combined to materialize in symbolically significant ways. Following occult tradition, he called such materializations from the psyche 'tulpoids'. He suggested that thoughts and imaginings are physically real, and remain in three dimensions separate from ours, but joined to ours by the common thread of time, until powerful emotions caused them to break through into our world. Bearden specifically linked the frequency of tulpoid UFO appearances to crises in the Cold War. The problem was that, once materialized, tulpoids took on a life of their own.

In the UK, Jenny Randles proposed something she called the 'Oz factor' – the sense of entering a separate reality that so many UFO percipients experience on the threshold of an encounter. She speculated that natural objects or events could trigger this state in someone who was not fully alert and so appear as UFOs or aliens. In some cases, the impression could be strong enough to generate tem-

Ellen B. Crystall took this photograph at 11:00 pm on 17 February 1981, at Wanaque Reservoir, New Jersey, USA, with the film exposed for 5 minutes. A triangular UFO reportedly passed overhead during that time, but did not appear on the film.

porarily real objects and entities that could be photographed or witnessed by others. The 'Oz factor', Randles thought, might be manipulated or created by aliens to contact us by purely psychic means.

The ufology of the Eighties was much preoccupied with new hypotheses. At the heart of all but the Earthlights Hypothesis and the Federal Hypothesis were the presupposition that UFOs and their occupants were beyond humanity's control – and the fear that they might, in fact, be in control of humanity.

THE EVENTS

According to Ms Hansen's accounts under hypnosis, two white-suited figures emerged from one of the UFOs and mutilated a cow in the field with an 18-inch (45cm) knife. She remonstrated with the aliens, but she and her son were captured and taken to separate ships. She resisted but was undressed and given a physical examination, including a vaginal probe that reportedly later produced a severe infection. This was interrupted by what appeared to be a tall, jaundiced human, who apologized and ordered the aliens to be punished. He then took Ms Hansen on a tour of this and possibly other UFOs. The last seems to have taken flight, as she was next led out into a landscape that she believed she recognized as being west of Las Cruces. She was taken into an underground base, where she was horrified by a room full of vats in which were floating human body parts. She and her son were both subjected to painful loud noises and blinding lights, before being taken aboard the UFO again and flown with her car back to the site of the abduction.

ASSESSMENT

The imagery here is unusually gruesome. The theme of underground UFO bases has recurred in many other reports and theories – a favorite candidate being under the Archuleta Mesa near Dulce, New Mexico, less than 200 miles (322km) from Cimarron.

FROM CIMARRON TO ALBUQUERQUE

The appalling experience of Paul Bennewitz

TYPE: Cover-up, disinformation
PLACE: Albuquerque, New Mexico, USA
DATE: Summer 1980 onward

BACKGROUND

Bennewitz investigated Myra Hansen's encounter for the Aerial Phenomena Research Organization and was present at her regressions. Parts of her account implied that American scientists were colluding with the alien abduction program. Bennewitz, who is president of Thunder Scientific Corporation and an accomplished electronics expert, was also aware of the rumored alien and UFO activity at Kirtland Air Force Base (AFB) near his home at Albuquerque. Kirtland itself contains a number of highly secret military installations, including the Manazano nuclear weapons store and a weapons test range. Despite the obvious risks, Bennewitz decided to monitor the AFB for signs of alien/human contact.

THE EVENTS

Bennewitz succeeded in taking many reels of 8mm film of what he believed were UFOs at Kirtland, and rigged up electronic surveillance equipment to eavesdrop communications. With this he picked up a number of apparently coherent but inexplicable signals at very low frequencies, and some unusual magnetic emissions – which he concluded were evidence of contact between the base and aliens. Kirtland electronics specialists became aware that Bennewitz was picking up their activities, and the Air Force Office of Special Investigations (AFOSI) was called in to discourage him.

Bennewitz saw this as proof they had something to hide – which they did, as he had tuned in to secret communications experiments. But they had nothing to do with UFOs, as he believed. He refused to co-operate. AFOSI then decided to feed Bennewitz a mass of misleading information about aliens, underground bases and anything else they could think of – so that, should he leak any technical details of their work, he would be discredited as a crank.

Bennewitz swallowed the bait, some of which was fed him by ufologist William L. Moore, who had been recruited by AFOSI for the purpose. Bennewitz became obsessed, believing that night rescue exercises by helicopters were UFOs on abduction missions, and repeated so many

FROM CIMARRON TO LAS CRUCES

One horror story leads to another

TYPE: Animal mutilation, close encounter of the fourth kind
PLACE: Near Cimarron, Colfax County, New Mexico, USA
DATE: Spring 1980

BACKGROUND

Driving home on a road near Cimarron one night, 28-year-old Myra Hansen and her 6-year-old son saw five UFOs descending into a cow pasture. Until hypnotically regressed, she had confused memories of a close encounter, and noted a time loss of four hours. She was regressed in sessions between 11 May and 3 June by Dr Leo Sprinkle, in company with Dr Paul Bennewitz, for whom the case was to have bizarre consequences.

of the bizarre claims passed on to him – for instance, that the animal parts taken during mutilations were used to construct humanoid bodies – that not even the most committed ufologists took him seriously. In the end, Bennewitz suffered a nervous breakdown. Moore's reward for his part in the deception, some say, was the Majestic 12 documents (described later in this chapter).

ASSESSMENT

Moore has publicly admitted his part in this deception, although strong doubts have been cast on the authenticity of his alleged reward. The case exposes the extraordinary – some would say completely unethical – lengths to which the military will go to guard its secrets, and confirms the principle of the Federal Hypothesis. But one result has been to make it even less likely that the reality or otherwise of the Cimarron case can ever be established.

AT HUFFMAN WITH HELICOPTERS

Three witnesses suffer vicious radiation poisoning

TYPE: **Close encounter of the second kind**
PLACE: **Near Huffman, Texas, USA**
DATE: **29 December 1980**

BACKGROUND

Betty Cash, Vickie Landrum and her seven-year-old grandson Colby Landrum were driving home to Dayton, near Houston, Texas, in the evening of 29 December 1980, after having had dinner together in nearby New Caney. At around 9:00pm the three of them, with Betty at the wheel, were traveling on Highway FM1485, which runs through a forest of oak and pine trees, near the small town of Huffman.

UFO caught by chance on film by Hannah McRoberts in British Columbia, Canada, on 8 October 1981. She, her husband and 19-month-old daughter stopped near the Eve River, north of Kelsey Bay, Vancouver Island, on a journey to Holberg. Mrs Roberts decided to photograph the scenery, and the couple were joking between themselves as she did so. Neither realized the UFO had been present until they saw the developed film. The frame is the only one on the roll showing a UFO. After various tests Richard F. Haines concluded that the image had not been faked nor the film damaged, and calculated that if the UFO had been directly over the mountain top, it would have been 123 ft (37.5 m) across. What, then, was it?

THE EVENTS

A bright light was moving over the trees ahead of them. It grew larger until it became 'like a diamond of fire' – while every so often flames burst from beneath it. Suddenly, it was right in their way, hovering about 60 yards (55m) away. Betty braked hard. Several times, from treetop level, the UFO sank to within 25ft (7.5m) of the highway, gave out a blast of fire, and rose again. The three climbed out to see the object more clearly. It seemed to be made of dull aluminum. The four points of its diamond shape were rounded, and a row of blue dots ran across its center. Now and then it emitted a beeping sound. A terrific heat was coming from the UFO, and Colby and his grandmother got back in the car, which was soon too hot to touch. Then a crowd of helicopters appeared from all directions, 'trying to encircle the thing'.

They drove on another 5 miles (8km) to where they could see the UFO in the distance, and the swarm of helicopters around it. One helicopter, a giant, twin-rotor CH-47 Chinook, roared right over them. They counted a total of 23 machines of various types.

Over the next few hours, the trio developed painful swellings and blisters on their skin and had severe headaches and stomach upsets. In time, Vickie's hair began to fall out, while Colby developed a sunburn-like rash. Betty's eyes became swollen so that she could not see, and she had to be hospitalized. In a few weeks all three had lost some hair and were developing eye problems. When their hair grew again, it was different from their original hair.

ASSESSMENT

The symptoms were consistent with exposure to intense electromagnetic radiation in the ultra-violet, microwave and X-ray bands. Other witnesses confirmed the UFO's flight path and appearance, and the presence of a large number of CH-47 helicopters in the sky that night. Local airfields and military airbases denied that such a fleet used their facilities or showed on their radar. Vickie Landrum was convinced that a secret military device was responsible for her injuries, and she and Betty Cash sued the US government for $20 million. In 1986, the case was dismissed on the grounds that 'no such object was owned, operated or in the inventory' of the US Army, Navy, Air Force or NASA. Thus the US government has not been obliged to admit whether or not it knows what the object was, irrespective of who owns it: the true nature of the Texas UFO remains unknown.

DOWN IN THE FOREST

Did US servicemen take part in an encounter in England?

TYPE: **Close encounter of the second kind**
PLACE: **Rendlesham Forest, near RAF Woodbridge, Suffolk, UK**
DATE: **27 December 1980**

BACKGROUND

At about 3:00am radars at RAF Watton in Norfolk registered an 'unknown' flying toward the coast over the North Sea. It disappeared from the scopes in the vicinity of Rendlesham Forest. At about this same time, next to the forest, security police at the Woodbridge gate of the USAF base RAF Woodbridge saw lights coming down from the sky into the trees. They were granted permission to investigate, and left the base in a jeep.

THE EVENTS

Because the forest track was impassable, the patrolmen abandoned their jeep and continued on foot. They came across a conical or triangular object 6-10ft (2-3m) across the base and 6ft (2m) high. The deputy base commander, Lt. Col. Charles Halt, described it in an official report as 'metallic in appearance'. It 'illuminated the entire forest with a white light' and 'had a pulsing red light on top and a bank of blue lights underneath. The object was hovering or on legs'. When the patrolmen approached, the UFO took off and disappeared among the trees. Nearby farm animals 'went into a frenzy'. When daylight came, various indentations were found on the ground where the UFO had been.

According to various accounts, the UFO was seen again; Lieutenant Colonel Halt made a tape-recording of his own observations and comments as he and several others watched strange lights darting about the sky. There are also simultaneous reports of aliens apparently floating in a beam of light beneath the UFO, and even a claim that the base commander, Colonel (now General) Gordon Williams, communicated directly with the aliens on board the unidentified craft.

ASSESSMENT

Many of the alleged witnesses' accounts contradict each other, particularly with regard to what was seen and how many people saw it. One witness maintains that before the second sighting a large number of personnel, including some British police officers, gathered to await the UFO's arrival in a prearranged spot. Skeptics have variously attributed these reports to exaggeration, misperception and attention-seeking, and they have proposed various mundane sources for the lights (including mirages). UFO researcher Jacques Vallée, however, has taken the most elaborate accounts as genuine, and he has proposed two possible explanations of the close encounter: either the US military has developed its own UFO-like weapons, and one of them touched down in the forest that night, possibly accidentally; or alternatively the object and the aliens were all deliberate fabrications designed to ascertain and monitor servicemen's reactions to an encounter with an apparent UFO – perhaps to gauge how enemy soldiers might react if confronted with UFO-like military craft. Nevertheless, for all Vallée's work on the subject, there is not yet a wholly satisfactory explanation of the events in Rendlesham Forest.

THE THIRSTY UFO

A giant tank of water goes empty

TYPE: **Close encounter of the second kind**
PLACE: **White Acres, Rosedale, Victoria, Australia**
DATE: **30 September 1980**

BACKGROUND

George Blackwell, a station hand and caretaker on White Acres, a 600-acre (240 hectare) property, awoke at about 1:00am to the sound of the farm's cattle going wild – accompanied by 'a strange screeching whistling'. He got up to investigate. There was no wind that night, and the moon was out.

THE EVENTS

Blackwell saw a domed object about 15ft (4.5m) high and 25ft (7.5m) broad with a white top and blue and orange lights. For a while it hovered over a concrete water tank about 450 yards (400m) from the house, then came to rest on the ground 20 yards (18m) further on. Blackwell drove a motorcycle to within 50ft (15m) of it. There was no effect on his machine, but the whistling from the UFO suddenly rose to deafening heights, there was a huge bang, and the thing lifted off. At the same time, a blast of hot air nearly knocked Blackwell over. The UFO dropped some debris and flew away eastward at no more than 100ft (30m).

Blackwell examined the site early the next morning. He found a ring of blackened grass, flattened in an anti-clockwise direction. Inside the ring was green grass, but the flowers that had been growing there had disappeared. In a line to the east outside the ring was a trail of debris – stones, weeds and cow dung. For days after the sighting Blackwell suffered headaches and nausea, and his watch refused to work normally. In addition, the tank over which the UFO had paused had been emptied of 10,000 gallons (45,500 litres) of water.

ASSESSMENT

There seems to be only the choice between a hoax – perhaps to cover Blackwell's negligence in not maintaining the water supply – or taking the witness's word for the events. There have been numerous other reports of UFOs taking on water.

NATURAL OR UNNATURAL, INDEED?

The curious experience of Monsieur Collini

TYPE: **Close encounter of the second kind**
PLACE: **Trans-en-Provence, France**
DATE: **8 February 1981**

BACKGROUND

At about 5:00pm, M. Collini, in the words of the French goverment's UFO study group GEPAN, 'was working quietly in his garden at Trans-en-Provence. Suddenly his attention was attracted by a low whistling sound that appeared to come from the far end of his property.'

THE EVENTS

The report continues: 'Turning around, [M. Collini] saw in the sky above the trees something approaching a terrace at the bottom of the garden. The ovoid object suddenly landed. The witness moved forward and observed the strange phenomenon behind a small building.

'Less than a minute later, the phenomenon suddenly rose and moved away in a direction similar to that of its arrival, still continuing to emit a low whistle. M. Collini immediately went to the apparent scene of the landing and observed circular marks and a clear crown-shaped imprint on the ground.'

ASSESSMENT

Gendarmes arrived the next day to take soil and vegetation samples. On 20 March, GEPAN investigators took some further samples and interviewed M. Collini. The tests showed that the witness 'had no psychological problems and that his testimony was internally and externally consistent' – in other words, he did not contradict himself, and there was evidence that something had landed at the spot he described. The soil at the landing site showed signs of having been been heated to between 300 and 600°C (570-1110°F), while the plants there were prematurely aged and had lost up to 50 per cent of their chlorophyll. There was no evidence of residual radioactivity.

Clearly, something physically real did land on M. Collini's property that evening. Was it an unusual natural phenomenon – perhaps an 'earthlight' – that scorched the earth, or was it an unknown kind of flying machine?

SPIRAL IN THE SKY

Hundreds see a UFO over China

TYPE: **Light in the sky**
PLACE: **Guizhou Province, China**
DATE: **24 July 1981**

BACKGROUND

In June, it was predicted that between 10 and 30 July UFOs would be sighted in China. A wise man said one UFO would appear in spiral form, rotating clockwise, and would be larger than the Moon.

French UFO magazine depicts the anomalous object that landed briefly in the yard of a M. Collini (sometimes identified as Renato Nicolai) on 8 February 1981. Although the UFO affected the ground and plants there, the witness suffered no ill effects. In 1989 Jacques Vallée had soil and plant samples analysed using electron microscopy and X-rays. The tests showed that no chemicals, cement powder 'or other surface contaminants' could have caused the effects on the plants.

THE EVENTS

On 24 July hundreds of people saw the promised spiral UFO – some viewed it by chance, while others had gone to outdoor viewing platforms specifically to watch the sage's predictions come true. A soldier thought it was the Moon until he realized it was in the wrong part of the sky. A university professor saw, and sketched, a classic 'flying saucer' with portholes. Some people panicked at the sight; others felt uplifted.

ASSESSMENT

The prophet in this case was a Chinese astronomer called Zhang Zhousheng from the Yun'nan Observatory. He in fact had no supernaturally clairvoyant powers – all he had done was use his scientific knowledge to predict accurately the appearance of a meteor shower. This case is a classic illustration of how witnesses can sometimes project their own imaginings onto a perfectly ordinary if relatively infrequent natural event.

CHANGING PLACES

Two Finnish boatmen lose seven hours

TYPE: **Close encounter of the second kind**
PLACE: **Cape Vaaraniemi, Lieksa, Finland**
DATE: **July 1981**

BACKGROUND

One summer evening, two 35-year-old vacationers were sailing a motor launch past Cape Vaaraniemi. There was a strong current and a considerable wind.

THE EVENTS

At 8:40pm they saw a black sphere in the sky surrounded by one large and several small lights. The large light approached them, and they stopped the boat. A black object bearing two lights then flew to the stern of the boat. The UFO was surrounded by some kind of fog. One of the men became paralyzed, unable to move his head, although he could still converse with his companion. Then the lights and the object all suddenly disappeared. At this point the two men realized they were sitting in different places in the boat from before. They checked their watches and found the time was 4:10am. Seven and a half hours had gone by since the start of their experience, and yet their boat was still off Cape Vaaraniemi, where it had been since they had first seen the mysterious black sphere.

ASSESSMENT

Two attempts to hypnotize the men – to get them to disinter memories of the incident that they might otherwise be unwilling or unable to recall – were completely unsuccessful. Whatever the reality behind the events at Lieksa, and whatever really occurred during the long period of missing time, the experience was painfully real to the witnesses themselves, who afterwards suffered from nightmares, a disturbed sense of balance, and bouts of uncontrolable shaking.

U F O

THE HESSDALEN LIGHTS

A long-term study of UFO phenomena

TYPE: **Lights in the sky, earthlights**
PLACE: **Hessdalen Valley, Norway**
DATE: **November 1981- December 1985**

BACKGROUND

In November 1981 the inhabitants of the rural Hessdalen valley began to report strange aerial lights performing unusual maneuvers in their neighborhood.

THE EVENTS

The lights came in various shapes – disks, eggs, cigars, and simple blurs – and some witnesses reported features such as port-holes and domes. No close encounters of any kind were reported. In 1985, the phenomena seemed to die away in frequency, although lights are still occasionally seen in the valley and may be on the increase.

ASSESSMENT

Radar, infra-red detectors, cameras, geiger counters, magnetometers and spectrum analysers were among the array of equipment brought to bear on the Hessdalen lights by the Scandinavian investigators of the case. They concluded that the lights were a rare natural phenomenon, if one as yet little understood by science, probably related to movements in the Earth's crust. The Hessdalen events immeasurably strengthened the suspicions of 'earthlights' researchers that unusual natural phenomena lay behind many UFO experiences.

SOVIET SPACE CENTER ATTACKED

UFOs put a key installation out of action

TYPE: **Close encounter of the second kind**
PLACE: **Baikonur Cosmodrome, Kazakhstan (then part of the USSR)**
DATE: **1 June 1982**

BACKGROUND

The enormous Baikonur Cosmodrome in Kazakhstan was one of the former USSR's foremost spaceflight centers and it was from here that the first Soviet space shuttle mission – the Eastern bloc's response to the US *Challenger* program – was launched in November 1988.

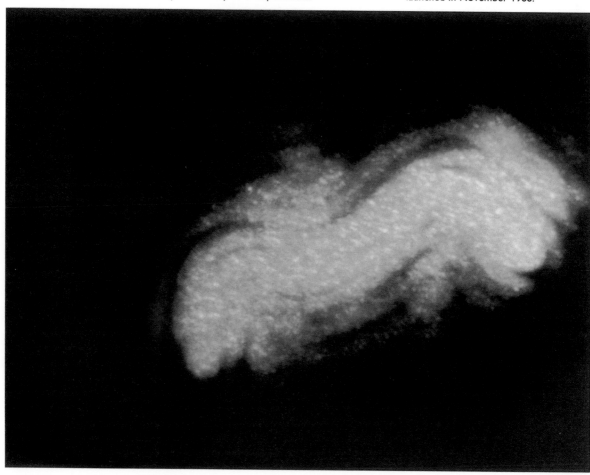

THE EVENTS

Scientists Dr Alexei Zolotov and Dr Vladimir Azhazha reported that on 1 June 1982 two UFOs hovered over the space center. One came down directly toward launch pad #1, while the other stayed near the center's housing complex. The gantries at the launch pad suffered from split welded joints, and rivets had apparently been sucked out of them. At the housing complex, thousands of windows were shattered or holed. The base was closed for two weeks for repairs.

ASSESSMENT

It is possible that UFOs were blamed for a launch pad disaster that the ever-secretive Soviets did not wish to admit. However, skeptic James Oberg confirmed that the Baikonur complex was out of action at this time, but he could not discover why. Welds are actually stronger than the sections of metal they join, so an unusually powerful force must have been behind the damage.

CHILDREN OF ALIENS

The astonishing claims of Debbie Tomey

TYPE: **Close encounter of the fourth kind**
PLACE: **Near Indianopolis, Indiana, USA**
DATE: **30 June-3 October 1983**

BACKGROUND

During the night of 30 June, Debbie Tomey (also known as 'Kathie Davis'), in her late twenties, saw lights seemingly

One of the mysterious lights photographed by the Hessdalen Project conducted in Norway in 1983. The lights temporarily faded in 1985, but in 1994 were appearing again. A new research project was being prepared to monitor the phenomenon.

searching the yard of her house. Next day she found a circular mark on the ground about 8ft (2.5m) across, and a swathe of dead grass 3ft (1m) wide.

THE EVENTS

Under regressive hypnosis conducted by New York artist Budd Hopkins, Tomey recounted how she had gone to investigate the strange lights, been hit by a blast of radiation, and abducted aboard a UFO. A probe was inserted into her abdomen during this time, an object was implanted in her nose, and some kind of suction device was applied to her. She was abducted again on 3 October 1983, while on a late-night trip to a store. The aliens showed her a child that she described as not looking 'like them, but she didn't look like us, either.... She looked like an elf, or an angel.' The girl, Tomey understood, was the result of her impregnation by the aliens during an earlier abduction in the Seventies. Following yet another apparent abduction in April 1986, Tomey maintained the aliens had told her that she she had been impregnated, and the fetus removed to be nurtured by aliens, no fewer than nine times.

ASSESSMENT

These are quite astounding claims, but the evidence for them rests solely on the unsubstantiated 'evidence' of a single person testifying under hypnosis. As such it would not be allowed as evidence in court in most US States. By her own account, Tomey has a long and varied history of physical ailments, which hardly suggests she would make the ideal surrogate mother. And if supposedly 'technologically superior' aliens wish to take advantage of human genes, why do they use gynecological techniques that are primitive even by Earthly standards? Or put 'implants' in the nose, one of the most heavily microbe-infested parts of the human body? If aliens are responsible for Tomey's experience and many similar abduction reports, it seems much more likely that they have been implanting such memories in their victims, for reasons we

can only guess at. There are, however, more cynical suggestions as to who has implanted these memories, albeit unwittingly, in the course of hypnosis.

THE ONE THEY THREW BACK

A fisherman escapes abduction

TYPE: **Close encounter of the third kind**
PLACE: **Basingstoke Canal, Aldershot, Hampshire, England**
DATE: **12 August 1983**

BACKGROUND

77-year-old Alfred Burtoo, with his dog, had settled down by the Basingstoke Canal, not far from a British Army barracks, for an all-night fishing session. He heard a nearby clock strike 1:00am, and was just about to drink a cup of tea from his Thermos.

THE EVENTS

Burtoo saw a brilliant light descending that at first he took for an Army helicopter. It landed on the canal towpath, however, some distance away, and the light went out. Within minutes he was approached by two beings, each 4.5ft (1.5m) tall, wearing greenish overalls and visors over their faces. His dog snarled defensively at them. They gestured to him to follow them, and he did ('I was 77 and didn't have much to lose,' he explained later). The trio came to a rounded object jutting out from the path over the canal, and Burtoo ducked inside the entrance.

Once within the craft, Burtoo was asked his age, and told in 'faltering' English to stand under an amber light, which he did. After some minutes one of the aliens told him: 'You can go. You are too old and infirm for our purpose.' When he returned to his fishing rod, his dog was acting normally but his tea was cold. Shortly afterward he saw the light of

127

September 24, 1947.

MEMORANDUM FOR THE SECRETARY OF DEFENSE

Dear Secretary Forrestal:

As per our recent conversation on this matter, you are hereby authorized to proceed with all due speed and caution upon your undertaking. Hereafter this matter shall be referred to only as Operation Majestic Twelve.

It continues to be my feeling that any future considerations relative to the ultimate disposition of this matter should rest solely with the Office of the President following appropriate discussions with yourself, Dr. Bush and the Director of Central Intelligence.

Harry Truman

Burtoo's wife is definite that he never altered a word of his account from the time he first reported the encounter to the day he died in 1985.

The first of the 'MJ-12' papers, a memorandum in which President Harry S Truman authorizes – or appears to authorize – the establishment of the Majestic Twelve Committee. Other MJ-12 documents purported to show that the Committee was set up to review investigations carried out into the supposed retrieval of alien bodies from the Roswell UFO crash.

the UFO rise up into the sky and fly away at enormous speed. The time was then about 2:00am.

ASSESSMENT

It may be significant that Burtoo went back to his fishing after his encounter and did not return home until 1:00pm the following day, when he told his wife about his sighting, but not (at first) about going aboard the UFO. Burtoo appealed for but did not find any independent witnesses to corroborate his story. Nevertheless

NIGHT SIEGE IN NEW ENGLAND

A giant 'boomerang' in the Hudson Valley

TYPE: **Lights in the sky, multiple witnesses**
PLACE: **Eastern New York State, western Connecticut, USA**
DATE: **31 December 1982 - 10 July 1986**

BACKGROUND

The sightings began in Putnam County, New York, and by the time the series was complete had been seen by a claimed 5000 witnesses. The area in which the UFO (or UFOs) appeared stretched from Peeskill and Ossining, New York, in the west to New Haven, Connecticut, in the east, and from Brookfield, Connecticut in the north to Westport in the south.

THE EVENTS

The objects as reported were gigantic, triangular or boomerang-shaped, and usually silent, although a hum was sometimes heard and, very occasionally, engine noises. An overwhelming percentage of witnesses estimated their size as at least 300ft (90m) in breadth. Speeds generally were said to be 'much slower than a plane'. All sightings were at night: the UFOs showed between five and 15 lights of various colors, which often turned on and off, sometimes changed color, and were sometimes bright enough to illuminate the ground below. The sightings came in distinct clusters at certain times, the most significant being in March 1983 and June and July 1984. The most widely reported event occurred on 12 July as the object traversed five counties. On 24 July, the UFO apparently hovered over the Indian Point nuclear reactor for some time.

ASSESSMENT

The case bears comparison with the 'Williamsport triangle' events of February 1992 (see Chapter Seven). Dozens of witnesses then saw a gigantic triangular or boomerang-shaped object flying at no more than walking pace in the Susquehanna Valley, Pennsylvania. The best explanation in these cases seems to be that they were all unadmitted night refueling exercises conducted by the USAF involving several tankers and many fighters at extremely high altitude. The formation gives the impression of a huge craft moving very slowly at low altitude. But even veteran skeptic Philip J. Klass admitted the Hudson Valley sightings 'could be unexplainable'.

THE MAJESTIC 12 FIASCO

The US government and the 'crashed saucer' saga

TYPE: **Secret UFO-related documents**

PLACE: **The White House and the Pentagon, Washington, DC, USA**

DATE: **Received on 11 December 1984**

BACKGROUND

The 'Majestic 12' documents were taken by many people as proof that a UFO had crashed at Roswell, New Mexico, in 1947 (see Chapter Three), and that the US government had conclusive evidence of alien contact with Earth.

THE EVENTS

On 11 December 1984 Los Angeles TV producer Jaime Shandera received a mail package that contained photographs of two documents, one dated 24 September 1947, the other 18 November 1952. The first was signed by President Harry S. Truman. The second was addressed to President Dwight D. Eisenhower by Admiral Roscoe H. Hillenkoetter. Both were marked 'TOP SECRET'.

```
TOP SECRET / MAJIC
           EYES ONLY
NATIONAL SECURITY INFORMATION
        • • • • • • • • • • • • •
        •  TOP SECRET  •
        • • • • • • • • • • • • •

EYES ONLY                                    COPY ONE OF ONE.




    BRIEFING DOCUMENT: OPERATION MAJESTIC 12

PREPARED FOR PRESIDENT-ELECT DWIGHT D. EISENHOWER: (EYES ONLY)


        18 NOVEMBER, 1952




WARNING! This is a TOP SECRET - EYES ONLY document containing
compartmentalized information essential to the national security
of the United States. EYES ONLY ACCESS to the material herein
is strictly limited to those possessing Majestic-12 clearance
level. Reproduction in any form or the taking of written or
mechanically transcribed notes is strictly forbidden.

        • • • • • • • • • • • • • •
        TOP SECRET / MAJIC       T52-EXEMPT (E)
EYES ONLY    EYES ONLY                 001
```

The first document purported to be a classified executive order from President Truman to Secretary of Defense James Forrestal, and it authorized him, after due consultation with nuclear scientist Dr Vannevar Bush, to establish a board of suitable persons, answerable only to the President, and to be known as 'Majestic 12'. Its job was to investigate the UFO that had crashed near Roswell, New Mexico, in July 1947.

The second document supported the first. It contained a briefing for the newly-

The cover sheet of the second set of 'MJ-12' documents – a 1952 briefing for the new US President, Dwight D. Eisenhower, on the work of the Majestic Twelve. The briefing seems unnecessary. Eisenhower was the senior serving US Army general in 1947, when the Roswell UFO crashed, and would surely have been kept informed of any related developments.

elected President Eisenhower on the members and progress of the MJ-12 group. It consisted of 12 eminent scientists, military men, intelligence experts, engineers and Harvard astronomer Dr Donald Menzel, who was ferociously skeptical about the existence of UFOs.

The first CIA Director, Hillenkoetter had retired from the Navy in June 1957 and soon after was appointed a governor of the National Investigations Committee on Aerial Phenomena (NICAP).

ASSESSMENT

On 29 May 1987 Jaime Shandera and his associates made the papers public, and claimed to know a 'highly placed military intelligence operative' who could authenticate them. However, the 'highly placed' intelligence source turned out to be a USAF sergeant who had previously been convicted of falsifying documents.

Philip J. Klass discovered that the machine used to write the 'executive order' was not produced until 1963. Hillenkoetter signed himself as 'Roscoe H. Hillenkoetter', a form that appears nowhere else in his voluminous correspondence. Klass showed that the Truman signature was photocopied from a letter he had written to Dr Bush on 1 October 1947. As the Hillenkoetter memo refers specifically to the Truman 'special classified executive order' of 1947, it follows that both are fakes.

ZOOMING OVER ZIMBABWE

UFO escapes two air force jets

TYPE: **Daylight disk, multiple witnesses**
PLACE: **Bulawayo, Matabeleland, Zimbabwe**
DATE: **22 July 1985**

BACKGROUND

Residents of six towns in the vicinity reported seeing a UFO over Bulawayo. At 5:45pm, two Hawk interceptors of the Zimbabwe Air Force (ZAF) were scrambled from Thornhill air base to investigate, making this the country's first ever military/UFO encounter.

THE EVENTS

Bulawayo airport had the UFO on radar, and it was visible to observers on the ground. It had a rounded shape with a small cone above it, and shone so brightly in the afternoon sunlight that other details were indistinct. The ZAF Hawks approached the UFO as it hovered at an altitude of 7000ft (2000m), but it then shot up to 70,000ft (21,000m) in less than a minute. The Hawks pursued it to 31,000ft (9500m) and then abandoned the chase as the UFO leveled off. It then followed the jets back to Thornhill before finally shooting away at high speed.

ASSESSMENT

The jets' gun cameras were not loaded, so no film of the UFO was taken. It seems certain from its reported behavior it was not a balloon, and it is curious that no sonic boom was reported when it ascended at a speed well over Mach 1. ZAF Air Marshal Azim Daudpota said: 'It was no illusion, no deception, no imagination.'

THE CURIOUS CASE OF WHITLEY STRIEBER

Was he abducted, or was he not?

TYPE: **Close encounter of the fourth kind**
PLACE: **New York State, USA**
DATE: **27 December 1985**

BACKGROUND

Science and horror fantasy novelist Whitley Strieber was staying with his wife and son in their isolated cabin in upper New York State. He had for some time been apprehensive of intruders, and before going to bed at about 11:00pm he set an elaborate alarm system.

THE EVENTS

Strieber was awoken in the early hours of the morning of 27 December by a strange 'whooshing' noise as if several people were in the room downstairs. The alarm had not sounded. A figure then rushed into the room. Strieber's next conscious recollection was of sitting in the woods outside his house. From conscious memories pieced together with those retrieved under hypnosis, it transpired that Strieber was floated from his house on a 'black iron cot' aboard a UFO. Here, in a messy chamber, he encountered entities of four different kinds: a small, robotic type; a short, stocky type, wearing blue coveralls; and two more, both about 5ft (1.5m) tall, 'very slender and delicate', one of which had 'mesmerizing black slanting eyes', the other black, button-like eyes. One of the

entities turned out to be hermaphrodite. The aliens inserted a needle into his brain, an 'enormous and extremely ugly object' with a network of wires on the end into his rectum, and made an incision in his finger. Under hypnosis Strieber recalled seeing comatose soldiers on tables inside the UFO, as well as his sister and his father.

ASSESSMENT

Strieber's hypnotist, Dr Donald F. Klein, wondered if the author was suffering from 'temporal lobe epilepsy', which can produce hallucinations. Strieber admits that many of the stories he has told about himself over the years were simply fantasies, but he rejected the doctor's diagnosis. In 1987, he was paid $1 million as an advance for his book *Communion*,

which recounts his abduction. In a foreword to Dr Kenneth Ring's *The Omega Project*, Strieber announced in 1993 that he had not been abducted by aliens.

UPROAR OVER SÃO PAULO

A fleet of UFOs versus Brazil's Air Force

TYPE: **Multiple radar visuals**
PLACE: **São Paulo and Rio de Janeiro, Brazil**
DATE: **19 May 1986**

BACKGROUND

Brazil has one of the highest rates of UFO reporting in the world. This is often ascribed to complex cultural and religious influences, which implies a high proportion of imaginative accounts. These events are less easily dismissed.

THE EVENTS

For about three hours after 9:00pm, military and civil radars showed numerous UFOs in the vicinity of São Paulo and Rio de Janeiro – about 200 miles (300km) apart on the coast – and in the state of Goias, in central Brazil. Pilots flying to and from airports here reported sightings and UFOs on their airbone radars. Among the sightings were the following:

- At 9:10pm, Ospires Silva, president of the state oil company Petrobras, was about to land his plane at São Jose dos Campos when he and his companion saw orange-red lights and gave chase to them. The lights blinked on and off, reappearing in a new location each time. After 30 minutes Silva abandoned the chase.

- At 10:23pm, three Norththrop F-5E Tiger fighters took off from Santa Cruz AFB near São Paulo. One came within 12 miles (20km) of a UFO changing color from white to green, which sped out to sea. Another Tiger pursued a UFO changing colors from red to white to green to red, but ran low on fuel before closing with it. Both UFOs were showing on both ground and airborne radar.

- At 10:50pm, a Dassault Mirage III fighter was surrounded by about a dozen UFOs, invisible except on radar until they climbed above the fighter at speeds impossible for conventional aircraft.

São Paulo, Brazil, one of the busiest UFO 'hotspots' in the world, apparently receives a visit from a UFO. The photograph was taken on 9 May 1984 by Amilton Vieira. It is striking that no one else in this clearly lively city failed to notice the huge glowing object overhead and also photographed it. Had the citizens of São Paulo been more alert, the pictures would surely have made front-page news around the world.

ASSESSMENT

UFOs playing cat-and-mouse games with interceptors sometimes turn out to be stars and planets. In these cases, the number of radar reports and eye-witnesses suggest structured objects were involved.

ON THE TRAIL OF A JUMBO JET

A massive UFO in Alaskan skies

TYPE: **Radar-visual**
PLACE: **Near Fort Ukon, Alaska, USA**
DATE: **17 November 1986**

BACKGROUND

Japan Airlines (JAL) Flight 1628, a Boeing 747 cargo plane with a crew of three, was en route from Iceland to Anchorage, Alaska. At 5:10pm the jet was flying at 35,000ft (10,500m) on a 215° heading over north-east Alaska.

THE EVENTS

At 5:11pm, the crew noticed lights to their left and below them. They first assumed they were from USAF planes. Then the lights suddenly swept up and in front of them, 'shooting off lights', so that the cockpit was lit up and, according to the captain, 'I felt warm in the face.' The lights, possibly a double array on a single object, first looked like two rectangular displays one above the other. They then switched abruptly to a side-by-side position. The crew contacted regional Air Traffic Control (ATC) for details of the unknown 'aircraft' in front of them. ATC had no sign on radar of the UFO. Radio communications in both directions now became garbled, but were restored to normality when the UFO moved away to the port side of JAL1628, but two white lights remained ahead, pacing the plane.

While ATC was contacting the USAF, asking if its radars had any returns from the vicinity of the freighter, the captain of the JAL 747 turned his weather radar sideways. It showed a large object about eight miles (12km) away. USAF and civilian ATC radars were now showing unidentified 'blips' around the plane. The white lights then dropped behind the plane and were lost to sight, disappearing from radar screens at the same time. At about 5:50pm, near Fairbanks, Alaska, the JAL captain checked what was happening behind the plane and saw a gigantic Saturn-shaped UFO. The crew was now definitely alarmed, and the captain requested permission to change course; this took some time to get through because of further radio distortion. The UFO followed the JAL freighter as it turned, and the captain asked to descend to a lower altitude. But there was no need. He turned the 747 sharply and the object disappeared.

ASSESSMENT

Most strange lights in the night sky turn out to be misidentified stars, planets, or aircraft. While the ground radar returns in this case are ambiguous and the UFO trailing the plane may have been a misidentification made under stress, it seems unlikely that the rectangular light arrays, in full view of the crew, were from any natural or man-made object.

STRANGE DAYS IN GULF BREEZE

A small town becomes the tourist center of the UFO world

TYPE: **Close encounters of the third and fourth kind**
PLACE: **Gulf Breeze, Pensacola, Florida, USA**
DATE: **November 1987– May 1988**

BACKGROUND

At about 5:00pm on 11 November 1987, builder and property developer Ed Walters and his son were alone in separate rooms in the family house. Mrs Frances Walters and their daughter were both out. From his office window Walters saw a UFO moving behind some pines across the street.

THE EVENTS

Walters grabbed a Polaroid and snapped several pictures. Running into the street to take more, he was 'zapped' by a blue beam of light and immobilized. There was a powerful odor of cinnamon, and his feet began to lift off the ground. He heard a

Aviation expert and UFO skeptic Philip J. Klass looks characteristically underwhelmed as he stands by a display of Ed Walters' UFO photographs from Gulf Breeze, Florida. The case generated enormous controversy in UFO circles for some time.

voice in his head say: 'We will not harm you.' When Walters continued to resist, his mind was filled with images of dogs. Then the light was gone, and he crashed to the ground. The UFO had vanished.

Walters had many more sightings, and took many more photographs, over the following five months. The UFO was always the same, about 12ft (3.5m) across and 9ft (2.7m) high, with a brilliantly-lit 7.5ft (2.5m) wide 'power ring' below. The UFO's arrival was generally preceded by a strange hum inside his head, which investigators speculated was produced by an implant in his head, put there during an abduction early in his life. Certainly he had had some strange experiences in his youth, and one could be interpreted as an abduction; the event also involved memories, or images, of dogs. On 2 December, he encountered an alien in his back yard, and chased it away. On 12 January 1988, he was in his pick-up truck and came upon the UFO hovering over the road, and photographed it. This time, a white beam of light paralysed Walters as he hid under his truck. Aliens emerged from the UFO and made for the truck, but Walters was somehow able to get into the vehicle and escape. On 7 February, the UFO visited the Walters' house again, and Frances Walters narrowly missed being 'zapped' by a blue beam – an event that Ed Walters managed to catch on film. At 1:10am on 1 May, Walters took his 39th UFO picture, was surrounded by white light, and blanked out. He came to at 2:25am. He has speculated that during this time he was abducted, and the implant that warned of an approaching UFO was then removed.

The case received massive national publicity, and as a result Gulf Breeze attracted enormous numbers of 'sky-watchers' intent on seeing UFOs if and when they came again, and indeed some people have seen repeat performances. But even before Gulf Breeze hit the headlines, several local people took photographs of UFOs or reported sightings that often coincided with the dates and times of Walters' experiences.

ASSESSMENT

Despite the multiple witnesses, Ed Walters' successful polygraph tests, the testimony of Frances Walters, and the endorsement of Budd Hopkins, photographic expert Dr Bruce Maccabee, and Walt Andrus of MUFON, the Gulf Breeze sightings generated an almost unprecedented furor in ufological circles. And with reason. On the one hand, Walters took high-quality pictures with sealed stereoscopic cameras as well as with his own Polaroid, sometimes in front of witnesses, although they never saw the UFOs themselves. On the other hand, Dr Maccabee had a financial interest in Walters' best-selling book about his experiences; and it is not impossible to fake 'special effects' with a Polaroid. Then, someone found a model UFO remarkably like the one in Walters' photographs in the loft of his house, and then a young man revealed he had helped Walters to fake his UFO photos, and produced film to prove it. Meanwhile, UFO tourists descended on Gulf Breeze, and many took pictures of UFOs; at the same time, pranksters were sending up brightly lit, miniature hot-air balloons into the Pensacola skies. It seems to have been one of these that Dr Maccabee himself photographed in May 1992. It looks as if it will be years before the dust settles and a properly informed assessment can be made of this case.

THE CAR THAT FLEW

An Australian family unwillingly takes to the air

TYPE: **Close encounter of the second kind**
PLACE: **Nullarbor Plain, near Mundrabilla, Western Australia**
DATE: **21 January 1988**

BACKGROUND

Fay Knowles and her three sons, plus two dogs, were driving from Perth east toward Mundrabilla across the Nullarbor Plain. At about 1:30am, their car radio began to malfunction. At about 1:45am, the quartet saw lights in the distance; as the car approached, it became clear that there was only one light.

THE EVENTS

The light was hovering by the side of the highway. Sean Knowles, who was driving, did not realize until the last moment that it was glowing down on another vehicle. He swerved violently to avoid a crash and then hung a U to see what was happening. The light flew on up the road, with the Knowles vehicle in hot pursuit. Then the light began to head back toward the car. Sean turned again, but the UFO caught up. Something landed on the car roof with a distinct thump, and the vehicle seemed to rise up. Fay Knowles rolled down a window and put her hand out to feel the object above. She said it felt 'warm and spongy'. Otherwise, there was chaos in the car. One son said that he felt as if his brains were being pulled out of his head. Sean, the driver, passed out briefly. The dogs were going berserk. Dust was swirling in through the open window, and there was a smell of decomposing bodies.

Then the UFO let go of the car. It crashed to the ground, bursting a tire. Sean brought it under control, stopped, and the family jumped out and hid by the side of the highway until the UFO flew off. They could now see that the light was about the same size as the car, white, with a yellow center. A kind of electrical hum came from it. When it had gone, one of the weirder effects of the experience emerged: for about 15 minutes, every-one's voice became very high-pitched, as if they had been breathing helium. In this state, the family changed the wheel and drove on to Mundrabilla.

ASSESSMENT

There have been strong suggestions that the Knowles case is a hoax, or at best an hallucination, brought on by driving late at night in the desert. Possibly the travelers fell asleep, and the car ran off the road and burst a tire. Possibly 'white line fever' brought about the same result. The motive for a hoax need be no more than a desire for fame, however brief. However, at about the same time, a fishing boat out for tuna off the Western Australian coast was also closely approached by a UFO that left the same after-effect on the crew – a short period of speaking in squeaky voices. Neither set

of witnesses was apparently aware of the other's experience when they reported their encounters.

A UFO WITH HUMOR

Cryptic banter with a British witness

TYPE: **Close encounter of the first kind**

PLACE: **Tetbury, Gloucestershire, England**

DATE: **24 March 1988**

BACKGROUND

At 10:15pm, the witness – known only as Mr R – was in the kitchen of his house in a remote rural location, looking out of the window. He saw a light cross a field some 300 yards (270m) away. He first thought it might be from a lamp carried by a shepherd rounding up sheep – this being the lambing season, with flocks vulnerable to attack by foxes – but it seemed too far from the ground. He went to the end of his garden to get a clearer view of the field, but the light seemed to have vanished. Then, without

An unusual pentagonal UFO captured on film by Akira Maezuka as it hovered over Shiogama City, about 190 miles (300 km) north of Tokyo, Japan. Two sets of people, a group of 16 adults and another of schoolchildren and their parents, witnessed the event. According to the first witnesses, the UFO first appeared as a black lozenge, then changed shape briefly. First seen at 11:30am, it hovered for a while and eventually rose and disappeared 25 minutes later. Its behavior was consistent with a well-controled kite in a good breeze – perhaps a kite set up to alter its appearance and capable of being released to fly free. The Japan Space Phenomena Society rejected this explanation of the event.

warning, he was surrounded by a glow that came from directly above. He glimpsed an object about twice the size of a football. Its glow did not light the ground around him.

THE EVENTS

Alarmed, Mr R cried out: 'What's going on?' To his amazement, he got a reply, in a voice that 'sounded tinny and unnatural,' and found himself in conversation with some unknown entity, who spoke rather stilted and sometimes ungrammatical English. The dialogue went as follows:

'*We are just observing your world.*'

'Well, you've come to the wrong part to see anything,' riposted Mr R.

'*We know where we are.*'

'When you say "we", who do you mean? Aliens or something?'

'*No – no aliens here. What you see is a probe, similar to how your scientists send out to observe other planets.*'

'How can you understand me?'

'*Your voice is recorded on the probe and relayed to us for reply.*'

'Oh, that's clever. But I'm not sure what's happening. Why are you observing us? What's the matter?'

'*You are gaining knowledge so fast and getting to the very basis of the structure of matter, and you could cause untold harm if you don't know what you are doing.*'

'Well, I don't know about that. I'm not a scientific man. I suppose it makes some sense.'

'*If your species don't learn some sense we will have to take measures against you.*'

'What do you mean? Are you going to exterminate us?'

'*No – nothing like that. We'd have to take action to reduce your activities.*'

'Could you do that?'

'*Oh yes, easily. Wouldn't take much to upset your order of things.*'

'What would you propose to do then?'

'*You are very susceptible to bacteria and viruses. Something like that would cause disorganization.*'

'You could introduce this into our world?'

'*Yes, of course.*'

'How will we know it's you?'

'*You won't know. We don't propose to tell you.*'

'Where are you operating from? Where are you?'

'*Ah, well, you're not clever enough to understand that, are you?*'

'I quite agree. I'm not an astronomer. Do you come from far away?'

'*Well – quite a distance.*'

'Are you in what we call our solar system?'

'*We may be.*'

'Farther afield?'

'*We may be. There's no point in asking such questions.*'

'What is really the problem? How come you are allowing it to go on? Why not just nip it in the bud?'

'*Explain what you mean by "nip it in the bud".*'

'Alter it before it gets too far advanced.'

'*Oh yes – we could do that.*'

The light around Mr R then went out. The encounter was over.

ASSESSMENT

Mr R thought the 'probe' had some connection with the nearby USAF base at Kemble. It is not known why he thought this but perhaps the thing spoke with an American accent. If so, was Mr R being manipulated as Dr Paul Bennewitz was?

GIANTS IN THE SUBURBS

Huge aliens seen in Russia

TYPE: **Close encounter of the third kind**

PLACE: **Perm and Voronezh, Russia**

DATE: **July 1989 and October 1989**

BACKGROUND

Two reports in summer and autumn 1989 confirmed rumors that a wave of sightings involving spherical UFOs with varying

numbers of giant occupants occurred at this time across Russia west of the Urals.

THE EVENTS

According to the news agency TASS, in July a milkmaid and other witnesses had seen two orange globes land near the city of Perm on the Volga River. Unusually tall entities with small heads had emerged. One globe was photographed.

In October, TASS reported that a spherical UFO had landed in a park in a suburb of Voronezh, 300 miles (480km) south of Moscow, and afterwards witnesses reported seeing two giant aliens, also with disproportionately small heads, nearby. With them was a small robot-like creature. Witnesses suffered from panic attacks for several days following the sighting. Russian scientists who investigated the site shortly after the events found what they thought might have been traces of some sort of aircraft landing – a depression that was 60ft (18m) wide together with four deep unexplained dents in the grass.

ASSESSMENT

Perm and Voronezh are 700 miles (1130km) apart, so the similarity of the sightings is intriguing. But details are scant, and the photos are poor. Also, folklore may have played a part in both events. Yet there are odd details in the Voronezh sightings. Some witnesses saw the UMMO symbol on the UFO, and there were reports of teleportations.

MANHATTAN TRANSFER

The Linda Cortile case and its witnesses

TYPE: **Multiple witness abduction**
PLACE: **Manhattan Island, New York, USA**
DATE: **30 November 1989**

BACKGROUND

In April 1989, 45-year-old New Yorker Linda Cortile (pseudonym: a.k.a. 'Linda

Linda Cortile, who claims to have been abducted from the 12th floor of an East Side apartment house in Manhattan at the end of November 1989.

Napolitano') began regressive hypnosis with researcher Budd Hopkins. She suspected that she had been abducted by aliens in her twenties.

THE EVENTS

On 30 November, Mrs Cortile reported to Hopkins that she had been abducted again – at around 3:15 that very morning. She had fragmentary conscious memories of what had happened. She had gone to bed at about 3:00am; her husband was already asleep. Almost at once she began to feel a paralysing numbness creeping from her feet up her body. From previous experience she knew this was a prelude to an abduction. She tried to wake her husband, but to no avail. She saw that a gray entity had appeared in the room, and threw a pillow at it. Then she became totally paralysed, and her mind went blank, although she vaguely recalled someone palpating her spine. The next thing she remembered was being back in her bed.

Under hypnosis, Mrs Cortile recollected that three or four aliens had come into the room. Then she had been 'floated' through the closed window of her 12th-storey East Side apartment by the aliens, had entered a blue beam of light, and was taken aboard a craft that was hovering above the building. She was given a medical examination, then taken back and dropped onto her bed from mid-air. Her violent return failed to wake her husband. Fearing he and her two sons had been killed by the aliens, she checked their breathing with a mirror held under their noses. They were unharmed.

About 15 months later, in February 1991, Hopkins received a letter from two men claiming to be police officers. They said that they had seen Mrs Cortile's abduction, from a car parked under the FDR Drive, just a few blocks from her apartment house. She had floated 'like an angel' through the air into the UFO, which was 'about three quarters the size of the builiding across'. Then the UFO had gained altitude, flown over FDR Drive, and plunged into the East River not far from the Brooklyn Bridge. They had considered visiting the block to find the woman and check the reality of what they had seen. They were particularly concerned to know if the victim were alive and well, for they had waited 45 minutes but not seen the UFO emerge from the river. The officers signed themselves Richard and Dan.

Hopkins warned Mrs Cortile that she might be visited by the pair. She was upset that an experience she had hoped was imaginary seemed to be all too true. Some weeks later she reported that Richard and Dan had called on her, and were visibly relieved to find her safe and well. They refused to speak to Hopkins in person, for fear of public exposure, but agreed to contact him.

Soon afterwards Hopkins received additional letters, drawings of the event and a taped account from one of the officers. He explained that they could not meet Hopkins because he and his partner were in fact Secret Service agents. On the night of the abduction they had been taking Perez de Cuellar, then Secretary-General of the United Nations, to a heliport after a secret meeting, when their limousine inexplicably broke down. They had pushed it to a safe place within a couple of blocks of Mrs Cortile's apartment house. De Cuellar had also witnessed the entire episode. Hopkins concluded that the aliens involved in the Cortile abduction had been deliberately demonstrating their powers and the reality of their presence on Earth, to a man of international standing and influence.

Linda Cortile experienced two more abductions in 1991, but not by aliens. One afternoon in April, Richard and Dan forced her into a car while she was out walking and asked her a series of bizarre questions. For example: was she an alien? They demanded that she remove her

shoes to prove she had toes because, they said, aliens had no toes. Mrs Cortile somehow noted that the car was being followed. Hypnosis later revealed the license plate numbers of the trailing car and the one she was in. Hopkins traced them to the British and Venezuelan missions to the United Nations.

On 15 October, she was kidnapped by Dan, who shoved her into red Jaguar and drove her to a beach house on Long Island. There, among other indignities, he made her disrobe and put on a white nightgown like the one she had been wearing when abducted. Mrs Cortile tape-recorded some of this encounter, which was cut short when Richard arrived and managed to sedate Dan. She later received a letter from Dan, written from a mental institution, that is clearly the product of an unhinged mind.

In November 1991 Hopkins received a letter and drawings from a grandmother, a retired telephone operator in her sixties whom he calls 'Janet Kimble', whose car had mysteriously, temporarily, failed as she crossed Brooklyn Bridge, within sight of the Cortile apartment about a quarter-mile away, on the night Mrs Cortile was abducted. The bridge lights had blacked out too, and the other cars on the bridge also broke down. Mrs Kimble claimed to have seen the UFO, the aliens and Mrs Cortile being floated into the craft, even though the UFO was shining so brightly that she had to shield her eyes from it. Drawings of the event by this witness and one of the 'Secret Service agents' matched in many details.

ASSESSMENT

Hopkins considered this the 'case of the century'. Other ufologists disagreed. For them it was too much to believe that four crucial witnesses should contact only Hopkins and no other investigators; that no one working at the busy night loading bay of the *New York Post*, right opposite the apartment, noticed anything unusual; and that there was never any corroboration of the statement that many cars simultaneously failed on Brooklyn Bridge.

 Budd Hopkins, the New York artist who conducted the program of regressive hypnosis on Linda Cortile.

It also seems unlikely that a breakdown of the UN Secretary General's car and its communications equipment would last so long without investigation. In fact, the UN insists that de Cuellar was not at a heliport at that hour on 30 November, and was at home in bed. Still more obscure is why the 'Secret Service agents' Dan and Richard waited more than 15 months to present themselves to Mrs Cortile when they were so concerned about her welfare, and what significance there is in the facts that they contacted Budd Hopkins first and have been met in person only by Mrs Cortile. Whether or not Linda Cortile was actually abducted by aliens that night, it seems reasonable to conclude that some people, if not Cortile herself, have been putting Hopkins on in order to strengthen or confuse the case, and he has believed them. (Hopkins is not a person, in this author's judgement, who would ever create a hoax, but he may be susceptible to one.) Further evidence may eventually reveal the truth of this matter. But it will be a long time coming.

CHAPTER 7

International Enigma

THE END OF THE COLD WAR BRINGS

A FLOOD OF INFORMATION FROM THE EAST

The collapse of the Soviet empire brought political and economic liberty to millions of people. No less fundamentally, it brought them freedom of expression. Information of all kinds at last flowed freely across the borders, and among it was up-to-date news of UFO experiences from the former Soviet bloc. Meetings were held between eastern and western ufologists to discuss scientific approaches to the enigma and to exchange data. At much the same time, the Chinese Communist authorities relaxed their former disapproving stance on ufology, and contacts between them and the West became more open than ever before.

The reports from the former Soviet bloc and China were intriguing indeed. For while they showed that UFOs were apparently visiting all parts of the world with striking frequency, many accounts from the East had a strangely dated feel to them. The phenomena often seemed to be less complex, less technologically developed, in the East. As the Nineties progress, this curious aspect of ufology promises to yield a rich controversy between those who believe UFOs are

An 'unknown aerial phenomenon' photographed by Rod Dickinson as it flew over Gould's Hill, Dorset, at 11:00 am on 21 December 1993.

'off-world' hardware and those who look for social and psychological explanations for UFO experiences.

The broad divisions among ufologists were becoming increasingly a matter of geography. British ufologist John Spencer called the USA 'the last bastion of the Extra-Terrestrial Hypothesis (ETH)', and noted that in Europe many different approaches to the problem existed side by side, largely in mutual respect – none was dismissive of the others, and each was largely complementary. In contrast, in the USA, research was dominated by abduction cases, and controversies tended to split those interested into 'believers' and those who shouted 'Hoax!' at the earliest opportunity. Reactions to the Gulf Breeze incidents of the Eighties (first reported in full in 1990) and the Linda Cortile case – which was still developing in 1994 – threatened to tear US ufology apart, polarising opinion and leaving few in the middle ground.

In Europe, skepticism toward the ETH took more forms than outright disbelief or debunking, for researchers there seemed to find it easier to accept the idea that there may be as many solutions to the UFO enigma as the enigma has facets.

Researcher Paul Devereux developed his 'Earthlights' hypothesis to include the possibility that abduction experiences resulted from a combination of electromagnetic natural phenomena – the initial

'UFO' sighting – and states of both consciousness and the biochemistry of the brain. Devereux was also planning a major research program to discover whether earthlights react to human consciousness. In a parallel move, Andrew Collins developed the work of James Trevor Constable in attempting to attract and photograph UFO-like entities that may be sentient and aware of a human presence. In Spain, Vicente-Juan Ballester Olmos and in France the government-sponsored study group GEPAN continued to investigate cases with solid scientific rigor. The most influential French ufologist, Jacques Vallée, published a mass of new data from his base in the USA to support his belief that UFOs represent a species of control system over human thought and action. Danish, Finnish, Norwegian and Swedish ufologists continued to add methodically to the carefully researched stock of data they had compiled over a number of years on the phenomenon in Scandinavia.

Such a variety of approaches, with the new internationalism of UFO reporting, will ensure that as the enigma thrives so will the search for scientifically convincing answers to it – well into the future.

UFO

UFOS OVER PUERTO RICO

Were they chased, or were they escorted?

TYPE: **Lights in the sky, daylight disk**
PLACE: **Various locations, Puerto Rico, West Indies**
DATE: **July 1989–April 1992**

BACKGROUND

Sightings from 1989 onward over Puerto Rico have often involved military jets, which seem sometimes to pursue and sometimes to escort the UFOs. Some

 **Below: An F-14 Grumman Tomcat, a supersonic multi-role aircraft that forms the backbone of the US Navy's strike force. Jets strikingly like F-14s, with wings swung back, were seen by José Antonio Valdés chasing a UFO across eastern Puerto Rico on 22 June 1990. Opposite page: Valdés' sketch of the UFO and a fighter in pursuit.**

investigators believe there is an alien base on the island. A selection follows of reports over the period.

THE EVENTS

At 8:30pm on 4 July 1989, F-14s from Roosevelt Roads Naval Air Station at Ceiba were seen by several witnesses from the nearby town of Luquillo, in hot pursuit of 'a very big and brilliant blue-white star' that performed several bizarre maneuvers near Mount El Yunque before heading south-east across the Sierra de Luquillo, with the jets still trailing it.

In the evening of 22 June 1990, three witnesses saw four F-14 Tomcats chasing 'a round ball of yellow light with a very bright red light in its center' flying south-west over the Rio Guyate near Route 52, in the eastern part of the island. The F-14s were followed in turn by an AWACS radar surveillance aircraft.

At 5:30pm on 19 December 1990, some residents of Caguas saw unmarked military helicopters in pursuit of a similar yellow and red light 'as big as a 747 [jumbo jet]' and 'flying totally noiselessly', which disappeared among the mountains.

At about 5:00pm on 28 April 1992 Freddie Cruz was repairing his truck near Lajas when a saucer-shaped, metallic UFO came in sight, hotly pursued by a US Navy F-14 Tomcat. The UFO, a little larger than the aircraft, stopped and started in the air then split in two, one half flying off to the south-west, the other to the east.

ASSESSMENT

The US Navy's Atlantic Fleet Weapons Training Facility (AFWTF) has its head-quarters hard by Roosevelt Roads Naval Air Station, and controls two ocean firing ranges – Alfa, some 120,000 square miles (195,000 sq km) in area, to the north and east of the island, and Bravo, 74,000 square miles (120,000 sq km) in extent, to the south-east. Among the hardware tested by AFWTF are cruise missiles and electronic warfare devices. The US Navy is also developing advanced fighters using unconventional airfoils – swept-forward wings, for instance. The Federal Hypo-thesis would suggest that these are either disguised as UFOs to cover tests that the local population might find objectionable (such as flying a cruise missile over urban areas) or could easily be mistaken for 'flying saucers', especially at dusk.

THE BELGIAN TRIANGLES

Unprecedented co-operation to identify UFOs

TYPE: **Radar-visual**
PLACE: **Belgian airspace**
DATE: **30-31 March 1990**

BACKGROUND

From November 1989 to March 1990 the Belgian authorities received over 2500 reports of triangular UFOs. The Royal Belgian Air Force (RBAF) agreed that if the local UFO research group, SOBEPS, co-ordinated reports at ground level, the RBAF itself would track and intercept.

THE EVENTS

On the night of 30-31 March, police and civilians linked to SOBEPS reported a UFO flying across Belgium. RBAF radars at Glons and Semmerzake confirmed the sightings, and two F-16 Fighting Falcons were scrambled to intercept. The UFO flew very slowly at 6500ft (1950m) until the F-16s' radar locked on to it. Then it accelerated hard and dived to below 650ft (200m), where it was lost to radar amid 'ground clutter'.

ASSESSMENT

The USAF may have been testing its 'stealth' aircraft. But F-16s can fly twice as fast as stealth aircraft. If the intruders were F-117s or B-2s, how did they manage to outpace the Belgian jets? It has even been suggested that both F-16 chase and radar images were an official hoax, designed to distract attention from the flight of a secret military probe: French radars allegedly picked up no trace of either the F-16s or the UFO.

ALIEN RETALIATION – OR SOMETHING ELSE?

Information or disinformation from Turkestan

TYPE: **Close encounter of the second kind**
PLACE: **Mary, Turkmenistan (former USSR)**
DATE: **25 May 1990**

BACKGROUND

Turkmenistan air space was controled by the Soviet 12th Air Defense Army. The war in Afghanistan made access strictly limited and closely monitored.

THE EVENTS

In daylight, a reddish-orange UFO with an estimated diameter of 1000ft (300m) hovered over the town of Mary at an altitude of 3000ft (900m). The commander of the local air defense division, Colonel Anatoli Kurkchy, ordered three SAM missiles to be fired at the UFO, which responded with three beams of light from its port side which destroyed the missiles. Two jet interceptors were scrambled but, as they closed on the UFO, they were hurled out of the sky. Both planes crashed and the crews were killed.

ASSESSMENT

Some details of the case are strikingly similar to those reported from Rybinsk, Russia, in summer 1961 (Chapter Four). It is possible that both are folklore stories. In November 1991, General Kremenchuk of the Air Defense staff of the Leningrad (St Petersburg) region denied that these events had occurred at all or that there was a Col. Kurkchy. However, a colonel on Kremenchuk's own staff asserted that the colonel did exist, and that he commanded the air defense of a nuclear proving ground on the island of Novaya Zemlya. Who was telling the truth?

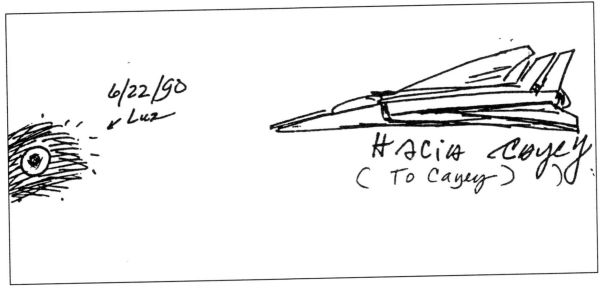

6/22/90
↙ Luz

HACia cayey
(To Cayey)

'NO CONVENTIONAL AIRCRAFT'

The mystery at Hoyt Lakes

TYPE: **Radar-visual**
PLACE: **Hoyt Lakes, near Skibo, Minnesota, USA**
DATE: **10 October 1990**

BACKGROUND

At around 9:00pm residents around Skibo began reporting unusual lights that had started appearing in the sky to the south-east of the nearby Hoyt Lakes. Two police officers sent to investigate saw, as did other witnesses, certain objects 'of indeterminate shape, alternately hovering and darting about.'

THE EVENTS

An hour after the first reports, Air Traffic Controlers (ATCs) at Duluth confirmed they had picked up radar echoes from the Hoyt Lakes area, and for more than an hour after that one of the ATCs at Duluth monitored the echoes. There were between three and five objects registering intermittently on the screen in roughly circular formation. The local National Air Guard radar also picked up the same returns.

Further confirmation that something strange was in the air that night came from the pilot of a commercial aircraft flying at 11,000ft (3300m) 45 miles (72km) west of Hoyt Lakes reported two steady, distinct, unidentified lights 1000ft (300m) below him. They were a few miles apart and a deep, glowing red.

ASSESSMENT

Investigators noted that no other conventional aircraft were in the area at the time, and 'no known weather factors accounted for anomalous radar returns.' There has been little further research into the causes and origins of the object and the lights, and so, despite the large number of independent witnesses, the incident remains unexplained.

THE ATTACK AT SAMARA

A triangular UFO destroys a military installation

TYPE: Radar visual, close encounter of the second kind
PLACE: Near Samara (then named Kuybyshev), Russia
DATE: 13 December 1990

BACKGROUND

At 12:07am the watch at the Kuybyshev (Samara) long-range radar tracking station saw a blip appear on their screens at a range of 60 miles (100km). They later described the blip as having been 'comparable to that of a strategic bomber.'

THE EVENTS

The station's automatic electronic Identify Friend or Foe (IFF) system failed, preventing the watch from identifying whether the aircraft was hostile or not. Two and a half minutes after its first appearance, the large blip then scattered into a host of smaller returns. By the time these were within 25 miles (40km) of the station, the largest had started to show as a triangular-shaped object, and was now heading straight for the radar post. As it approached, a team of soldiers was

A UFO shows off its legs. This photo was taken at about 2:00pm on 4 February 1990 by Dima Girenko, near Solnechnoye, in the Achtyrka district of Sumy, Ukraine. A report from the Moscow Aviation Institute declared the photograph 'no hoax', although an experienced analyst could easily show how the picture might have been faked. The object slightly resembles a miniature 20 inch (50cm) UFO, also displaying legs, reported in the USA by two independent witnesses from Yorba Linda, California, and from Wapello, Iowa, in the early part of 1967.

scrambled to find out what was going on: the thing shot over their heads, at a height of less than 30ft (9m), as they came out into the open. Then it stopped, and began hovering about 300ft (90m) beyond a barbed-wire barrier that lay less than 150ft (45m) from a mobile, short-range radar array known as Post No 12. There was a flash, and No 12's paired aerials caught fire; as a result, shortly afterwards the upper aerial collapsed to the ground.

Later inspection by Soviet government analysts revealed that all the steel parts of Post No 12's aerials had been melted, presumably by the flash. Witnesses – among them both officers and enlisted men – described the mysterious triangle they had seen as black and 'smooth... not mirror-like – it was like a thick layer of soot'. According to their accounts, the sides of the object were about 45ft (14m) long, and it was about 10ft (3m) thick. There were neither openings nor portholes on the craft. The machine remained hovering for about 90 minutes after destroying the radar. Then it took off again and disappeared completely into the night sky.

ASSESSMENT

A Soviet Defense Ministry commission investigated the Kuybyshev site on 18 September 1990, and removed from it the wrecked upper aerial of radar array Post No 12 for detailed scientific analysis. Unnamed military sources later claimed to have examined the site and to have seen tapes of the first radar returns. The description of both these on-screen radar effects and the craft itself suggest all the characteristics of known 'stealth' technology. And yet no known stealth aircraft can hover, and it is difficult to believe that any American stealth aircraft would have perpetrated such a provocation, particularly given the danger of a resulting nuclear confrontation between the two superpowers who – even at this late stage in the history of the USSR, almost immediately before the union dissolved – were still in Cold War mode.

THE FARIBAULT RECTANGLE

UFO and mystery planes in Minnesota

TYPE: Light in the sky
PLACE: Faribault, Minnesota, USA
DATE: 2 April 1991

BACKGROUND

At about 7:00pm, Dick Feichtinger was driving to work in his car when he saw above him a curious, white, long and narrow rectangular object apparently hanging vertically in the sky above the town of Faribault.

THE EVENTS

The object was still there when Dick Feichtinger returned from work later that evening. It was now colored red and green. Feichtinger called his wife and children; as they watched, it changed color from red to green then went back to its original solid white. Neighbors also watched the weird rectangle – which 'seemed to be intelligently guided.'

At this point two aircraft cruised low over the houses. Said one neighbor: 'I thought they were going to land on my house.' And they were flying so slowly that Feichtinger said, 'I couldn't figure out what was keeping them up there.' He waved at them as he stood under a street light, and one of the planes seemed to acknowledge him by briefly turning on 'a set of floodlights.' More aircraft came on the scene. Witnesses counted up to 11 planes, including helicopters and two large aircraft.

ASSESSMENT

The local military had no knowledge of any aircraft in the area besides two National Air Guard C-130 Hercules cargo planes – one of which, a spokesman admitted, had turned on its landing lights. However, the C-130 pilots did not report seeing any strange lights in the vicinity of Faribault town.

UFO

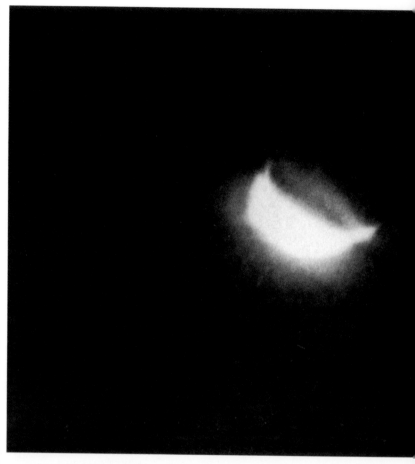

Professional photographer Evgeny Gridnevsky took this picture at about 2:30am in Kok-Jar, Kirgistan. The unknown, light-emitting aerial object remained in place, apparently revolving, until 4:30am.

THE EMERALD SPHERE

Sightings by an Aeroflot crew

TYPE: **Light in the sky**
PLACE: **Voronezh to St Petersburg, Russia**
DATE: **20 August 1991**

BACKGROUND

Aeroflot aviation mechanic Igor Yadigin took Flight 2523, which left Voronezh at 1:35am for St Petersburg. At about 2:05am he was invited to join the crew on the flight deck.

THE EVENTS

The crew pointed to a huge milky-white hemisphere of light just below and to the right of the Great Bear (Plough) star constellation, which was visible on the starboard side of the aircraft. At the centre of the sphere was an emerald-colored object that none of the crew could identify. From this object, a beam of light emerged and pointed to the ground. The witnesses saw the lights of another aircraft as it apparently changed course to avoid the unidentified object. 15 minutes later, the object vanished.

ASSESSMENT

The crew estimated the size of the UFO at 1250-2500ft (375-750m), and its distance at 30 miles (48km). But how could they have arrived at these figures, given the lack of comparable objects at 33,000ft (9900m)? Nor is it clear why they did not track the UFO on radar, why they did not contact the other jet, or why no one else on board the plane saw it.

Yadigin later claimed that he had been abducted by aliens in September 1989. So was he on the level, or another hoaxer leading investigators up the garden path?

SIGHTING AFFECTS ANIMALS

UFO and helicopters over Kentucky

TYPE: **Close encounter of the second kind**
PLACE: **Prague, Oklahoma, USA**
DATE: **7 January 1992**

BACKGROUND

During the night a rancher, his wife and his daughter, together with another couple staying on the property saw two large white lights hovering between the ranch house and a nearby microwave relay tower.

THE EVENTS

A small red ball appeared for a while. After about 45 minutes, a large fleet of helicopters appeared and split into two formations. At this time, animals on the ranch began to behave strangely. One group of helicopters approached the UFOs while the other flew out of sight. The UFOs remained stationary until the second group of choppers reappeared and headed towards them, whereupon they flew away.

ASSESSMENT

Mysterious helicopters are recurrent features in UFO reports, as are mystery aircraft, like those in the Faribault case.

path from Sunbury across Williamsport between 6:00 and 7:00pm and twice again between 8:00 and 9:30pm. Red and green lights seemed to move erratically around it. Estimates of its size varied from 100-600ft (30-180m) across, and estimates of its altitude also varied widely, from 50-500ft (15-150m). While the UFO was overhead, a deep rumble 'like the Niagara Falls' was heard. The UFO then disappeared over Bald Mountain, to the south of Williamsport. No commercial or military aircraft were known to have been in the area at the time.

ASSESSMENT

The size and altitude of lights seen against a night sky are notoriously difficult to estimate with any degree of accuracy. British ufologist Jenny Randles has suggested the lights were from a formation of USAF tanker aircraft, flying at perhaps 40,000ft (12,000m), on a secret refueling exercise with flights of strike aircraft. This explanation would account for the speed, sound and shape of the UFO, and the erratic movement of the red and green lights, which some witnesses actually identified as small aircraft. It would also help to account for the lack of physical reactions in witnesses.

THE WILLIAMSPORT TRIANGLE

Strange rumblings over Pennsylvania

TYPE: Light in the sky, multiple witnesses
PLACE: Williamsport, Susquehanna Valley, Pennsylvania, USA
DATE: 5 February 1992

BACKGROUND

Dozens of witnesses reported a gigantic triangle or boomerang flying along the Valley at no more than walking pace.

THE EVENTS

The UFO, showing white lights, was first seen moving roughly north to south on a

RETURN OF A CLASSIC STYLE

Long sighting by Russian military pilots

TYPE: Light in the sky
PLACE: Komsomolsk-Na-Amure, near Khabarovsk, Russia
DATE: 18 April 1992

BACKGROUND

This report of an inexplicable light in the sky originally appeared in the Russian military journal *Red Star* in June 1992. It was a plain account, with no attempt being made at interpretation or analysis of the significance – if any – of the strange events described.

THE EVENTS

The pilots of a military transport aircraft flying in the far east of Russia watched a UFO perform 'a series of acrobatics, such as figures of eight and loops' as it apparently flew for over an hour directly ahead of them. The UFO emitted beams of light that varied in color from light green to pale blue. At no time did either ground radar or the radar on the aircraft pick up any echoes from the UFO.

ASSESSMENT

This sighting is an illustration of the slightly dated style of many UFO sightings in the former Soviet Union. Was it a star or a planet? The account is too short and too lacking in detail for judgment to be made, and there has been no scientifically rigorous follow-up research that would be able to finally confirm or deny the authenticity of this light in the sky. In the absence of better and further particulars, the incident must remain unexplained.

MORE FROM THE MEN IN BLACK

A sighting, a circle and surveillance

TYPE: Close encounter of the second kind
PLACE: Raeford, North Carolina, USA
DATE: 27 June 1992

BACKGROUND

At about 12:30am on the night of 27 June, a noise like a passing freight train rattled the trailer where Mrs Diane Messing lived with her daughter, a nurse's assistant. Shortly before this happened, the light outside their own and their neighbor's homes had suddenly failed. The Messings went outside to see what was happening.

THE EVENTS

Outside, the pair saw something 'like a fire burning in the woods' in a hayfield about 300ft (90m) from the trailer. The object was spherical in shape and about 15ft (4.5m) across; it had orange windows, and it was entirely silent. The women approached closer, then went to phone the sheriff's office. When they returned, the object had vanished, and the six deputies who arrived to investigate saw nothing; but the outside lights were working again. The following day, the pair found an area of grass in the hayfield that had been swirled, flattened and discolored. When their sighting was investigated by ufologists, they were visited by a man claiming to be a US military officer, whose questions seemed distinctly odd and irrelevant and whose identity was never established.

ASSESSMENT

The case looks like a classic 'earthlight' visitation of the kind believed to create genuine crop circles. The mystery here, as in all such cases, is the mechanism behind the earthlights, and the real origin and identity of the creepy 'Man In Black'.

THE MISSILES RETURN

Air-to-air sightings in the Nineties

TYPE: **Close encounter of the first kind**
PLACE: **European and US airspace**
DATE: **April 1991-August 1992**

Mystery missiles plagued Scandinavia in 1946 (see Chapter Three). In December 1993, Swedish ufologists Clas Svahn and Anders Liljegren published a survey of unknown missiles seen mainly by civil airline passengers. Sightings of this type seem to have increased in the Nineties.

THE EVENTS

- 21 April 1991 – Achille Zaghetti, the captain of an Alitalia McDonnell Douglas MD-80 approaching the English coast, said that he and his co-pilot spotted a 10ft (3m) long, brown-colored missile cross their line of

vision. They were at 22,000ft (6750m), descending at 1200ft (365m) per minute at about 380 knots (640km/h) toward London Heathrow when the sighting occurred at 8:00pm (some reports say 9:00pm). The missile was heading east-south-east. Capt. Zaghetti estimated that it was 1000ft (300m) above him. He immediately contacted Air Traffic Control (ATC), who said they had an unknown target 10 miles (16km) behind him. This indicates that the UFO was traveling, not stationary. Capt. Zaghetti estimated that 40-60 seconds elapsed between his call to ATC and the answer, which makes the UFO's speed 200-500mph (320-800km/h) – if what he saw was making the radar return.

- 1 June 1991 – Both pilots of a Britannia Airways Boeing 737 flying from Dublin to London Heathrow saw 'a very short object' for a second or two at 2:38pm. The aircraft was on final approach on a 110° heading, at about 8000ft (2450m). The 'missile' streaked by its port side. It was about 10ft (3m) long, yellow-orange in color and with a 'wrinkled' appearance.

- 17 June 1991 – At 6:30pm, four passengers on a Dan Air flight from London Gatwick to Hamburg saw a wingless projectile below them. It was just above the cloud layer, at about 4000ft (1500m), and left no contrail. German engineer Walter Liess said: 'The object was slender, gray, and... cigar-shaped. Its flightpath was on a parallel with ours but diametrically opposed.... [It] seemed to oscillate in altitude. It's possible [it] was standing still and only gave the impression of movement.' The UFO was visible for 2-3 minutes. None of the crew saw it. The aircraft was at 5000 ft (1500m) at the time, ascending over Essex. There was no radar return from the UFO.

- 15 July 1991 – At 5:45pm, a Britannia Airways Boeing 737 from Crete was at 15,000ft (4600m), descending toward London Gatwick. The co-pilot spotted a 'black lozenge-shaped object' about 1.5ft (0.5m) long, at about 1600ft

(500m) above and ahead. In two seconds it had passed within 300ft (100m) of the 737, and less than 30ft (10m) above it. London ATC picked the 'missile' up as it flew away at 100mph (60km/h), and warned another aircraft that it had turned toward it. But the crew of this plane saw nothing.

- 5 August 1992 – At 1:45pm a United Airlines Boeing 747 was at 23,000ft (7000m) about 50 miles (80km) north-east of George AFB, California. The pilots saw 'an unusual aircraft without wings but with a tail of sorts' about 50ft (15m) long, flying directly toward them at supersonic speed. It was in sight for several seconds, and came within 500-1000ft (150-300m).

One of a series of pictures taken over a period of an hour on 4 November 1991 by 17-year-old Alexandr Pavlov. He and 14-year-old Alexey Vasilyev, were on the Migalov Quay on the Volga River at Tvev, Russia, at 1:00pm when the UFO first appeared. The pair said that while they watched, the object changed shape from the disk seen here to a dark ball.

1:10am on 31 March, against a clear sky, they saw two brilliant yellow globular objects traveling at speed in a north-west to south-easterly direction. The UFOs left long vapor trails and made no sound. Estimates of height varied from 2000ft (600m) to 30,000ft (9000m). Local air traffic control radars had no unidentifieds on their screens at this time.

Between 1:10am and 2:40am, a UFO of 'some considerable size' was seen first over North Devon, then at 2:00am over Bridgewater (Somerset), then in Shropshire and finally over South Yorkshire – thus following first an easterly and then a north-easterly route. The most detailed report came from Bridgewater: a number of fishermen saw a 'very large catamaran-shaped object' fly toward them, passing overhead in complete silence about 800ft (240m) up. Two very bright white lights showed at its rear, and two orange lights at its center. A similar UFO was reported from 8:00pm to 11:00pm the previous evening (30 March) from locations in Cornwall, Somerset and North Devon.

ASSESSMENT

It is difficult to lump all these reports together. The Zaghetti/Alitalia report is unreliable, partly because there were no reference points to judge the UFO's color, size and distance by, and partly because there is no guarantee that the London ATC's radar image and the UFO report referred to the same thing. Similar objections can be raised to some of the other reports. One or two of the UFOs – 'wrinkled', very small, or stationary ones – could be escaped kites or balloons. All the UFOs were officially classified as 'unknowns'. The USAF denied any knowledge of the 'missile' over California, but added, 'We're not the only ones with strange projects.'

A GIANT CATAMARAN

A bizarre mixture of IFO and UFO

TYPE: **Lights in the sky**
PLACE: **Wales and England, UK**
DATE: **30-31 March 1993**

BACKGROUND

The author of this book was a witness to one of the events that occurred this night – see the Introduction for details.

THE EVENTS

Numerous witnesses from west and south Wales and the west of England reported that between 1:05am and

ASSESSMENT

At about 1:05am on 31 March the casing of a Russian Tsyklon rocket, which had put the Cosmos 2238 radio satellite into orbit, re-entered Earth's atmosphere over Ireland, broke in two, and passed over the UK at a height of 145 miles (233km). It passed over Land's End at 1:10am. This accounts for the sightings in Wales and the west of England at that time. But the British Ministry of Defence could not explain the earlier or later sightings, and classified the UFO as an 'unknown'.

CHAPTER 8
The Modern Era

A SHAPESHIFTING ARRAY OF CONSPIRACIES, LEAKS, COVER-UPS AND DATA BLUR THE FACTS

Communication technology, and the internet in particular, has had an enormous effect on UFO sightings and UFO research. Whereas in the past events were spread by word of mouth and were occasionally investigated by the police or picked up by curious journalists, in the internet era sightings can be reported immediately, uploaded for all to see, and instantly be either debunked or hyped. Now everyone can be an expert and everyone can be a skeptic.

Adding to this ease of communication is the fact that our skies have never been so full, with the use of unmanned aerial vehicles growing rapidly – from recreational drones to agricultural delivery vehicles to covert aerial spies and weather-mapping cameras.

The proliferation of reports has coincided with an explosion of information and topics that were once

The use of camera phones in the 2000s has led to UFO sightings becoming more commonplace. Here an object was caught in the sky above Canary Wharf, London, in March 2011. Meanwhile, a new branch of Ufology has flourished, studying UFOs in found images and on NASA's live video feed from the International Space Station.

seen as outré conspiracy theories – such as the storage, examination, and reverse engineering of crashed alien spacecraft at Area 51 – becoming mainstream.

THE CHANGING SHAPE OF UFOs

Science fiction says more about the time in which it was created and the politics that people are living through than it does about the future, particularly on the topic of alien intelligence. In times of conflict, aliens are potential enemies; in times of peace, they are messengers with warnings to protect our dying planet or refugees from their own dying civilization. To some degree this is the same with UFO sightings: whereas once we largely feared the possibility of an invasion from distant galaxies in strange saucer-like ships, UFO sightings are often looked on in the 21st century with benevolence and wonder, something like spotting a pod of dolphins while at sea.

On a more practical level, the types, shapes, and behavior of crafts seen in UFO sightings change with the times too and reflect current technology. In this chapter there are only a few occasions where sightings do not conform with technology we can easily imagine. One such example is the experience of the Navy pilot who reported a huge churning in the ocean being created by something vast and indescribable beneath the surface

of the water. However, while cigar-shaped crafts, saucers, and orbs remain among the most commonly spotted phenomena, the 21st century has become the age of the triangle. From the Belgian UFO wave, from Phoenix to Dudley and dozens of other cases, mysterious black triangles are increasing curiosity.

The reason for this is clear: although people are familiar with the shapes created by a regular aircraft, the size, speed, and shape of newer military aircraft seem bizarre and otherworldly – and in some cases possibly are. Matters are not helped by the military in the USA and UK covering up their maneuvers; most black triangle sightings are at night. There are several existing fighter planes that could be responsible for the wave of triangle-shaped UFOs, but there are also believed to be many classified jets, including the notorious TR-3B – a 'black project' aircraft constructed using reverse technology from a crashed UFO.

FREEDOM OF INFORMATION

Freedom of information laws emerged as a response to increasing dissatisfaction with the secrecy surrounding government policy development and decision-making, and are increasingly easy to request. They have been used to unlock doors that some thought would never be opened, including to UFO files. As society has

149

BACKGROUND

Kelly Cahill and her husband were driving home from their friends' house along an unlit rural road surrounded by fields when she saw what looked like a blimp with circular orange headlights hovering over the road ahead.

THE EVENTS

Cahill had seen the same craft at the same location on their 90-minute drive to their friends. On the return journey, at around midnight, she and her husband saw it again; shortly afterward, they were dazzled by a bright white light that caused their car to slow down. The pair blacked out. On returning home, they looked at the clock and realized that about 60 minutes of their journey time were unaccounted for.

In the days following the incident, Cahill, who was 27 at the time, believes that she was visited by unknown entities during the night. The tall, black-cloaked figures stood over her bed and she felt as if she had some kind of suction device attached to her body. She said it was as if they were trying to take the life out of her. She was hospitalized for stomach pains and also noticed a small triangle-shaped burn mark on her navel.

Cahill then had a series of flashbacks that, over time, explained the missing 60 minutes. She says that during the drive, she and her husband pulled over shortly after seeing the white light. They crossed the road into the field, where they witnessed a large saucer-shaped craft with beams of blue light beneath it hovering over the grass. Then she remembers seeing a number of tall, skinny, black figures with bulging red eyes appear in front of the UFO and approach them.

She started screaming, she told Australian TV show *Today Tonight*. 'I felt this blow to my stomach and went flying in the air and I heard my husband say "let go of me" and this male voice that said, "I mean you no harm".'

Incredibly, Kelly and her husband were not the only people who saw this event.

TV show *The X Files* mixed fact and fiction when Australian abductee Kelly Cahill was referenced by Mulder and Scully in a 2016 episode. The mention prompted new interest in the mysterious 1993 case.

become more open, so too has the knowledge that governments, and in particular the USA, take UFO sightings far more seriously than they would like us to think. In 2017, the existence of the Pentagon's top-secret Advanced Aerospace Threat Identification Program was revealed. Operational between 2007 and 2012, with a budget of $28 million, it was tasked with researching UFO activity and paranormal events.

UFO data is no longer limited to planet Earth. Thanks to the limitless release of photography by NASA, there is a sub-strata of UFO researchers investigating UFOs landing on Mars.

Amid the noise and hypothesizing, there is something incredibly pure and innocent about one of the first sightings in this chapter: the mass experience by children at a private school in Zimbabwe, Africa, who saw a silver flying saucer and two large-eyed, big-headed aliens. In the Ariel School event, there was no covert military weaponry, no police conspiracy, hysterical social media reaction, or officials making jokes; just a group of shocked children trying to comprehend the incredible things they had seen. Even 25 years later, they are still trying to explain it.

THE KELLY CAHILL CASE

Australian housewife in time loss abduction

TYPE: **Contactee, close encounters of the first, second, third, and fourth kind**
PLACE: **Belgrave, Australia**
DATE: **8 August 1993**

Another car with three passengers had stopped behind them and also crossed the road to look into the field. Their drawings depict the same craft as that described by Cahill.

ASSESSMENT

Kelly Cahill wrote a book about her experience, *Encounter*, and appeared on national TV, where she revealed that she felt uneasy about what she had seen and realized she sounded ridiculous. It is perhaps because of this fear that neither Cahill's husband nor the occupants of the other car have ever come forward to tell their version of events. 13 years

South Africa became a hotbed of UFO activity in the 1990s. One of the biggest stories was of some strange shape-shifting lights in Sasolburg.

later, with Cahill's book long out of print and the story largely forgotten, interest in the case was resurrected when it was mentioned in detail during an episode of *The X Files*.

RAINDROP-SHAPED CRAFT

A strange shape-shifting UFO is spotted over Free State

TYPE: **Lights in the sky**
PLACE: **Sasolburg, South Africa**
DATE: **18 November 1993**

At 10:15pm, two residents of Sasolburg, South Africa, observed a strange silent craft in the sky. As they tried to make out what it was, the object left in a flash but returned after three minutes.

The craft was similar in appearance to a water droplet, but changed to a cigar shape. It glowed yellow and orange and also emitted a downward blue light before darting off again.

The pair thought they had been seeing things until, two months later, another resident of the town claimed to have discovered imprints of the craft's landing gear in their field.

VISITORS WITH A MESSAGE

62 school children witness landing

TYPE: **Contactees, close encounters of the first, second, and third kind**
PLACE: **Ruwa, Zimbabwe**
DATE: **16 September 1994**

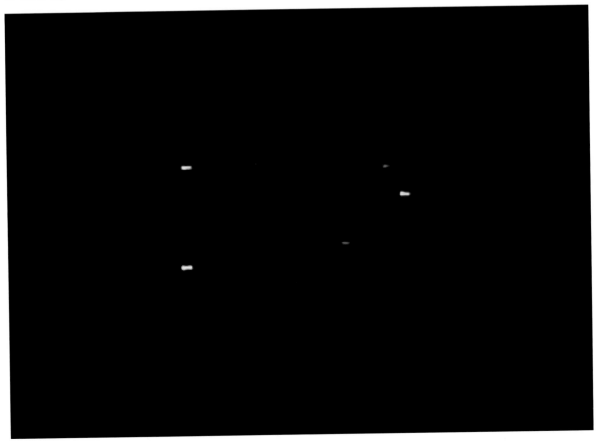

UFO

BACKGROUND

Ariel Primary School is in the town of Ruwa, around 15 miles (24km) from the capital city of Harare. The children were aged between 8 and 12. At 10:15am, the eldest children at the school were in an exam and the teachers were in a staff meeting. The rest of the children were on recess. The children had access to a large open play area, the outer boundary of which was marked out by logs. It was just behind these tree trunks that the children first heard a high-frequency noise, saw some strange lights, and then two saucer-shaped silver objects land, out of which appeared at least one being.

THE EVENTS

The children first observed three 'silver balls' in the sky above some distant hills. The balls disappeared in a flash of light, then reappeared. This happened three times before one of the balls landed among the trees and scrub beyond the children's play area. The children were not allowed in this area because it was considered dangerous, but they went to the edge of the forbidden area to investigate the silver objects they'd seen. The children then say they saw two small men, approximately 3ft (90cm) tall and wearing black suits, appear on top of a saucer-shaped ship and walk a little way across the rough ground. Some of the children were scared and ran away; others were mesmerized by what they were seeing. One of the children said that the men's movements appeared to be mirroring their own and there was a strange energy that seemed to freeze time. One group of children said that they received messages from the beings through their eyes, which they described as being black, large, and rugby-ball-shaped. Others just said they were scared.

A day after the incident, a BBC cameraman visited the school, together with UFO investigator Cynthia Hind, who requested that the school's headmaster ask the children to draw what they had seen. The drawings, depicting a large-headed black being beside a saucer-shaped ship, were all remarkably consistent

and detailed. In the accompanying TV interview, the children seem shocked by what they had witnessed the day before.

The event became a huge national news story. Around a month later, renowned child psychologist John Mack, from Harvard Medical School, who was visiting Zimbabwe at the time, went to speak to the children. He discovered that a few weeks on from the event the children were still displaying signs of shock. His approach differed to the initial TV interviews and he delved into the children's feelings, discovering that they had felt that the beings were attempting to communicate with them. One described flashing images of technology, and two children described a sense that the beings were trying to tell them that the world was ending.

There were reports of a UFO sighting in Zimbabwe on 14 September linked to this event.

ASSESSMENT

The most compelling feature of this event is the large number of witnesses. The fact that they were all children has fueled skepticism from some, but there is also a strong argument that the children – who were all polite and articulate – lacked the capability to lie in such extraordinary detail. UFOs or sci-fi were not a strong part of Zimbabwean culture at this time and it is unlikely that the children had any concept of such things. Indeed, they described the visitors as men, one even thinking that the strange visitors were gardeners. The children's testimonies and descriptions are convincing, and even among the more cynical teaching staff there was recognition that the children had seen 'something'. As John Mack puts it: 'These are people of sound mind telling me something that's very real but that they fear might make people think they're crazy so they question themselves.' 25 years on from the event, the children who attended this school and witnessed this event are still profoundly affected by it.

Mack was killed by a drunk driver in London in 2004. Prior to his death, in a

BBC interview, he said: 'I would never say, yes, there are aliens taking people. I would say there is a compelling powerful phenomenon here that I can't account for in any other way.'

MOTHERSHIP OR FLYING CAR?

Farmer annoyed by noisy UFO

TYPE: **Close encounter of the first kind**
PLACE: **Warrenton, South Africa**
DATE: **September and October 1994**

There was a huge amount of UFO activity in South Africa in the early 1990s. One case that received some publicity was a farmer who claimed to have made repeated observations of a noisy, nighttime craft traveling at incredible speeds, besides a mothership. The man compared the loud noise the craft made to the sound of a helicopter or a Volkswagen Beetle engine. The farmer's claims were supported by four independent observers.

FLIGHT 564 MYSTERY

Huge UFO spotted by passenger plane crew

TYPE: **Light in the sky**
PLACE: **The sky above Texas**
DATE: **25 May 1995**

BACKGROUND

America West Airlines Flight 564, a Boeing 757 piloted by Captain Eugene Tollefson and First Officer John J. Waller, was passing near Bovina, Texas, at 9:25pm from Dallas to Las Vegas at an altitude of 39,000ft (11,900m).

THE EVENTS

There were thunderstorms and lightning flashes, but the crew noticed something else in the night sky. A flight attendant

An F-117a stealth jet investigated a UFO above Texas in 1993 after the crew of a passenger plane reported seeing strobing lights. The pilot saw it too and ruled out a weather balloon. It remains a mystery.

was the first to observe a line of regularly flashing lights in the sky to the north and below the airliner. The first officer noticed them too, together with a horizontal row of eight strobe-like lights, flashing on and off in sequence from left to right. The lights were an extraordinarily bright white, tinged with blue. Captain Tollefson left his seat to look, and he saw the left to right sequence of lights also. As lightning flashed behind the lights, it silhouetted a cigar-shaped object approximately 500ft (150m) in length. Recordings of the first officer talking to Albuquerque Air Traffic Control Center have subsequently been made public. Concerned about what he is seeing, Waller tells the controller that

the object is traveling at about 30,000ft (9100m). Unable to detect the object, the air traffic controller says, 'the length is unbelievable... it has a strobe on it... this is not good'. At the same time, an F-117a stealth fighter jet from Holloman Air Force Base was alerted to the report and the pilot radioed that he had seen something passing by very close to his left side.

In their conversation with the air traffic controller, the pilot and first officer speculate about what the object could be and rule out that it was a weather balloon. The air traffic controller speculates that it could be a reflection from something on the ground such as a beacon. The following day, the controller checked with the North American Air Defense Command (NORAD) and was told they had been tracking an unidentified object the previous evening.

ASSESSMENT

While there is no doubt that the crew of Flight 564 saw something extraordinary

during a thunderstorm and their sighting is backed up by the recordings, there is no evidence of what NORAD told the curious air traffic controller. A freedom of information filing discovered nothing and NORAD denied that they had tracked anything unusual on 25 May.

A STINKY VISITATION IN BRAZIL

Three women meet a strange and smelly creature

TYPE: **Close encounter of the first kind, crash**
PLACE: **Varginha, Brazil**
DATE: **20 January 1996**

BACKGROUND

Ten years after the end of the military junta, there was still much distrust and dislike of the military across Brazil. By the mid-1990s, the armed forces were so cash-strapped that instead of firing their rifles

 In Varginha, Brazil, there were multiple reports of a UFO crash and of a dazed alien captured by the military. Strange denials from the army helped increase the mythology surrounding the case.

during training exercises, troops were told to shout 'bang!'. The uneasy relationship between the people in this coffee-producing region and the authorities is a backdrop to a story that gripped Brazil.

THE EVENTS

Out on a Saturday morning stroll, three young women – sisters Liliane and Valquíria and their friend Kátia – took a shortcut through a vacant lot in the small Brazilian city of Varginha, when

something stirred in a clump of weeds. The trio encountered a creature like nothing they had seen before. 'It wasn't a man or an animal – it was something different,' Kátia told reporters later, describing it as looking like the outside of a heart. It had, she said, oily brown skin, rubbery limbs, and three rounded horns sprouting from its oversized head. The creature seemed muddled and in pain. But what affected the women the most – and caused them to flee – was the creature's unbearably strong ammonia-like smell. The women ran home and told their families they had seen 'the devil'.

The sighting coincided with reports earlier on the same day of a cigar-shaped craft hovering above a farm and crashing on the outskirts of Varginha in the early hours. According to some, the creature

that the women had seen had crawled from the wreckage. Two days later, rumors circulated that the military had loaded a bizarre creature found at the side of the road into a truck. A janitor at a zoo also reported seeing a strange being and linked its appearance to the unexplained deaths of several animals. There were also claims that people had witnessed the army conducting an autopsy at a local hospital.

ASSESSMENT

Stringent denials from the military that they had anything to do with covering up the Varginha incident only served to inflame public suspicion. The military had a lengthy record of abuses against the Brazilian population – if they could make people vanish, went the reasoning, then they could do the same to aliens. The legend surrounding the incident has only grown. The author of a book on the case also claimed that a 23-year-old soldier had died after coming into contact with one of the beings.

The official account of the crash site – a fallen piece of debris from a satellite – seems plausible. According to the National Oceanic and Atmospheric Administration, on average between 200 and 400 tracked objects enter the Earth's atmosphere every year, but most burn up on reentry or land in the sea. On the night of the incident, NORAD reportedly warned the Brazilian authorities that an object had entered their airspace.

However, the military's initial explanations of the various alien sightings only fueled the conspiracy. It was not an alien being poked and prodded at the hospital, they said, but an expectant dwarf couple, while the confused being that the three women had seen was a homeless man nicknamed 'Mudinho' who covered himself in mud while hunting for cigarette butts in the undergrowth.

In the 21st century, Varginha had become famous for this alien visitation, hosting UFO conventions and becoming the subject of TV documentaries. Prior to the event, few people knew of the small municipality, but the city has embraced its reputation as the UFO capital of Brazil to such a degree that the events of January 1996 have become irrefutable in the minds of its inhabitants.

THE TENTACLED TORMENTOR

Police chase glowing disk

TYPE: **Close encounter of the first kind**
PLACE: **Erasmuskloof, South Africa**
DATE: **28 August 1996**

BACKGROUND

Two police officers were on their regular beat in a patrol car in the Pretoria suburb, 40 miles (64km) north of Johannesburg, in the early hours of a Wednesday morning. There was a full moon, but otherwise their shift had been exceptionally dull when Sgt Nico Bekker spotted a brightly glowing disk in the sky.

THE EVENTS

When Sgt Bekker left his vehicle, he realized he was seeing more than a strange light but a flying disk-shaped object emitting green tentacles of light. When the policemen on duty first called for backup they were laughed at, but then, as more reports from across the region came into the police station, they took the event seriously. In total, 200 police officers and a canine team were deployed. Another police officer filmed the light; in the videotape, one can see the steering wheel of the police car and a bouncing ball of light through the front windscreen. Over the buzz of the police radio, one of the officers says that the light is pulsing like a heart.

A radar operator at Johannesburg (now O.R. Tambo) International Airport confirmed the presence of an object and a police helicopter was scrambled. It began to pursue the craft at a height of 10,000ft (3000m). The pilot described it as moving in an undulating pattern at great speed. He had to give up the chase when he ran out of fuel and the object made a sharp vertical ascent.

ASSESSMENT

Although the local media jokingly linked the sighting to the release of the *Independence Day* movie, the presence of 200 police officers indicates how seriously it was taken. The most compelling evidence comes from the helicopter pilot. Superintendent Fred Viljoen was a UFO cynic and had initially considered his callout a prank, but admitted that he and his four passengers had witnessed something beyond their comprehension. The first newspaper reports of the sighting described Viljoen as looking 'as if he'd seen a ghost' as he recalled the 'unusual flight pattern' of the disk.

A CONE ALONE

Bizarre UFO the size of a soccer stadium

TYPE: **Close encounter of the first kind**
PLACE: **Pelotas, Brazil**
DATE: **5 October 1996**

BACKGROUND

Harold Westendorff was a Brazilian businessman who ran a rice-processing company and flew a single-engine Piper airplane as a hobby. He had around 20 years of flying experience and knew the area around Pelotas well. At around 10:15am, he was a short time into a recreational flight over a lagoon, approximately 10 miles (16km) from Pelotas Airport, flying at an altitude of 5000ft (1500m), when he encountered an immense UFO.

THE EVENTS

Westendorff described a cone-shaped craft. Its base was the size of a soccer stadium, about 325ft (100m) in diameter, and around 170ft (60m) high. It was rotating slowly on its axis. The businessman flew around the UFO for approximately 12 minutes and observed that it was made from something like metal, and had eight side panels, all of which had three bubble-like protrusions. The ship was moving slowly toward the coastline as Westendorff continued to fly close by. As he circled the craft, he called the control room at Pelotas Airport. He told the operator that he reached what was happening, gave him his position, and asked him to look in his direction. 'I looked out and saw on the horizon an object in the shape of a gray triangle with rounded edges,' said the operator. The craft was also spotted by several sunbathers.

On his third loop of the craft, Westendorff says that the tip of the cone disappeared, revealing an opening out of which emerged a saucer-shaped ship that

U F O

speeded rapidly upward. The disk had a diameter of 32ft (10m) and the pilot estimated that as it sped away it moved ten times faster than the speed of sound. At that point, the mothership emitted a red ray from its tip and ascended out of view. The pilot says that he feared a shockwave from the sudden movement of the UFO, but experienced no turbulence. Shocked, he returned to Pelotas Airport.

ASSESSMENT

The fact that this huge craft was also spotted by the official at Pelotas Airport and by a group of people at the beach adds to its believability. So too do the actions of Westendorff after landing: After reporting the encounter to the nearest military air base, he immediately took off again and went in search of the UFO. He did not find it, but on the ground local media were waiting for him when he landed. In the TV news shows on which Westendorff subsequently appeared, he does not seem like an attention-seeker – more like a man who has been reluctantly thrown into the limelight.

The case against the sighting's authenticity is that the military airbase and the much larger Curitiba airport had no evidence on their radar equipment of any large flying object or unusual activity.

OUTER SPACE DANCE

A ring of orbs filmed by space shuttle cameras

TYPE: **Lights in space**
PLACE: **Space, 240 miles (386km) above Earth**
DATE: **1 December 1996**

BACKGROUND

STS-80 was the 80th orbital space shuttle flight. There were five astronauts on board Space Shuttle Columbia, whose main objective was to deploy two satellites. The 17-day mission was the longest in space shuttle history and also included the deployment of the Wake Shield Facility. The shuttle featured four external cameras controlled remotely by NASA ground control. On the 12th day of the mission, between the first two days of December, the low-light cameras picked up several strange events.

THE EVENTS

At around midnight, the crew is asleep as the shuttle circles Africa. The cameras – which NASA control and usually use to look at weather patterns – pick up an initially out-of-focus orb that comes from behind the shuttle and appears to hover in the upper atmosphere above Earth. This is then joined by around a dozen other translucent circular objects that form a loose ring. Next, another orb comes, travels toward the center of the circle, and then, when it reaches the middle, begins to glow, triggering a dance of pulsing lights from the other orbs.

Another strange phenomenon was captured during a thunderstorm over Africa. As lightning flashes over the land, viewed from space by the shuttle cameras, an orb travels toward the heart of the storm and retains a stationary position.

Both these events were the subject of much excitement among the UFO community. The first was described as evidence that alien intelligence was attempting to communicate with humans. The second was taken as an example of alien planets harvesting energy from electrical storms.

Adding to the sense of a NASA conspiracy was the choice of wake-up-call music played to the STS-80 Columbia crew on the twelfth day of the mission: 'Break On Through (To the Other Side)' by The Doors.

ASSESSMENT

While it is tempting to believe the conspiracy that NASA is somehow withholding evidence of alien life, this camera footage does not support it. Astronaut Tom Jones, who was a member of the five-person STS-80 crew, and veteran of three other space shuttle missions, explained in a blog that seeing objects during missions is common: most of it is debris released by the shuttle's payload bay that drifts along with the shuttle for days after launch. In the case of this particular event, Jones has said that the low-light cameras had captured ice particles in the very near field of 10–20ft (3–6m) and that the objects are tumbling ice flakes captured in the sun as they move out of the shuttle's shadow.

Perhaps the most damning thing to dispute the theory that STS-80 encountered a mass visitation of alien craft is – as shown in a cutaway of the footage – how uninterested NASA ground control is by the flickers and pops of the dozen space orbs.

THE PHOENIX LIGHTS

Mass sighting of boomerang-shaped lights

TYPE: **Lights in the sky, multiple sightings**
PLACE: **Nevada and Arizona, USA**
DATE: **13 March 1997**

BACKGROUND

Over the space of four hours, a group of lights was spotted flying above Nevada. On the same evening, there were multiple sightings of other lights in the sky across a 300-mile (480-km) radius. The sightings became known as 'the Phoenix Lights' due to the large number of sightings above the city.

THE EVENTS

The first sightings, at 6:55pm, described a V-shaped object with large lights on its leading edge above Henderson, Nevada.

The craft had six lights and, according to the witness, was the size of a Boeing 747 and sounded like 'rushing wind'. In his report to the National UFO Reporting Center, he said that it moved in a straight line southeast before disappearing over the horizon.

This was the first of many sightings of lights that evening. The next reported one was from a former police officer at 8:15pm, 200 miles (320km) away from Henderson in Paulden, Arizona. He was driving when he noticed a cluster of five orange lights.

Within minutes, there was a blitz of sightings reported to TV stations, newspapers, and police departments, mainly from communities to the north and west of Phoenix.

John Kaiser was outside with his wife and sons in Prescott Valley when he saw lights travel in a V-shaped formation, but other reports were different: some saw five lights, others seven; some reported that they were red, others yellow or white. One report from a mother and four daughters in Phoenix described an object shaped like a sergeant's stripes. A driver on Interstate 10 said that one of the objects came so close to him that it blocked out the sky above their car.

Among those who reported seeing the lights above Phoenix was Fife Symington, the governor at the time. Prior to the sighting he had mocked the idea of alien life, but called the lights 'otherworldly'.

Most of the sightings in the Phoenix area occurred at around 10pm. They included the teams and spectators of a Little League baseball match, who stopped to watch the phenomena. Thirty to 40 motorists on the I-17 toward Flagstaff pulled over to the side of the road and watched the craft flying along the canyon.

A repeat of the lights occurred on 6 February 2007 and 22 April 2008. The 2008 incident was widely reported, with residents in North Phoenix seeing a group of lights form a diamond shape. The incident was later revealed to be a hoax.

The Phoenix Incident is a 2015 movie based on the mass **UFO sighting in Arizona in 1997, where hundreds of witnesses spotted a group of lights traveling at speed.**

to this explanation, the flares would have been visible in Phoenix and might have appeared to hover due to rising heat from the burning flares creating a 'balloon' effect on their parachutes, which slowed the descent.

EASTERN CAPE FLYPAST

Family of five film golden triangles

TYPE: **Lights in the sky**
PLACE: **Graaff-Reinet, South Africa**
DATE: **27 December 1998**

On 27 December 1998, at about 3pm, Jacques Laubscher was editing video footage of his family's Christmas celebrations when one of his children ran into the house shouting that there were UFOs in the sky. Laubscher grabbed his video camera and began filming the skies.

In the resulting videotape, the family can be heard discussing the objects they see in the sky, ruling out airplanes and paragliders. What they saw were eight to ten golden objects that flickered red and blue when stationary. Laubscher filmed the activity for five minutes, but sadly, due to the automatic focus on the camera failing to lock onto the objects, the footage is unclear. However, analysis of the film determined that the objects were 8ft (2.5m) in diameter, rounded and triangular-shaped, and flying at an altitude of 25,000ft (7620m) at speeds between 200 and 600mph (320–965kmh). Fearing ridicule, the businessman kept the footage locked away for a month before a friend persuaded him to show it to the media. The resulting news story

ASSESSMENT

Despite the fact that this event was viewed by hundreds of witnesses, disappointingly, there is no good film footage of either the craft or the light formations.

Investigators may never be able to reassemble all of the facts surrounding the events that took place, but the most logical explanation is that the sightings were the result of secretive Air Force maneuvers at the Barry M. Goldwater Air Force bombing range 150 miles (240km) southwest of Phoenix. The first round of sightings could have been jets flying in formation; the second the release of their payload of decoy flares. The US Air Force explained that slow-falling, long-burning LUU-2B/B illumination flares were dropped by a flight of four A-10 Warthog aircraft on a training exercise on the evening of 13 March. According

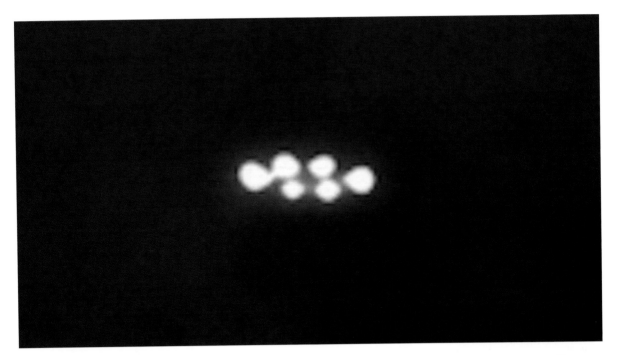

 Traffic stopped on the Jersey Turnpike in 2001 as motorists exited their cars to observe a V-shaped group of bright lights moving slowly across the night sky.

led to several other witnesses saying they had seen the same phenomena too.

FLARES OR UFO?

Light show stops traffic

TYPE: **Lights in the sky**
PLACE: **Carteret, New Jersey, USA**
DATE: **14 July 2001**

BACKGROUND

In the township of Carteret, 20 miles (32km) south of New York City, hundreds of people reported seeing an array of 16 bright yellow lights traveling very slowly in a V-formation across the night sky. Newark Airport said there had been no unusual flight patterns in the area at the time.

THE EVENTS

This sighting was seen by hundreds of residents during a warm summer evening. The lights stopped traffic on the Jersey Turnpike with motorists leaving their cars to get a better look at the sky.

Although 15 people called 911, several witnesses who spoke to the local TV news channel said that they found the vision strangely calming. One said it was 'very peaceful and serene, I think we witnessed some kind of miracle.'

ASSESSMENT

The description sounded very much like the Phoenix Lights, another V-formation that appeared in the sky near Phoenix in March 1997. News Channel 4 sent video of the phenomenon to NASA, who confirmed that the lights were not space debris or meteorites. Their theory was that they had the appearance of being airborne flares released by a National Guard unit or as a prank from a private airplane.

NASA's flare theory was backed up by one witness who claimed that he saw smoke after the lights disappeared.

NARCO HUNT BECOMES UFO CHASE

Mexican Air Force film UFO pursuit

TYPE: **Radar visual, lights in the sky**
PLACE: **Campeche, Mexico**
DATE: **5 March 2004**

BACKGROUND

A Mexican Air Force airplane was traveling at an altitude of 11,500ft (3500m) using infrared equipment to search for drug-smuggling aircraft when the pilots encountered 11 unidentified objects over southern Campeche.

THE EVENTS

A week after the incident, Mexico's Defense Department issued a press release accompanied by videotape. The footage shows the bright objects, some sharp points of light and others like large headlights, moving rapidly in the late-evening sky. Only three of the 11 lights appeared on the plane's radar system. The plane pursued the lights until they

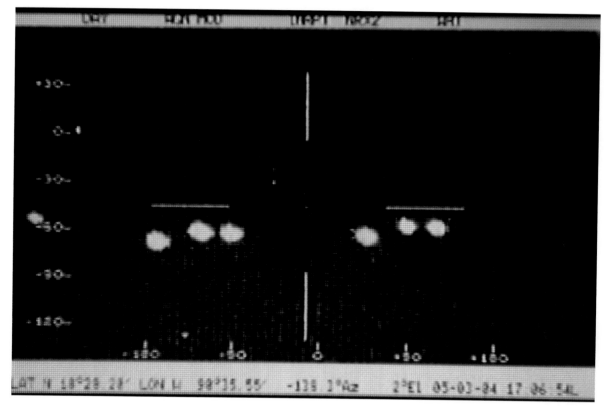

disappeared. In an interview about the incident, the captain, Maj. Magdaleno Castanon, said: 'I believe they could feel we were pursuing them.' Indeed, whatever it was the crew encountered, it seems as if it was playing with them. 'There was a moment when...the screens showed they were behind us, to the left and in front of us,' said the captain. 'It was at that point that I felt a bit tense.'

ASSESSMENT

This event made worldwide news bulletins thanks to the videotape and the testimony of the flight crew. Sightings such as this were not rare, but this incident appeared to have the backing of the Mexican military. However, subsequent investigation suggests that what the witnesses saw could have been burn-off flares from the Bay of Campeche Cantarell oil platforms. These would not have shown up on the plane's radar system but would have been picked up by infrared cameras.

THE TINLEY PARK LIGHTS

Mass sighting in Chicago suburbs

TYPE: **Lights in the sky**
PLACE: **Tinley Park, Illinois, USA**
DATE: **21 August 2004**

BACKGROUND

Tinley Park is a quiet suburb 30 miles (48km) south of Chicago. The night of the event was a clear, warm Saturday evening. Residents were enjoying block parties and barbecues, and Ozzy Osbourne's Ozzfest was in town at the Tweeter Center. The first reports of unusual activity in the sky came at around 7pm.

THE EVENTS

Around 25 separate video recordings exist of the event and they all show the same thing: three orange-red lights glowing in

In-flight recorders captured the moment a Mexican Air Force pilot on a mission tracking narcotics traffickers found himself in pursuit of a 'bright light' that darted around before vanishing at incredible speed.

the night sky. The lights form a triangle shape and appear to be connected in some way, either through some invisible force or through a structure that is not visible to the human eye. Analysis of the video calculated each side of the triangle to be 1500ft (460m) and its altitude to be 4000ft (1220m). The lights were traveling west to east. Although the initial reports were from Tinley Park, the lights were also spotted above the neighboring communities of Frankfort, Orland Park, Mokena, and Oak Forest as well as by concertgoers leaving Ozzfest. The lights were traveling at a slow speed and each sighting lasted approximately

A US navy pilot on the USS *Nimitz* spotted several strange objects during a military exercise in the Pacific Ocean, including an enormous craft beneath the water. A Pentagon leak of the incident became global news.

12 minutes. One Tinley Park witness said that the lights stopped above his home in a straight line, then reformed into a triangle and moved away. He said that the lights were completely silent.

Multiple similar sightings made on or around 21 August in British Columbia, Canada, and Melbourne, Australia, were linked together to promote a theory of a worldwide visitation.

The identical pattern of lights was seen above Tinley Park on two other occasions: 31 October 2004 and 1 October 2005. Tinley Park had also been the location of a UFO sighting in the early 1960s.

ASSESSMENT

The lights were too slow to be traditional aircraft: indeed, one piece of footage shows a helicopter also in the night sky moving five times faster than the lights. (The pilot was contacted by the History Channel show *UFO Hunters*, which investigated the sighting, but refused to comment on what he had seen because he feared for his job.) Suggestions that it could have been weather balloons, computer fakery, or weather phenomena were all disproved. Theories that this event could be explained as military flares – just like the Phoenix Lights event in 1996 – have also been ruled out. The airspace over Tinley Park and its neighboring suburbs are part of the immediate operating area of both nearby Midway International Airport and Chicago O'Hare International Airport, and is a controlled, Class Bravo airspace. The controlled status of this airspace makes scheduled military exercises of any type unprecedented, unsafe, and unlikely.

THE USS *NIMITZ* INCIDENT

Sightings and pursuit by US Navy pilots

TYPE: **Radar-visual, close encounter of the first kind**
PLACE: **Pacific Ocean, 100 miles (161km) off the coast of southern California, USA**
DATE: **14 November 2004**

BACKGROUND

Two US Navy pilots revealed details of a November 2004 sighting of an 'unidentified flying object' over the Pacific Ocean after a Pentagon report into the incident was leaked.

THE EVENTS

The USS *Nimitz* was one of several ships deployed on training exercises in the Pacific Ocean, off the coast of California

UFO

 A saucer-shaped craft was reported by ground staff at Chicago O'Hare Airport. Despite delays and multiple sightings, officials denied the reports.

and Mexico. In early November, one of these ships, the Ticonderoga Class Guided Missile Cruiser USS *Princeton*, began tracking some strange signals on its SPY-1 radar. On several occasions from 10 November, two experienced officers detected multiple returns of an object rapidly descending from 28,000ft (8530m), hovering approximately 80ft (24m) above the water, then disappearing at impossibly fast speeds.

At around 11am on 14 November, the *Princeton*'s radars again picked up the bizarre object and this time called in two F/A-18 Hornets that were returning to the USS *Nimitz* from a training exercise. Pilots Navy Cmdr. David Fravor and Navy Lt. Cmdr. Jim Slaight were instructed to investigate the objects by the radio operator on the cruiser. Initially, Fravor and Slaight could see nothing on their radars or in the air. But then Fravor looked down to the sea and noticed that the waves were breaking over something

below the surface, causing the sea to churn. Hovering about 50ft (15m) above the churn was a craft that was described by Fravor as being white, 46ft (14m) long and oval in shape but otherwise featureless. In an interview with the *New York Times* in 2017, he said that it was jumping erratically but not moving in any specific direction. In drawings of Fravor's account the craft looks a little like a giant Tic Tac. Fravor circled back and descended from 20,000ft (6100m) to 3000ft (915m) for a closer look, but as he approached the craft accelerated and disappeared at rapid speed. The *Princeton* radioed the jets that the radar target had reappeared 60 miles (96km) away – a feat that *Popular Mechanics* calculated meant the craft was traveling at 2400mph (3860kmh). Meanwhile, whatever was beneath the surface of the water had disappeared too as the ocean was now calm.

When asked by another pilot about the sighting, Fravor said: 'I have no idea what I saw. It had no plumes, wings or rotors and outran our F-18s.' His superiors did not investigate further.

The incident only came to light following a leak of an unclassified Pentagon report from 2009. In December

2017, infrared footage of the encounter was released to the public.

In an interview with the *Boston Globe* in January 2018, Fravor said he was surprised at the lack of curiosity the Defense Department had shown about the encounter. 'I figured someone would come out,' he said. After all, they had been tracking the objects for two weeks and surely a debriefing would be in order. But no one ever did.

ASSESSMENT

It would be hard to find a more reliable witness than David Fravor. He is described by everyone who knows him as level-headed and the complete opposite of someone who would make up a sighting. Indeed, he had to suffer ridicule from his colleagues when he reported the sighting and only came forward when prompted by Luis Elizondo, the man who once headed the Pentagon's UFO program. Although the incident is clearly not a hoax, there are plenty of skeptics ready to pour cold water on the sightings. Defense and security writer Kyle Mizokami suggested two alternative possibilities: equipment failure and classified government technology. The churning water could be explained as a submerging nuclear submarine.

ALIENS AT THE AIRPORT

Saucer checks United hub

TYPE: **Close encounter of the second kind**
PLACE: **Chicago O'Hare Airport, Illinois, USA**
DATE: **7 November 2006**

BACKGROUND

In 2006, Chicago O'Hare was the world's second busiest airport, serving around 76 million passengers a year.

THE EVENTS

At approximately 4:15pm, federal authorities at Chicago O'Hare International Airport received a report that a number of airport employees were witnessing a revolving, gray, metallic, saucer-shaped craft hovering over Gate C-17 at an altitude of 1900ft (580m). Some said it looked like a rotating Frisbee, while others said it did not appear to be spinning. The object was first spotted by a ramp employee who was pushing back United Airlines Flight 446, bound for Charlotte. The employee informed Flight 446's crew of the object above their aircraft. It is believed that both the pilot and co-pilot also witnessed the object, which disappeared into the clouds. According to *Chicago Tribune* reporter Jon Hilkevitch, 'The disc was visible for approximately five minutes and was seen by close to a dozen United Airlines employees, ranging from pilots to supervisors, who heard chatter on the radio and raced out to view it.'

ASSESSMENT

Drones have increasingly become an issue at airports around the world, particularly in London, where departures were halted at Gatwick Airport for two days in December 2018 when a drone was spotted close to the runway. However, the O'Hare incident was clearly something much larger and stranger than a drone.

According to the Federal Aviation Administration (FAA), nothing was detected by radar, and official channels denied that anything unusual had happened. The event was not in the United duty manager's log. The *Tribune* filed a Freedom of Information request that uncovered a call by the United supervisor to an FAA manager in the airport tower concerning the sighting. The FAA concluded that the event was a weather phenomenon, an explanation that has caused controversy. Regardless of whether or not this was a UFO, any objects seen close to aircraft pose a safety risk. However, to some at O'Hare the incident provided a chuckle.

'To fly seven million light years to O'Hare and then have to turn around and go home because your gate was occupied is simply unacceptable,' said O'Hare controller and union official Craig Burzych.

Witnesses interviewed by the *Tribune* were upset that federal officials declined to investigate the matter further.

CHANNEL ISLANDS SIGHTING

UK airline pilot spots two giant yellow UFOs

TYPE: **Close encounter of the first kind**
PLACE: **The Channel Islands, UK**
DATE: **23 April 2007**

BACKGROUND

Captain Ray Bowyer, the pilot of an 18-seat Trislander passenger plane, had been flying the same route from Southampton,

A pilot and passengers on board a small passenger plane flying to the Channel Islands spotted a huge yellow-colored cigar-shaped craft.

UFO

England, to the island of Alderney, off the coast of northern France, for eight years. But on this particular spring afternoon, his flight was anything but routine.

THE EVENTS

Captain Bowyer first noticed something unusual when a bright yellow light, approximately 50 miles (80km) away, caught his eye. His initial thoughts were that it was the reflection of the sun off a glasshouse. However, as he approached the Channel Islands, he realized it was something far more unusual. With the plane cruising on autopilot, he looked through his binoculars and saw that the lights were emanating from two cylindrical objects that were stationary in the air. Scared of a collision, he contacted Jersey Air Traffic Control. Their radars could only track moving objects, but they did pick up a faint primary return radar signal. A passenger sitting behind the captain confirmed what he was seeing, while another passenger plane 25 miles (40km) to the south reported seeing the same yellow light. As he prepared to descend, Bowyer got a closer look at the objects, describing them as cigar-shaped and about a mile wide with a pulsating interface where sparkling blues, greens,

A misfired Bulava missile led to peculiar formations in the sky above Norway caused by the dispersement of its propellant gases and explosives.

and other hues were strobing up and down about once a second. The entire encounter had lasted 15 minutes.

There was also a ground-based observation of the objects. Two tourists on the neighboring island of Sark enquired at their hotel as to what two bright yellow objects in the sky might be. They had seen the objects during an afternoon walk in the direction of Alderney.

ASSESSMENT

It is not uncommon for pilots to witness strange phenomena, but this report is unusual. Twenty minutes after landing, Bowyer had filed his flight log, including a report of the sighting, with the British Civil Aviation Authority. Often in the US, flight crews fear they will be ridiculed if they report events, but in this case the captain received the support of his airline to discuss his experience on British TV. As he matter-of-factly put it: 'I did not feel that I was in any danger of being ridiculed because all I did was to report what actually happened as was my duty as operating aircrew.'

THE INDIAN FIREBALL

The burning orb in Bengal

TYPE: Lights in the sky
PLACE: Kolkata, India
DATE: 29 October 2007

A fast-moving fireball was spotted across Bengal between 3:30am and 6:30am. The object, seen by thousands on Indian TV, seemed to alter its shape from an orb to a triangle to a straight line. It emitted a bright light with a halo effect around it and radiated a range of colors. As word spread about the mysterious object, hundreds gathered along a highway to catch a glimpse of the scene in the early-morning skies.

Some believed it was a meteor, but the length of time for which it was observed counted against this.

THE STEPHENVILLE SIGHTINGS

Mass sighting in cowboy country

TYPE: Lights in the sky
PLACE: Stephenville, Texas, USA
DATE: 8 January 2008

BACKGROUND

A group of three friends was out admiring the Texas sunset at around 6:15pm when they saw some lights in the sky that none of them could explain. Among them was Steve Allen, a pilot with more than 30 years of flying experience.

THE EVENTS

The group of men were among the first, but not the last, to see a group of lights above a corner of the world that likes to call itself the 'cowboy capital'. What they saw was a group of flashing lights about 3500ft (1070m) above ground level, which were part of a large ship that Allen estimated to be about a mile and a half (2.5km) across. The lights went from corner to corner. It was directly above Highway 67, traveling toward Stephenville at a speed of 3000mph (4830kmh).

Allen says that the craft disappeared in an instant but returned ten minutes later, this time pursued by two F-16 jets. The craft seemed to play with the military aircraft, slowing down and then speeding up again.

The trio were not the only people to see the lights or the pursuit by the jets. In all, 40 people reported the sighting, with several residents describing a craft the size of a football field. Among the witnesses were two policemen from Dublin, Texas, who used their patrol car dashboard cam to film the event. Hunter Ricky Sorrells, also in Dublin, observed the lights through the scope on his deer rifle. He described what he saw as a 'huge gray object' the color of galvanized metal, with no rivets, bolts, or seams.

ASSESSMENT

A great deal of secrecy and obfuscation surround this event, not least from the military. On 23 January, after initially denying that any aircraft were operating in the area, the US Air Force said that it was conducting training flights in the Stephenville area that involved 10 fighter jets. The Air Force said they were F-16 Fighting Falcon jets conducting night flights from NAS JRB Fort Worth, leading many to believe that what people saw above Stephenville were military flares.

There was also suspicion among some of the witnesses that once the media arrived in town, some began to make up tall stories about what they'd seen. Allen says that he regrets describing the craft as 'the size of a Walmart', as he is still teased about it. But others insist there is no denying they saw something. 'I didn't call them flying saucers or extraterrestrials,' James Huse, a former Air Force navigation specialist who had observed the lights, told *Popular Mechanics*. 'All I said was that it was unidentified flying objects, and I'm sticking to that. I couldn't identify them. People in Erath County aren't nuts or hicks. We are just ordinary people who happened to look up.'

THE NORWEGIAN SPIRAL ANOMALY

Fireworks in the fjords

TYPE: Lights in the sky
PLACE: Norway
DATE: 9 December 2009

An incredible spiral white light that appeared in the skies above Norway was preceded by a stream of luminescent blue light. At first, many thought they were witnessing a UFO event or something supernatural. The spiral span around for several minutes before eventually disappearing in on itself as if into a black hole. The incredible light show was captured by hundreds. There were

 The usual tranquility of the Newfoundland village of Harbour Mille was disturbed in 2010 by two streaks of light. Canadian authorities denied they were missiles and joked that the area was a 'UFO landing strip'.

several wild theories, including one that proposed that the strange sight was a wormhole that had been caused by the Hadron Collider.

The mystery was apparently solved on the following day. On 10 December 2009, the Russian Ministry of Defence admitted that it had run a Bulava missile test that had failed. According to a spokesperson's statement: 'The missile's first two stages worked as normal, but there was a technical malfunction at the next third stage of the trajectory. The visual phenomena was created as the malfunctioning missile arrived in the upper layers of the atmosphere and went into a spin.'

THE HARBOUR MILLE INCIDENT

UFO or stray missile?

TYPE: **Lights in the sky**
PLACE: **Harbour Mille, Newfoundland, Canada**
DATE: **25 January 2010**

BACKGROUND

Harbour Mille is a small fishing village of around 200 residents on the south coast of Newfoundland. Darlene Stewart was taking photographs of the sunset when a flash of light came into view.

THE EVENTS

Stewart, her husband, and her neighbor watched three more objects speeding through the sky at one-minute intervals. They looked almost like missiles, and their trajectory suggested they had come from the water. Photos show a rocket shape with a long, fiery tail soaring skyward. Stewart's neighbor, Emmy

Pardy, watched the objects through her binoculars. 'I zoomed in and I saw a humongous bullet, silver-gray in color and it had flames coming out of the bottom and a trail of smoke,' she said.

Stewart reported her sighting to the police. Royal Canadian Mounted Police initially said that the reports were due to a missile launch, but later retracted the statement. The incident went all the way to parliament, with the Office of the Prime Minister stating that the objects were not missiles. Military experts discredit the possibility of ballistic and cruise missiles. DND's Directorate of Scientific and Technical Intelligence (DSTI) assessed the images and reported: 'The object is not a ballistic missile, not a cruise missile in boost phase nor a cruise missile in-flight phase. It is also

 UFO sightings have led to the closure of several Chinese airports. In 2010, Xiaoshan Airport closed after a craft was spotted hovering above a runway.

not a licensed model rocket launcher.' As media speculation grew that a UFO had been spotted in Newfoundland, Canada's Defense Minister, Peter MacKay, confirmed during a speech at a funding announcement that there had been no reported missile tests. Jokingly, he announced funding for an alien landing strip at Harbour Mille.

Another minor report of this incident came from Calgary, where boys playing hockey reported seeing similar objects.

ASSESSMENT

If the objects were not missiles then what were they? Björn Borg, a UFO researcher from Finland, believed that he could provide the answer to the mystery. What people were really seeing was the effect of jetliner vapor trails catching winter sunlight, he claimed. 'The sun is shining on the vapor trail. In winter time, the color of the trail will show up in very strong yellow or even red. It looks like fire.'

AIRPORT CLOSURE

Chaos in China

TYPE: **Lights in the sky**
PLACE: **Xiaoshan Airport, Hangzhou, China**
DATE: **7 July 2010**

BACKGROUND

At about 8:40pm, an object was reported by a flight crew preparing to land at

Hangzhou's Xiaoshan Airport. Air traffic controllers could not see the object on their radar, but as a precaution they decided to close the airport. Departures were delayed for four hours and 18 incoming flights were redirected to other airports.

THE EVENTS

This is a very confusing sighting, as, although there is no doubt that something happened at the airport, Chinese TV reports showed footage that did not tally with the description of a craft hovering over the runway. Instead, they showed video footage that had been captured by several Hangzhou residents of an object shooting above the city and the airport that was bathed in golden light and trailing a comet-like tail behind it.

Reporting of the event was not helped by the fact that a passenger had circulated photographs of what he claimed to be the UFO but were later clearly revealed to be of a regular aircraft.

ASSESSMENT

There have been an increasing number of accounts of UFO sightings taking place at airports during the 21st century, many of which have remained unexplained. In 2010, there were eight sightings within a three-month period, with three of the events taking place in China. The decision to shut down Xiaoshan Airport, albeit temporarily, indicated that, unlike with previous events such as the one at Chicago O'Hare in 2006, this issue was being taken seriously and would be properly explored.

A team that was made up of about half a dozen government and aviation organizations formed a joint committee to investigate the incident. Unfortunately, their official conclusion was rather vague, to say the least. Although the report revealed that two – not just one – flight crews had seen the mysterious object, they decided that it had 'resulted from the activities of private or military aircraft'.

THE DUDLEY DORITO

A chip-shaped UFO haunts the UK

TYPE: **Lights in the sky**
PLACE: **West Midlands, UK**
DATE: **14 November 2010**

BACKGROUND

Munesh Mistry and Neil Martin, both 21, spotted something unusual in the night sky above Tipton near Dudley in the West Midlands on a Sunday evening.

THE EVENTS

The two friends initially thought they were observing some unusual bird activity before they realized it was actually a craft of some sort. Mistry told the *Daily Mail* that what they saw was a 'fast-moving and silent craft in the shape of a triangle made up of what appeared to be three lights flying across the sky at a mind-boggling speed.' The craft was nicknamed the 'Dudley Dorito', after a popular brand of tortilla chips. Although there were no other sightings on that particular evening, a very similar craft has been reported on dozens of occasions since. There were three more sightings in 2010, all near to Dudley. In 2011, three pub-goers saw a black triangle-shaped craft with white lights in each corner flying at a low level. Gary Nock and his family were in the car park of the Badgers Sett pub, Hagley, when they noticed what they presumed was an experimental military aircraft. After a five-year absence, there was another sighting. In October 2016, a dog walker took a photo of the mysterious craft.

ASSESSMENT

While its nickname makes these sightings sound like a comical hoax, the large number of them suggests that there is an odd craft that keeps returning to the West Midlands. Experimental aircraft are recurrent features in UFO reports and here the triangular shape led some

to suggest that the craft could be a McDonnell Douglas A-12 Avenger II fighter jet. The triangle-shaped stealth bomber was nicknamed the 'Flying Dorito' during its development prior to cost overruns leading to its cancelation. Could a prototype somehow have made it to Central England?

A RETURN VISIT?

Fast-moving lights

TYPE: **Lights in the sky**
PLACE: **Sasolburg, South Africa**
DATE: **27 February and 29 November 2013**

BACKGROUND

Almost exactly 20 years since a previous sighting, there were two events of a very similar nature to the famous Sasolburg UFO incident of 1993.

THE EVENTS

In February, five fast-moving lights, each one a different color, crisscrossed in random patterns very rapidly. There was no sound – just these lights moving very quickly. The witness managed to take two pictures before the lights just vanished. Then, in November, two witnesses described seeing an orange light moving from the east to the southwest at a rapid speed. Just like the previous sightings, the craft sped off after a while, and was completely silent.

ASSESSMENT

While these sightings remain a mystery, it is possible that they are connected in some way to the vast petroleum refinery in Sasolburg. The plant was once seen as so vital that it had its own regiment.

YOU CANNOT BE SIRIUS

Dancing diamond in the Maritimes

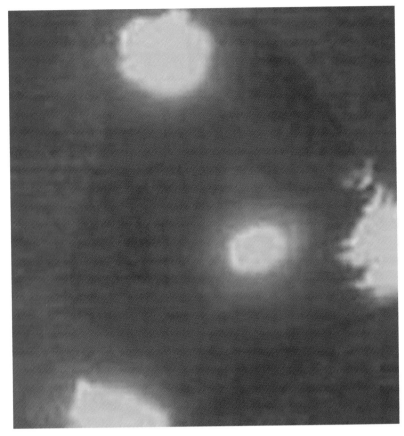

Sightings of triangular-shaped craft grew more common in the 21st century. Among the most famous was the so-called Dudley Dorito, seen above towns in the West Midlands of the UK.

BACKGROUND

In the middle of a rainstorm, some odd lights were photographed above the city that is home to the Johnson Space Center, headquarters of NASA's Mission Control.

THE EVENTS

A circular group of lights were seen by a driver to be maneuvering and changing their configurations in the sky. His footage shows what appears to be a spinning circle of eight lights. As a UFO frenzy took over social media, dozens of other photos appeared, capturing similar lights – and in some a circular craft surrounded by lights.

ASSESSMENT

Twitter and Instagram can cause hysteria, and that appears to be what happened here. A day after the event, and following a flurry of TV news reports, UFO researchers questioned the validity of many of the photographs that had been posted online. One video was dismissed as the reflection from a shopping mall; another as flares due to a trail of smoke behind them. For a city that is synonymous with space exploration, it was all a little ignominious.

DRONE OR UFO?

Reverse engineering in action?

TYPE: **Daylight disk**
PLACE: **Iranian airspace**
DATE: **11 November 2014**

BACKGROUND

Iran was the location of one of the most famous incidents where the military

---

TYPE: **Lights in the sky**
PLACE: **Kensington, King Edward Island, Canada**
DATE: **4 June 2014**

BACKGROUND

John Sheppard was camping at Twin Shores campground, near Kensington, with his wife. At around 11:30pm, he left his tent to put out a fire when he noticed a strange light over the Gulf of St Lawrence.

THE EVENTS

Sheppard had seen a diamond-shaped light dancing about 250ft (75m) above the water, around half a mile offshore, for several minutes. A flashing light on the object flickered on and off. Sheppard, who recorded the event on his cellphone, described the movement as being something like a spinning top.

Around three minutes later, a second light appeared.

ASSESSMENT

A vast number of purported UFO sightings that are reported in Canada are actually of Sirius, also known as the dog star. The bright star is particularly prominent on the east coast of Canada. However, Sheppard reported his sighting to Mutual UFO Network, who ruled out a star-spotting error.

THE HOUSTON RING

Strange lights over Space City

TYPE: **Lights in the sky**
PLACE: **Houston, Texas, USA**
DATE: **11 August 2014**

engaged with a UFO when, in 1976, two F-4 fighter jets pursued an object the size of a Boeing 707 and attempted to take fire (see Chapter 5, page 113). Perhaps because of this event, the nation is also the location of one of Ufology's wildest conspiracy theories. In 2012, the Iranian military successfully shot down an RQ-170 stealth drone likely to have belonged to the USA. The Iranians proudly displayed the 65 by 90ft (20 by 27m) craft in a public hall. Capturing the highly advanced drone cannot have been easy, and many theorists have suggested that the Islamic Revolutionary Guard did so using reverse-engineered alien technology. This theory was given some veracity when, to the alarm of the US administration, Iran announced that it would be reverse-engineering the Lockheed Martin developed machine – a feat they achieved two years later.

THE EVENTS

In November 2014, video footage emerged taken by a passenger on board a plane flying over the Alborz mountain range in northern Iran. As he films out of his window, a small circular craft can be clearly seen traveling at speed several thousand feet beneath the passenger plane.

ASSESSMENT

The 30-second footage definitely shows something moving at a steady pace through the cloud cover. It could be tempting to believe that it is Iran's reverse-engineered stealth drone on a test flight.

CALIFORNIA ORBS

Circular orbs in the sky

TYPE: **Daylight orbs**
PLACE: **Pasadena, California, USA**
DATE: **13 January 2018**

BACKGROUND

At 12:45pm, an unnamed man and his family had just finished eating a meal when they stepped outside into the bright sunshine and noticed a group of circular orbs in the sky.

THE EVENTS

The man's initial thought was that he was seeing seagulls behaving in a strange manner, but he then realized they were looking at a group of five or six white orb-like objects at an altitude of approximately 20,000ft (6100m).

There were several other similar sightings across the USA on the same day. 90 miles (145km) to the south of Pasadena, in Carlsbad, California, five oval or circular orbs were seen in the sky at around 2:30pm by a man testing out a new pair of binoculars. Then, at around 8pm the same day, more than 2000 miles (3220km) away in Hollywood, Florida,

It makes sense that aliens would want to visit America's 'Space City', but some people believe that the mass sightings in Houston were a hoax.

there was another sighting of 'numerous orange lights above the coastline' by a law enforcement officer, who says they glowed and then disappeared completely.

ASSESSMENT

Although all three of these sightings were linked together by the National UFO Reporting Center, they do not constitute a mass sighting. While the California sightings could be connected, the lights in Florida seem to be an entirely separate event and sound as if they could have been Chinese lanterns.

A CLOSE SHAVE ABOVE IRELAND

Three airline pilots spot a high-speed object

TYPE: **Lights in the sky**
PLACE: **Ireland**
DATE: **9 November 2018**

BACKGROUND

The pilot of a British Airways flight from Canada to London called air traffic control in Shannon to report seeing an object moving at incredibly high speed past her aircraft, and asked if there were any military exercises taking place off the west coast of Ireland.

THE EVENTS

A recording of the pilot talking to air traffic control was circulated after the event. 'It was moving so fast,' she says. 'It came up on our left-hand side and then rapidly veered to the north. It was a very bright light that disappeared at very high speed.'

UFO experts Ron James, Earl Grey, Bill Crowley, Tamara Scott, and Harold Burt discuss global UFO sightings and first contact experiences at the science event **AlienCon in Pasadena in June 2018.**

The pilot feared that her plane was on collision course with a military jet. Two other commercial pilots reported a similar sight of a very fast object ripping through the skies above Ireland.

ASSESSMENT

This object, traveling at Mach 2 speeds according to one report, is highly likely to have been a meteorite. It is not uncommon for meteorites to come in at a low trajectory into the Earth's atmosphere. It is very rare for them to be spotted above a land mass, however.

Glossary

Abduction: 'Close encounter of the fourth kind'.

Advertising Plane: Light plane or helicopter carrying a commercial message; its bright lights are sometimes mistaken for UFOs.

Aliens: UFO occupants; sometimes called *extra-terrestrial aliens*.

Altered State of Consciousness: State of heightened sensitivity to psychic phenomena; often reporterd before UFO experiences; see *Hypnogogic/Hypnopomic States, Oz Factor*.

Android: Robot with human appearance; see *Humanoid*.

Angel: False echo given by radar; also called a *ghost*.

Angel Hair: White, gossamer-like substance that falls from the sky during or immediately after a UFO sighting, but rapidly 'evaporates'.

Animal Mutilation: Mysterious physical attack on animals; associated with UFO sightings, these attacks are often carried out with a surgical precision.

Autokinesis: The apparent movement of a small, bright light (such as a star) against a dark background; caused by normal, involuntary, rapid movements of the eye.

Autostasis: The apparent stopping of a small or distant moving object, also caused by normal, involuntary, rapid movements of the eye.

Close Encounter: Term coined by J. Allen Hynek for when a UFO comes within 500ft (150m) of the witness.

Collective Unconscious: Psychologist C.G. Jung's term for unconscious images and symbols that he believed were common to all humankind and the source of much UFO imagery

Condon Report: Common name for the Scientific Study of Unidentified Flying Objects, headed by physicist Dr Edward U. Condon.

Contactee: Person claiming to have had repeated contacts with aliens. See Chapter Three.

Crash-Retrieval Syndrome: Term coined by Leonard H. Stringfield for reports of crashed UFOs and the retrieval of their wreckage and alien bodies by the military.

Crop Circle: Crop patterns, often circular, ascribed by some to UFOs.

Cultural Tracking: The tendency for UFOs to echo current Earth technology or beliefs.

Daylight Disk: Coverall term for any UFO seen in daylight.

Drone: Also known as a *Remotely Piloted Vehicle (RPV)*; aircraft or missile controled from the ground and used as a target in combat exercises, and for reconnaissance and surveillance.

Earthlight: Ball of light generated by stresses within the Earth's crust.

Extra-Terrestrial Hypothesis (ETH): Proposal that UFO phenomena are generated by visitors from outer space.

Fireball: Exceptionally bright meteor; also known as a *bolide*.

Flap: Local, intense, usually brief series of UFO sightings. See *Wave*.

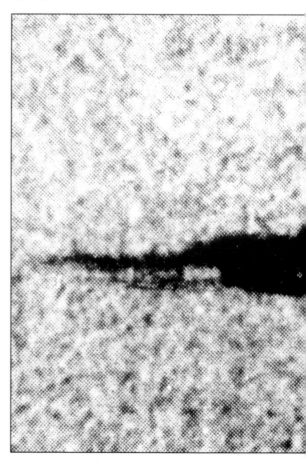

Foo Fighters: Balls of light seen by aircrew pursuing combat aircraft during World War II and the Korean War.

Gray: Alien entity reported in abduction cases.

Hoax: Deliberate fabrication of evidence.

Humanoid: Alien with generally human form.

Hypnagogic/Hypnopompic States: Drowsy states in which the mind can generate images and other sensations that seem objectively real.

IFO: Acronym for Identified Flying Object.

Inner Space Hypothesis: Proposal that UFO experiences are manifestations of psychic energy of human, animal or alien origin.

Lenticular Clouds: Disk-shaped clouds that have occasionally been mistaken for UFOs.

Light in the Sky: Luminous, usually nocturnal, UFO.

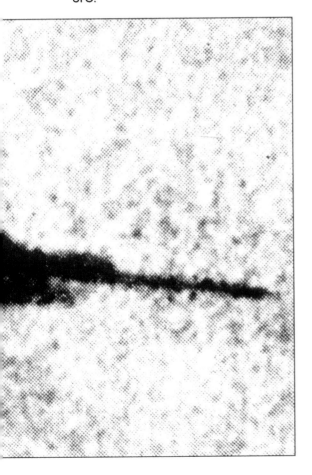

Men In Black (MIB): Mysterious visitors to UFO witnesses. See Chapter Five.

Mass Hysteria: Also called *hysterical contagion*; when a group of people share a (false) belief that an (unreal) event is occurring.

Oz Factor: Sense of entering an alternate reality or 'cone of silence' that precedes close encounters and abductions. See Chapter Six.

Parhelia: Luminous patterns or balls of light, a.k.a *mock suns* and *sundogs*, caused by refraction of sunlight on ice crystals in the atmosphere.

Plasma: Volume of air carrying exceptionally high electrical charges, appearing as a brightly-glowing ball of light in a variety of shifting colors.

Polygraph: Electronic equipment measuring physical stress in response to questions. Also known, less accurately, as a 'lie detector'.

Project Blue Book: Code name for US Air Force UFO investigation founded in 1952 and closed after the Condon Report (q.v.) in 1969.

Radar-Visual: UFO sighting by radar returns.

Regressive Hypnosis: Controversial hypnotic technique to recall forgotten events.

Sundog: See *Parhelia*.

Temperature Inversion: Layer of cold air above a layer of warmer air; may cause spurious radar returns and bizarre visual effects around bright stars and planets, leading to UFO sightings.

Uncorrelated Target: False radar return or *angel*.

Wave: Extended period of high UFO activity over a wide area; see *Flap*.

Window Area: Tightly defined locality where UFO experiences repeatedly occur. Some alleged window areas also show a very high incidence of a wide variety of other paranormal phenomena.

This UFO – which looks strikingly like an aircraft – was photographed in Brazil in the early 1950s. According to the witness, however, the object, though like an airplane, was flying sideways, and it was this bizarre movement that first drew his attention to it.

Index

INDEX